WHILE YOU ARE SINGLE

A Guide to Finding and Keeping the Right Mate for Your Life

REVISED AND UPDATED

O. J. TOKS

Author of *Rejected for a Purpose: How God Uses Rejection to Help You Find and Fulfill Your Destiny*

ELEVATOR GROUP
• FAITH •

Helping People Rise Above™

While You Are Single:
A Guide to Finding and Keeping the Right Mate For Your Life

Published by

The Elevator Group Faith
Paoli, Pennsylvania

Copyright © 2016 by O.J. Toks

Trade paperback ISBN 13: 978-09820384-4-4

E-book ISBN: 978-0-9820384-7-5

Jacket and interior design by Stephanie Vance-Patience

Published in the United States by The Elevator Group Faith.

This book was printed in the United States.

To order additional copies of this book, contact:

The Elevator Group Faith
PO Box 207
Paoli, PA 19301
610-296-4966 (p)
610-644-4436 (f)
www.TheElevatorGroup.com
info@TheElevatorGroup.com

This book is dedicated to Dana, Capt. Johnson, Mrs. Eunice, Damilola, Gboyega, Rotimi, and to all the individuals looking for the right mate to share a lasting, wholesome and meaningful relationship.

Acknowledgments

I thank God for granting me the opportunity and privilege of writing this book. I thank Him for the inspiration, direction, and revelation that gave rise to it. I am also grateful to Him for the relationships that will be birthed, revamped and confirmed because of it. I'm honored to be a ready writer for His words.

To my lovely wife Dana, thanks for coming into my life. I found you 4 years after I first published this book. But I was too distracted and incapable of comprehending the gem that you are. Thank God for His grace which opened my eyes to behold your virtue and graciousness. Though it took me another 4 years after we met, to realize that you were the one for me, you are more than worth the wait.

My gratitude also goes out to my parents, Captain J.N. & Mrs. E.O. Adeoye whose love and ceaseless prayers helped me be who I am today. I honor, appreciate, and love them for supporting me spiritually, socially and financially. I thank them for truly being my parents. I also thank my sister, Damilola, for her love, support and resilience, which helped me through tough times. Likewise, to my brothers, Gboyega and Rotimi, I thank them for loving and encouraging their big brother too. Special thanks to Sheilah Vance and the Elevator Group for embracing me, and for their invaluable contributions to this work. Their efforts on this project, editorial and otherwise, cannot be overemphasized. My gratitude also goes out to Pastors Joel & Victoria Osteen for giving me hope and encouragement. Thanks to Pastor Steve Parson for helping me learn how to apply God's Word to life; and to Pastors Calvin & Barbara Duncan for their support, mentorship and friendship. The same goes to Pastors Michael & Raquel Maye, Adeolu & Alison Adejokun, Arthur & Claire Modeste and Pastor Todd & Melisa Hull. They all supported me lovingly with open arms, open houses, open refrigerators and open wallets.

I'm also very grateful to Pastor John Bowman, Pastors Geoffrey and Margarette Stirrup, Ron and Diane Geyer, Pastor Barbara Curtis, Pastor Steve Austin, Reverend Gwendolyn Young, Elder Lillie Gaines, Reverend Rhonda Hickman, Dion & Belinda Woods, Deacon Ajai Blue-Saunders, Pastor Sean Randall, Dr. Melba Williams, Sheila McNair, Barbara Johnson, Ezekiel Adewale, Eric Larkin, Cavell & Vanessa Phillips, Tim Neville, and Daniel Dutka for their suggestions which helped in all aspects of this book. Much thanks to Elder Gloria Randolph for allowing me to print all those drafts from her printer.

Thanks also to Kwaku & Charyl Nornoo, Yolanda Medina, Yemi & Bunmi Otusemade, Wesley & Ijeoma Ekeruo, Patricia Mobolade, Ndidi Ananaba, Debbie Mingo, Pamela Jayne Davis, Lisa Soto, Gracie Estrada, Fernando & Leslie Villanueva, Titus & Nora Benny, Craig & Naisha Ford Jr., Joseph & Schande Villareal, Rigel & Jenna Garcia, Rudy Morales, Violet Hernandez, Alex DiSaggio, Javier Nieto, Bonny Olvera, Felipe & Jessica Casarez, Apple & Steve Fierros, Delsena Tarr, Sonia Gonazalez, Neakia Payton, Javier & Nohemy Santos, Christine & Angela Laredo, Meisha Smith, Karen McMillan, Lee & Nicole Hardy, Adrienne Bridges, Timothy Hines, Robert Valdez, Kim McNeil, Patricia Medina, Roberto Leyva, Martin Davis, Goreti Okello, Sarah Carrion, John Kay, Eleanor Delgado, Kemi George, Edward Jones, Rebecca Benson, Antonio Schjang, Stephanie Edwards, Erica Palin, Briana Butler, Laura Halperin, Kim Farrah, Brandy Anderson, Nicole Mason, Dewayne & Chinyere Seay, Line of David and Sir Walter & Patience Scott III, for all their prayers, encouragement and support.

Thanks also to you, dear reader. Congratulations for picking up this book. You just made a huge leap of faith in the right direction. I wish you the best in your quest for the right mate for your life.

Table of Contents

Also by O. J. Toks

Rejected for a Purpose:
How God Uses Rejection to Help You Find and Fulfill Your Destiny

Introduction

This book was first published 12 years ago—*while I was single*. While I was updating this book I was engaged to a one-of-a-kind, rare gem of a lady. Before this revision was published, I married her. Thanks to God's grace, I have practiced the guidelines I present in this book. My wife and I are still practicing them.

I have learned a great deal these past 12 years. I have included them in this update. Therefore, you have a more concise guide that will help you in your search for your mate. This revision reinforces the truths I discussed in the first edition. It also includes information that addresses new trends in the search for love, as well as insights that expose lingering issues that often hinder relationships from moving forward.

The idea for this book was conceived in my heart close to 14 years ago. I was asked to speak in a True Love Waits, Bible study event hosted at Virginia Commonwealth University by *VISION*, a student organization. I sought God to direct me on what to speak about and I believe He inspired me to discuss what I learned from my failed attempt at establishing a relationship with a certain damsel whom I had cherished. It became clear that my disappointment was actually the trigger that propelled me to seriously evaluate my readiness to be in a relationship. It was also a blessing that gave rise to the lessons for my discussion in the event and this book.

This work started after I was infected by what I considered to be the love bug. The infection didn't invade me rapidly; rather, it gradually inched its way through my heart and weakened me. The source of the infection was a lovely young woman whose body was gracefully sculpted and glossed with a buttermilk complexion. This lady had the kind of smile that sold toothpaste and real estate; the kind of smile that landed million dollar accounts; the kind of smile that companies placed on the cover of their brochures and the front pages of their websites.

The love pathogen's progress on my heart was reinforced each time the image of the lady rested on my retina and floated in my thoughts. I considered asking God to give me another dose of breath as I fantasized that she took my initial supply away. In essence, this "mama" was h-h-h-ot! Perhaps that explains why my heart burned so for her.

Unfortunately, my excitement and anticipation in establishing a relationship with her was dealt a hard blow when she tactfully declined my feelings. I was distraught. My affection for her, which I had conserved for a few months before unveiling them to her, seemed to be flushed down the toilet in a single instance. I felt as if I had been knocked out of a boxing bout before the bell rang for the first round. That notwithstanding, its effect was not a rude awakening but a good awakening for me. I couldn't have asked for a better position sprawled, with my back on the canvass like the alphabet, "X." In that stance, and at that point, I had nowhere else to look but up. Moreover, "up" was my source of help. I reached out to God who pulled me up and sustained me through that emotional distress.

Although she understandably turned me down because her feelings were not congruent with mine, she inadvertently turned me on, and I've not been able to locate the "off switch"—not that I tried looking for it. I was impassioned to write about my frustration and disappointment regarding the unrealized relationship, and in doing so, I channeled the energy she inspired in me.

In all fairness, I realized that the issue wasn't whether she was the right one for me; it was whether *I* was the right one for her. Was I good enough for her—or for anyone else? If I was not, what should I do to make myself a prime candidate for the description, "The right one"? Whatever I needed to do, I had better start doing it now while I'm single rather than later, when I'm married.

Scripture and other sources helped me identify appropriate guidelines helpful for finding the right person with whom to share a lifetime. I first discussed some of these guidelines in the true love event. While discussing them with my peers, truths were unveiled that effectively addressed major issues that singles, at large, were wrestling with. Several months later, after much deliberation I concluded that the information disclosed in that Bible study was too important to be confined within the walls of the red-bricked, Baptist Student Union building where the program was hosted. I felt charged with the responsibility to spread the word.

Therefore, the guidelines are presented in their entirety as the chapter titles of this writing. This book's title was coined from the realization that preparation for a mate should take place before marriage. This will help save an individual from the consequences of ending up in a relationship, ill-prepared, with wrong expectations—and with the wrong person. With this in mind, this was written to help you avoid unfruitful relationships and the heartache that goes along with them. It was written to help you learn from mistakes that, perhaps you, and others, have made in relationships, and to prevent you from repeating them. It was written to help you maximize your singleness by conserving the time and energy you'd have otherwise exhausted in such relationships.

This was also written to *forewarn* you while you are single to *forearm* you when you are married. It assists you with taking advantage of your life *now* as a single person, to help prepare you for your life *ahead* as a married person. It helps you learn what you can know now about marriage before you get married, to help you handle what you might not know later when you do get married.

In a nutshell, this book will help you make the most of your singleness, prepare you for holy matrimony, and guide you in finding the right person to share it with—an outstanding mate for you. This will facilitate a relationship that will emulate in reality, the idea of a marriage made in heaven. Having and applying all the information relevant for securing and cultivating a healthy relationship prior to wedlock will go a long way in helping you maneuver your upcoming marriage in the sea of life without it hitting the rocks.

Oftentimes in the search for a mate, people place most of their emphasis on finding someone who *looks* right for them. If you have tried this and discovered that your incessant efforts proved to no avail, perhaps, you might need to have a paradigm shift by changing your focus from the other person to yourself. Have you ever thought of being *the right one* for someone else? Maybe you should not be trying to find the right person; but rather, be the right person to be found.

Before you can become right for someone else, it is sensible for you to find out what makes a person right for any other person. Learn how you can become that right person. After you have done this, and developed yourself to be suitable for someone else, you will put yourself in a better position to find the right person—since you will now know who to be on the look out for. Someone like you. Someone who will emanate qualities that you developed in yourself. Qualities that will complement and be compatible with yours. Qualities that characterize the right mate for your life.

While you are single, the investments that you make in yourself pertaining to matrimony will determine the returns you will get in marriage. Your lifestyle as a single person is a seed that will determine the harvest you will reap as a married person. It is important for you to see that your singleness is an opportunity for you to train for marriage. Your singleness is an excellent time for you to work on yourself so that when you meet and marry the love of your life, you will have something of value to contribute to the relationship. Although people have survived and still survive marriages on the brink of destruction, you do not have to go through a divorce or have a disastrous relationship, before you learn what you can do to avoid being in one.

It is with great pleasure that I *re-present* this book to you. Rest assured that this book will be especially helpful to those who desire to tie the knot—and perhaps, to those who desire to retie theirs, to those who desire not to untie theirs, as well as to those who desire to keep theirs taut. Come with me and let us journey through the pages of this writing. While I drive as the designated chauffeur, relax, buckle your seat belt, and open your heart to receive the information that will take you on the quest of what it takes to obtain and retain God's best—the right mate for your life.

CHAPTER ONE
Understand What You Are Getting Yourself Into

I find it interesting that relationships are like investments. If you want to get great returns from a relationship, not only do you need to invest wisely, you also need to *find the right* investment. This is what smart investors do. I learned that smart investors generally look at five things to help them make smart investment decisions. For example, before they invest in a stock, they look at the fundamentals of the stock. They call this fundamental analysis. This analysis deals with evaluating a stock by looking at the financial health of the company offering the stock, their management, their gains, losses, debts, etc.

The second thing they look at are the technicals of the stock. This is what they refer to as technical analysis. Here, they use mathematical computing formulas and charts to help them project whether the stock will go up or down. The third thing they look at is the economy. This approach involves noting what is happening in the economy and how this affects the stock. The fourth thing they consider is sentiment, which has to do with listening to analysts or financial experts' views of the stock. Finally, they pay attention to any news about the company offering the stock. Is the company going bankrupt, merging with another company, facing a lawsuit, releasing their quarterly profits or loses, or bringing in a new product?

These five things: fundamental analysis, technical analysis, economy, sentiment and news, help wise investors decide whether or not to invest in a stock. As a result of applying these techniques smart investors choose the right stocks and reap good to great returns. Every once in a while, they lose money. But, because they did their homework, they don't lose money as badly and as often as unwise investors do.

Unwise investors don't perform due diligence to their stocks. They often do what everyone else is doing. They invest in stocks that are popular, and they are quick to follow stock tips from anyone from anonymous emails to the guy in the barber shop. Consequently, they lose big. Sometimes an arm and a leg.

That is kind of what happens in a lot of relationships. People are doing what everyone else is doing. A plethora of individuals are going about relationships based on what is popular. They receive tips from any and everyone about relationships. They invest in relationships like unwise investors. Therefore they end up disappointed and distraught when the person they invested in did not yield returns. Rather, the only "returns" they get are their love interests *returning* home to their parents. Some others return to being single. Others return to the volatile singles' market, hoping and scoping to invest in another prospect. Others quit completely. Mad at the world. Mad at marriage. Mad at the opposite sex. Even mad at God.

A vital key to being successful in a relationship, especially one that leads to marriage and stays in marriage, is to approach the relationship like a smart investor. This approach will more than likely help you end up with the right person and experience a wholesome relationship. This does not mean that you won't encounter losses in the form of finding out that the person you thought was the one for you turned out not to be. However, it means that should you encounter a loss, you encounter it *before* the altar rather than after you've said your vows. It also means that your losses will be parting with a *few* prospects as opposed to going through a whole bunch of prospects before you end up with the right person for you. Even if you have already gone through an annulment or a breakup, learning to think and act like a smart investor will help you in your next go around toward the altar.

Just like smart investors educate themselves on the investments they are about to put their money into, we should also educate ourselves on *who* we're planning to share our lives with. We should also understand a *fundamental* aspect of healthy relationships necessary for us to find and keep that person. This aspect, which we need to understand but is often misunderstood, is love.

There are all kinds of love today. There is the one night stand love, midnight love, thug love, puppy love and popcorn love—none of which is really love. It is imperative and advantageous for you to understand what true love is—especially while you are single. If not, you are likely to end up in a relationship that will end up in disaster.

My people are destroyed from lack of knowledge.... (Hosea 4:6)

A lack of knowledge of anything in any area that is relevant to you leads to your failure that area. For example, not knowing the material on which you are being tested in an examination leads to your failure in that test. Not knowing that you should not microwave any food wrapped in aluminum foil can lead to fire. This fire can destroy the microwave, the food and the aluminum foil in the microwave, the kitchen, the house, and the realtor's confidence in your ability to handle domiciliary responsibilities.

Prior to marrying him, a lack of knowledge of who Benson really was, left Janet with the impression that *he's charming*. But not long after their wedding she found out that *he's harming*—harmful. She didn't know that when he said he had a job as a freelancer he meant that he was free from not having a job. She also didn't know that he had incurred huge amounts of debt as he owed Wells Fargo, the local credit union, Wal-Mart's layaway department, Home Depot, Best Buy, child support, and three women. These women were the mothers of his five kids for whom he owed child support. Kids that Janet didn't know about. All these led to her depression, destruction of her credit, her dignity and her marriage.

A lack of knowledge of who Isabella really was, left Richard befuddled and feeling manipulated when he discovered that without makeup she transformed from looking like *Halle Berry* to looking *hardly pretty*. Her alluring rosy colored manicured nails were artificial. Her Miss Piggy eyelashes were synthetic. Her vivacious hair was just a wig that she bought for five dollars at the local thrift store. And her beautiful teeth were actually dentures which she obtained from her Dentist. Subsequently, on the night of their honeymoon, when she took them out of her mouth in an *attempt* to consummate her marriage vows, Richard was appalled by her façade, and his romantic intentions were abruptly extinguished.

Not knowing that the non-citizen married her because he only wanted to reside legally in the country left Dorothy devastated, dispirited, and in a dilemma after the individual obtained the immigration papers, served her with the divorce papers and of course, nullified the marriage paper. Regardless of how ludicrous these examples are, I don't want you to miss the main point. The issue is not the chaos faced by these fictitious characters. The issue is the lack of the proper knowledge that would have either prevented the individuals from being in those situations or prepared them to handle them better.

A lack of knowledge of the true meaning of love has lead droves of bachelorettes and bachelors to search for it in night clubs, astrology, tarot cards, reality shows, soap operas, twitter, facebook, myspace, your space, outer space and every other space. As a result, countless numbers of relationships have been short-lived. This was inevitable since one or both individuals involved in the relationship didn't really know what love is. Subsequently they didn't know what to look for. And even if they did know what to look for, they didn't know where to find it. So they were left in a quandary of either looking for the right thing in the wrong place, or looking for the wrong thing in the wrong place, and worst still—in the wrong person. Whichever case, the results were still the same: disagreement, disappointment, discontentment, and even divorce.

There are different perspectives about love. One of those views about love is put forth by Dr. Pat Love. The relationship consultant categorized love in four stages: infatuation, post-rapture, discovery and connection. What I found particularly interesting in her discussion of love was the physiological aspects of it, which she began to elaborate in the infatuation stage. She describes this stage as the one in which we find ourselves very attracted to someone. Our euphoric affection for this individual is often characterized by having those bizarre "I'm so in love with you, I can't do without you" feelings. Hmmm, sounds familiar. However, she cautioned that what we often think is love, is actually an aftermath of the influence of a mix of chemicals, which she labeled the love cocktail.

According to Dr. Love, when we are in contact with the person we are infatuated with, these chemicals aggressively alter our brain chemistry. Some of the culprits that comprise this chemical mix are phenylethylamine (PEA) also known as the love molecule, dopamine and norepinephrine. These work in unison and boost us with excitement and energy, which inspire us to do whatever it takes to please the objects of our affection. This naturally-produced love potion is so powerful that it inhibits the amygdala, the inhibition center of our brain from helping us to be reasonably cautious about getting involved in a relationship with the person we are attracted to.

Unfortunately for us, these hormones don't tell us when they take a break, a vacation, quit, resign or retire. Neither do they give two weeks notice before they take their typical undisclosed hiatus. And when these chemicals go "AWOL" and if we don't know any better, as we often don't, so does our relationship with our beloved; because, it is now up to us to *willfully* duplicate what the chemicals did for us. Dr. Love also revealed that the infatuation stage lasts for about six months to two years.

That is when reality hits and this is when true love begins according to the marriage therapist. She designates this impasse as the post-rapture stage. She said that this second stage of love can be marked with huge arguments or gradual and subtle changes. Like, couples not hanging out and conversing with each other like they used to. Couples not as excited about each other, and even noticing things about each other that they thought were cute and overlooked, but are now getting on each other's nerves.

If these individuals survive the post-rapture stage, then they progress to the third stage of love. The discovery stage. Here, they truly begin to discover each other by gathering information from each other about each other. They begin to understand each other and work out ways of meeting each other's needs. They begin to find out what says "I love you" to each other—each individual's unique love language, and express it appropriately and accordingly.

Having done this successfully, couples can now connect and usher themselves to the fourth stage of love. The connection stage. In this stage, she emphasized and expounded on the invaluable and healthy results of commitment to a relationship, which in the long run promotes and illustrates true love.[1]

I found Dr. Love's research on the truth about love very insightful. Her discovery on the truth about love had always and continues to be epitomized by another physician. In charismatic circles, this individual is known as *The Great Physician*. He has "been there done that" in all aspects of all relationships. Therefore, this Physician knows how you feel and what you deal with in any relationship: whether you are single, married or divorced. While others can only claim that "there is no mountain high enough" to keep them from their respective heartthrobs as an expression of their love for them, this Physician spoke to mountains to move and told them where to relax.[2] I hope you know whom I'm talking about. The Doctor of Love— Jesus.

"Why Jesus?" You might ask. Well, He personifies what true love is all about.

Jesus answered, "I am the way and the truth and the life. No one comes to the Father except through me. (John 14:6)

Amongst numerous and equally profound insights revealed from that verse of scripture, Jesus is the perfect embodiment of love as He is the *way* to love, He is the *truth* about love, and He is the *life* of love. Since no one comes to the Father except through Christ, and the Father is God, and God is love, then no one can come to love (God, the Father) or know what love is except through Jesus. Therefore, Jesus is the *way* to love. He is the direction, pathway or guide to love. In Him is the understanding of how to love. The *way* He loves is the *way* we're to love, too. Not only is He the guide to love, He is also the guide to finding and keeping the right mate for your life.

He is the *truth* about love. He indeed is. Do you want to know real love? Know Him. He is the perfect example of love. In the name of love, He humbled himself, left His throne, and came down to earth as a man and died for the world.

He said:

Greater love has no one than this, that he lay down his life for his friends. (John 15:13)

He didn't just say this, He demonstrated it when He died for us. And He did not just die for his friends, He died for His enemies as well. He is definitely the *truth* about love. He is also the *life* of love, or the life that His love gives. This sheds more light to this statement:

For God so loved the world that he gave his one and only son, that whoever believes in him shall not perish but have eternal life. (John 3:16)

In demonstration of His love for us, God gave His Son to die for us. We obtain eternal *life* by believing in Christ. Notice that eternal life was made available to us by believing in Jesus who died for us in demonstration of His *love*. In other words, we have *life*—eternal, through God's love shown by giving His Son's life for us.

To truly know love it is best for you to know Jesus. To know Him, it's necessary to know what He said about Himself. He reveals Himself to us through His Word, which is one and the same with Him.[3] His words to us are in the Bible. Since we should understand love based on Him it's pertinent for us to find out what He says about it in His book. Thus:

Love is patient and kind; it is not jealous or conceited or proud; Love is not ill-mannered or selfish or irritable; Love does not keep a record of wrongs; Love is not happy with evil, but is happy with the truth. Love never gives up; and its faith, hope, and patience never fail. (1 Corinthians 13:4-7 GNB)

True Love is all of the above. Love is universal and applicable to all situations. Love is applicable to our enemies and friends alike; how much more the person we each choose or chose to marry. Our desire and obligation to marry or stay married to whomever God has brought before us respectively, gives us an incentive to love them.

The way love was described above is very concise; however, I would like to draw even more from what we just read. In doing this, I'll disclose six things that love is. Let's begin in the next chapter.

CHAPTER TWO

Understand What Love Is

1. *Love is unconditional.*

The Greek word "agape" is used to describe true love.[4] This is the God kind of love, an unconditional, unselfish love as stated in *1 Corinthians 13:5.*

> *But God demonstrates his own love for us in this: While we were still sinners, Christ died for us. (Romans 5:8)*

God loves us unconditionally. Even when we don't meet conditions to be loved, He still loves us. He does not withhold His love from us when we are unworthy of it. If we don't think about Him or care about His values, He still loves us because His love is unconditional. I like the way Pastor and cofounder of the Los Angeles Dream Center, Tommy Barnett, described unconditional loving. He said:

> *When we love unconditionally, we can never be imprisoned to a man or woman. But when we demand that somebody love us, we become their slave and are easily imprisoned by their lack of love toward us.*[5]

In essence, when you love your mate unconditionally, you are not in the bondage of wanting him or her to love you back. You make the decision regardless to love your beloved just as God loves us despite our shortcomings. He just decided to love us without any conditions whatsoever.

Perhaps you are familiar with the premise that if you believe in God then you should marry someone who also believes in Him. Considering that love is unconditional, you might argue that you can marry anyone you want regardless of his or her religious beliefs—or lack of it. You can contend that you will not be demonstrating unconditional love by marrying someone on the *condition* that the person share a belief system of God like you do. You can feel that since love is unconditional, then anyone is game.

If that is your argument, I have to admit, you have a valid point—and one that should not be overlooked. It looks like a contradiction to be told to love unconditionally but marry someone as long as the individual meets certain conditions, religious or otherwise. Although this argument sounds reasonable, it is misapplied in this case. The best way I can clarify this perceived contradiction is to say this:

Your choice of who to marry is conditional; loving the person you marry should be unconditional.

You should love unconditionally the person you conditionally choose to marry. We should love *everyone*, including your mate, unconditionally. However, the person you choose to share the rest of your life with should be selected conditionally and wisely. For couples in uninspiring and chaotic marriages, this is a very hard pill to swallow. However, for the person who is still single, swallowing this pill is not as difficult. Therefore, while you are single, take your time to ensure that the person you choose to share the rest of your life with meets certain realistic and relevant guidelines before you marry him or her. I will be sharing some of such guidelines later.

2. Love is a decision you make.

I once attended a men's conference dealing with relationships with women at the University of Richmond, Virginia. I was intrigued by a comment made by one of the speakers in the seminar. He said that love is a decision you make.

Good decisions are made based on good information. More so, God decisions—Godly decisions are made based on God's information. God just informed us in *1 Corinthians 13:4-7* what love is. Based on this information we can make a firm decision to love or affirmatively decide to express all the attributes mentioned in that passage. In essence, love is a choice you make. It is an act of your will. It is a decision you make to treat someone in a Godly way.

Psychiatrist Dr. Scott Peck put it this way:

Genuine love is volitional rather than emotional. The person who truly loves does so because of a decision to love. This person has made a commitment to be loving whether or not the loving feeling is present. If it is, so much the better; but if it isn't, the commitment to love, the will to love still stands and is still exercised.[6]

There is this concept of *falling* in love. Maybe this is the problem. Without taking away from the excitement that love brings, love is not something we fall in. It's something we *walk* in. You see, when you fall you injure yourself. When you fall, this means that you had an accident. When you fall, this means that you were unaware of the thing that tripped you. While true love is a trip of a life time, it does not "trip" you. Loving someone should not be an accident; it should be deliberate. We are not supposed to "fall" in love; we are to walk in love. Love is not an illusion; it's a decision you make.

3. Love is an attitude.

If you make a firm decision to love by displaying its characteristics, then it can be said that you have an attitude of love. Therefore, we can deduce that love is an attitude. Distinguishing from bad attitudes, love is a be-attitude or an *attitude to be* expressed. It is a good attitude; better still, a God attitude— God's attitude. It's a Godly attitude or an attitude that God displays.[7]

If you understand and employ the attitude of love, its way of thinking, its mentality or mindset, your *mind* should be *set* to wait for the right mate for your life. Your mind should be set to be patient with your mate. Your mind should be set to treat your mate kindly. Your mind should be set not to be jealous, conceited, or proud to your mate. You've made up your mind not to be ill-mannered, selfish or irritable to your mate. You're determined not to keep the record of wrongs you suffered from your mate. This explains why Jesus epitomizes love. He displayed this attitude toward us.

4. Love is a sacrifice.

I believe that you, like me, realize that love is a sacrifice. Love costs. To truly love your beloved, to bear him or her, to not take account of wrongs suffered and be patient with his or her shortcomings, is a sacrifice. Do you recall that Jesus sacrificed himself for us? The greatest expression of love is shown when someone lays down his or her life for his or her friends. Considering that your mate should also be your friend, the greatest way to show your love to that person is to sacrifice or lay down your life for him or her. By laying down your life, I mean dying to yourself to benefit the individual just like Christ died to himself by laying down his life to benefit us. When you get married you are supposed to lay down the rest of your life for your mate in demonstration of your sacrifice of love.

In the best interest of your matrimony, you might have to lay down your momma's way of cooking unless you are going to do the cooking for yourself and for her—without making her feel incompetent. You might have to lay down your poppa's way of fixing the house or the car—unless you're going to fix or make arrangements to get the house or the vehicle fixed without making your hubby feel like he's less of a man. You might also need to lay down your honorary awards and achievements, your opinion, your need to be right, your paycheck and of course, your ego—especially if you are male.

Marriage is a different ball game. It is not just about you; it's about you *two*. The way you lived your life will have to change in order for you to adapt to your new life with your new wife or husband who was probably raised differently. And as a result, your spouse had a different perspective on life. In order to make your new life conducive for each other, in order to merge your varied, independent and perhaps contrasting respective views on life harmoniously and peacefully, you will need to lay down the rest of your life for him or her. You'll need to sacrifice some, if not all of the ways you did things. "Me" becomes "us," "mine" becomes "ours," "what I want" becomes "what we want." To stress the unselfish, sacrificial nature of love even further, sometimes "me" becomes "you," "mine" becomes "yours," and "what I want" becomes "what do you want?"

5. Love is an investment.

Since love is a sacrifice, since love costs, then love is an investment. No wonder why we need to think and act like wise investors to succeed in this matter of the heart. Genuine love is at the core of successful relationships, and so is its sacrificial nature. Make no mistake about it, love is an investment—the biggest investment and most important investment that can, and should be made in any relationship.

Differentiating from bad investments, love is a good investment. Usually a bad investment yields a loss instead of a profit. For example, assume you bought a thousand shares of a particular stock at $77 each. This means you invested $77, 000 in the stock. And let's say you expected each share of the stock to go up from $77 to $154 so that you could sell it for a profit. Unfortunately, due to circumstances beyond your control, the stock went down to $6 per share, and never went back up but kept spiraling down. Having no other choice, you sold it for a loss, and got back only $6000 or less of your original investment, depending on how far down your stock dipped.

That is a bad investment. The investment is not bad because of the $77, 000 you invested in it, but because of the stock in which you invested your money. Furthermore, you invested in a bad stock most likely because you were fed wrong information about the stock (remember lack of proper knowledge), which you either obtained from a misinformed or incompetent stockbroker, anonymous email, or by taking matters into your own hands.

Bearing this in mind, it is beneficial for you to be mindful of whom you invest your good love investment. Ensure that it is not invested in a bad stock or the wrong person. Yes, love is a sacrifice and endures everything. But, it's better, wise, and very lucrative to love the person God has for you than the person the devil brings your way through ungodly opinions, misinformed individuals, and your lack of knowledge. It's beneficial for you to have God as your stock broker. He's the best financial and "relational" manager. Check His track record. The "returns" He helps His clients (His children) obtain are exponential—as long as His clients follow His guidance (conditions) by investing in the stock He recommends for them.[8]

Within the financial community you can invest in bonds, mutual funds and stock options. For illustrative purposes, I'll like to use options to represent the person in which you are to invest your love. An option is a contract that gives the owner the right, but not the obligation, to buy or sell an underlying stock at a specified price on or before a specified date.[9]

I prefer options because as the name implies, you have the *choice*, not an obligation, to invest in the "option" God "brokers" or brings to you. Notwithstanding, if God recommends an option, be it a man or a woman, you better accept him or her! He or she is worth your love and is your best investment. Moreover, there is also a specified *price* and a *timing* factor which should not discourage you since Jesus already *paid* the price of love which is available for your investing if you solicit Him as your "Romance Manager." And His *timing* is the best.

While I like to use options to represent the right person for you, I prefer to use mutual funds to represent marriage. Why? Because marriage should constitute two people who are *mutually fond* of each other.

With any good investment there is a good return. God invested Himself in His Son through His death on the cross that we might have a good return of eternal life by believing in Him. A good investment is like a good seed since such investments yield good returns like good seeds in good grounds yield a good harvest. With regard to this frame of reference, God's love for us inspired Him to plant Christ (One Man) as a seed, which resulted in His innumerable—exponential harvest of children which includes me and hopefully you, and others to come. It's interesting and relevant that this scripture reads:

We love Him because He first loved us. (1 John 4:19 NKJV)

In essence, God's investment or seed of love in, and for us, yielded a return of love from us to Him. In order for God to get love from us He gave love to us. Therefore, in loving the person God has for you, especially if you are a guy, you're supposed to love her first so that she can love you in return. Do not wait for her to express love to you first. Take the initiative like Jesus did and watch what your investment of love yields.

"...to have love, you don't seek it—you give it."[10]

A man in particular should invest love to his wife or have a mind set to invest love first to the woman he's about to marry.

Husbands, love your wives, just as Christ loved the church and gave himself up for her. (Ephesians 5:25)

Notice that the passage addressed husbands to love their wives and not the wives to love their husbands. Please don't misunderstand me. It doesn't mean that wives shouldn't love their husbands. To me the passage suggests that wives are not responsible for loving their husbands *like* Jesus loved the church *and* gave Himself for her. It's the husbands' responsibility to love their wives that way. When husbands love their wives like Jesus did the church, the wives in turn are to love them back in response to their respective husband's love.

Notice that the church is referred to as "her" and not "he." Also, notice that Christ loved her *and* gave Himself for her. Husbands are to love or invest love like Christ. Wives, "her," as represented by the church, are supposed to be the recipients of the love *investment* which should motivate them to yield a love *return* to their husbands, just like God's children love God because He loved them first.

The husbands are the ones responsible for loving their wives like Christ loved the church, not the other way round. Unfortunately, in some marriages it seems like the reverse is the case. It is the women that are loving their husbands unconditionally. It *seems* like some women love their husbands unconditionally while some men love their wives conditionally. Some women love their husbands whether they look like a receiver from the Pittsburgh Steelers or look like the Pillsbury Doughboy. On the other hand, some men only love their wives as long as they look like *Eva Longoria*. If they look like *Eva no longer*, their love for their wives takes a hike. This should not be the case.

Jesus Christ giving Himself for the church means sacrificing Himself for her. He did this ultimately on the cross. I tell you what might be a sacrifice for a guy akin to Christ on the cross; keeping his ego in check when he's wrong and she's right. In the best interest of the relationship and in demonstrating his love for her like Christ did for the church, he should lay down his pride by apologizing and admitting that he's wrong—and his queen should not twist the knife on his wounded ego further by letting him know how wrong he was. Even if she's wrong and he's right, he should crucify his ego by not taking account of her wrong and not being conceited, but by being patient and kind to her.

Hopefully, as you understand more about love you begin to realize that love is not a *fairy tale* but *very real*. Love is serious. Not a joke! It is better for you to know this while you are single, than to have you and a possible Cinderella-type mentality of love crushed in a relationship that wasn't of love, but of bluff.

I don't mean to frighten you but enlighten you about true love. If you're beginning to realize that you had a false understanding of love and as a result conclude that you're not ready to truly love, sacrifice or lay down the rest of your life for whomever God has for you, I respectfully suggest you change the title of this book from, *While You Are Single* to *Stay Single a While*.

6. Love is a fruit.

I said love is an investment; a seed. Investments should grow. Seeds should grow too. Investments or seeds should come to fruition. Investments should yield returns and seeds should yield a harvest. In this token, love is a fruit. I believe the first part of this scripture corroborates this conclusion.

But the fruit of the Spirit is love.... (Galatians 5:22)

If you've received Jesus as the Lord and Savior of your life, then you have the fruit of love deposited in you by the Holy Spirit. Thus, the later part of this passage reads:

...because God has poured out his love into our hearts by the Holy Spirit, whom he has given us. (Romans 5:5)

I once heard Bible Teacher and host of *Enjoying Every Day Life*, Dr. Joyce Meyer, say that love is the fruit of the spirit, whereas the other attributes mentioned alongside it are derived from love, since *Galatians 5:22-23* completely reads:

But the fruit of the Spirit is love, joy, peace, patience, kindness, goodness, faithfulness, gentleness and self-control....

Pastor and Author Dr. Creflo Dollar gave me more clarity to her infer-
ence when he pointed out that the scripture said "fruit of the Spirit" and not
"fruits of the Spirit." This implied that there was one fruit of the spirit since
the word "fruit" used in that passage is singular not plural. The fruit is love.
Whereas, the others mentioned with it are its ingredients.

Therefore, if you're truly in love with your mate, you should be *unconditionally* in joy with the person—and you should enjoy the person.
You should have made the *decision* to be at peace with your beloved. You
should be longsuffering or suffer long as a gesture of your *sacrifice* for
your mate. You should emanate an *attitude* of kindness to God's gift to
you. You should *invest* goodness—and good things in, and for, the object
of your love. When your love *fruit* is squeezed, you should also spurt juices
of faithfulness, gentleness, and self-control for your mate.

Since love is a fruit, this suggests that just like fruits develop, love grows
or leaves room for development. Ever heard some married couples say that
they have more love for themselves than when they first got married? This
took place because they nurtured their love for each other to grow. Since
love grows, then in the words of Author and Speaker Matthew Kelly:

We shouldn't fall in love; we should rise in love.11

If you had any anxiety about how inadequate your perception of love
was, I hope this revelation alleviates this. As long as you are connected to
Christ and you allow Him to develop His fruit of love which He deposited
in you through His Spirit in you, you are on your way to getting married.
However, don't send out the invitations just yet.

*I am the vine; you are the branches. If a man remains in me and I in
him, he will bear much fruit; apart from me you can do nothing. (John
15:5)*

That passage goes in line with what I just said. God's Spirit in us came with a deposit of the love fruit which can be developed as we remain and maintain our connection to Him. As we allow ourselves to know Jesus as the *way* to love, the *truth* about love, and the *life* of love, then through His help we can cultivate our love and allow it to grow to the point where it displays its true nature as exemplified by Christ to whom we remain connected.

Drawing from Dr. Pat Love's research and my discussion of love gleaned from the scriptures, we can conclude that love is not a feeling. Love is not an emotion. Yes, love is expressed through emotion; but it is not an emotion. I first came to this understanding of love when Apostle and Author Dr. Frederick Price mentioned it while teaching in his *Ever Increasing Faith* telecast. He also stated thus:

Love is not an emotion; love is expressed through emotions. But it is much more than emotion. We have gotten the idea that if you do not have the emotion of love, then there is no obligation on your part to be involved with someone, even with your children, parents, mate, or other Christians. You do not really relate to other people, because you do not have any emotional feeling for them. Well, that is a fallacy.[12]

Just because you have feelings for someone doesn't mean you really love the person. Your feelings for the individual might be purely sexual or chemical—biochemically induced. In other words, you might not be in love but in lust—or you might just be infatuated. Please don't get me wrong. I strongly believe that you will have feelings for whomever God has for you. In fact, I believe that He'll see that you do. Nevertheless, love is not based solely on emotions. Just because you have feelings does not mean you are in love; however, when you are in love you will have feelings.

I believe Matthew Kelly said it beautifully:

...feelings are just the aroma of the flower we call love...and flowers are not always in bloom.[13]

Feelings are fickle. Sometimes you feel good, and sometimes you feel bad. Feeling bad about a relationship that you felt good about previously does not mean that you cannot love your mate anymore. I am in no way advocating that anyone stay in a tumultuous relationship. I am rather deliberating on situations where the baby of love is thrown out with the dirty baby bath water of feelings.

You should not stop loving just because you are not *feeling* it. Jesus was not feeling it in the garden of Gethsemane prior to going to the cross. He opted for a way out of dying for us, but his love for us, which was not based on his distressing feelings, overcame his distraught emotions, endured his melancholy, and never gave up. He didn't abort His mission for giving us life just because He didn't feel like it. He sacrificed himself as He endured long and hard from the time they spat on Him, beat him, and ripped his flesh apart. He persevered through the whips on his body, and crown of thorns on his head, until He said "it is finished."[14]

I believe emotions have a place in our expression of love; however, they are not love, but a means of expressing love. I also believe that you should be attracted to your mate. Though, just because you are attracted to someone does not mean you're in love with the individual. You might just be attracted to the person superficially.

In any case, I still believe that you should be attracted to whomever God gives you. There is no doubt in my mind that Adam was attracted to Eve. After God created Adam, I noticed that Adam did not say much except give names to the animals. But when Eve showed up, the cat that got his tongue suddenly vamoosed! All of a sudden the poet in Adam resurrected himself as he declared her bone of his bones and flesh of his flesh.

Sounds like he said, "Whoop there she is!" Kind of sounds like what a guy would do when he sees a lady he is attracted to. All of a sudden he wants to talk to her. All of a sudden many a man's morality commits suicide as it flies out the window! Maybe Adam's attraction to Eve contributed to his disobedience.

I often wondered what Adam was thinking when he blatantly disobeyed God. God hooked him up big time. God created him, breathed life into him, and gave him a job as the COO while God remained as the CEO of the Garden of Eden. He also gave him a wife. God gave him an instruction. A simple uncomplicated instruction. To stay away from the tree of the knowledge of good and evil. God had given him a previous assignment, which was to give names to the animals. Which set of instructions do you think were more difficult to follow? I think this is a no-brainer. I believe it's harder to give names to animals that you are seeing for the first time than restraining yourself from barking on the wrong tree.

What on earth would make a guy disobey such a God given order? *A beautiful woman*! Kind of makes sense. You know how some guys begin to act when they see an attractive lady. Some begin to act like they have no morals. Perhaps when Adam saw Eve he was so taken by her beauty and uniqueness that he voluntarily forgot what God instructed him not to do. After all, he was standing right there when the devil tempted Eve.

...She also gave some to her husband, who was with her, and he ate it. (Genesis 3:6)

Since he was *with* her, then he must have been present when the devil coerced Eve to eat the fruit from the forbidden tree. Perhaps Adam had a point when God called him on the carpet. Absolutely not a valid point, but a point nevertheless.

The man said, "The woman YOU put here with me—she gave me some fruit from the tree, and I ate it" (Genesis 3:12) Emphasis mine.

In essence and in his defense, he blamed Eve and God for his transgression. He might have been saying that it was Eve's fault because she looked so h-h-hot! that she melted the commandment God gave him into oblivion. And it was God's fault because He gave him such a ravishing woman— since he was in his right mind before she showed up. God fired him! Since He is the CEO, and dismissed Adam and his "alleged" cause of his disobedience out of His garden.

I hope you're not taking my version of this story too seriously. All I'm trying to stress is that God will give you someone that you are attracted to. Sometimes you might not be attracted to the person at first, but as you yield to God's purpose and begin to see through His eyes, you might become overwhelmed by the glamorous person He placed before you.

Even Jacob's attraction to Rachel further substantiates that God will give you someone desirable. Jacob was talking to a bunch of shepherds and kind of telling them how to do their job, but when he saw Rachel he stopped telling them how to do their job and undertook their job for them (perhaps those hormones altered his brain chemistry). All of a sudden he became motivated as a spirit of machismo rose up in him and he moved a "large" stone from the mouth of a well, drew water from the well, and watered Rachel's father's flock (sounds like the love concoction did a serious number on him). After showing off to impress Rachel, he kissed her and wept.[15]

When a guy decides to do an odd job for a woman in his own expense, she must be something. It's one thing for a guy to flex his muscles for a lady like Jacob did for Rachel, but it's another thing when he gets emotional and cries. How often do you hear some men say that men are not supposed to cry? I doubt if Jacob had that mentality; however, if he did, Rachel sure erased it.

Of course, saying that men are not supposed to cry is not true! There is no man more real than Jesus, and the Bible says:

Jesus wept. (John 11:35)

Wow! Jacob undertook a job for Rachel, and even cried aloud with no shame whatsoever. As I will expound on later, he even worked for her father for fourteen years because of her (so, if he was infatuated with Rachel, he went way beyond that stage of love, authenticating his love for her). For him to do all these, the dude must have been very endeared to her.

This passage probably explains why he was attracted to her:

...but Rachel had a beautiful figure and a lovely face. (Genesis 29:17 NLT)

In other words, baby girl was "thick!"

Wouldn't it be nice in this day and age to see an attractive lady and just walk up to her and plant your lips on hers? I'm sure the fellas are with me on this one. That would be hilarious wouldn't it? At least—until she smacks you back into the Old Testament.

CHAPTER THREE
Understand What Love Does

In the previous chapter I discussed six things that love is. Not only do we need to know what love is, we also need to know what love does. And it's with this in mind that I address four things that it does, in this chapter.

1. Love Forgives.

Knowing that love is not a feeling or based on emotions, and knowing that love does not take account of wrongs or hold grudges, it is fitting to say that love forgives. Since true love is not based on conditions, love already has made the decision and portrayed the attitude to forgive just like Jesus did for us. True love does not hold on to past or present offence. Love forgives any wrongdoing whether the perpetrator of the offence asks for forgiveness or not.

Above all things have intense and unfailing love for one another, for love covers a multitude of sins (forgives and disregards the offenses of others). (1 Peter 4:8 AMP)

Hate stirs up trouble, but love forgives all offenses. (Proverbs 10:12 GNB)

2. Love Gives.

Not only does love forgive, it also gives. I said that love is a sacrifice, an investment and a fruit; all of which are given. When you sacrifice your life for someone you are giving your life for the person. When you invest your money you're giving your money to garner a profit. The fruit of love was given to us by God's Spirit in us. Therefore, love gives. *"For God so loved the world that he gave...."*

The amount of love you have is directly influenced by how much love you give. It's a paradox, but it's true: The only way to hold on to love is to give it away.[16]

If you operate in true love, just like our Father who art in heaven gave us His only Son's life as a gift, and Jesus in turn gave us grace, faith, salvation and the Holy Spirit as gifts, then you should also give gifts in demonstration of your love to your mate. You should give gifts such as yourself, your time, and your touch. Give your undivided attention, affirmation, encouragement and support. Give your money, even your reading glasses—if you wear them.

You should also share your straw with your mate to have the last sip of virgin piña colada. If applicable, share your dentures to help your beloved eat the last piece of granola bar. Sometimes "give-in" to the one you love. The only thing that your love for your mate should not give—is "up"; because love does not give up.

Although love gives, you should be mindful that just because someone gives you gifts, it doesn't mean the person loves you. Perhaps you know that some men, and women, too, give gifts with strings attached. Like a guy who gives gifts just to get under a lady's Victoria's secret, and divulge her secret to his peers as a way to express his bragging rights.

Anybody can give without loving, but nobody can love without giving because true love gives.

3. Love Communicates.
Love also operates on the premise that:

...'It is more blessed to give than to receive.' (Acts 20:35)

Give, and it will be given to you.... (Luke 6:38)

The last statement supports the investment nature of love, as giving to someone will result in someone giving back to you. And in reference to the subject of love, giving love to your mate should lead your mate to reciprocate love back to you.

If you want to be inundated with love, become a love waterfall, always pouring it on other people.[17]

Since love gives and receives, this means that love is a two-way street. More so, when you consider that communication also involves giving and receiving, speaking and listening, sending and returning, then communication is also a two-way street. Therefore love communicates. In communicating, love does something to elicit a response. Paraphrasing and revisiting *1 John 4:19*, God communicated His love to us first, which elicited a response from us in loving Him back.

4. Love Waits Patiently.
According to the *Today's English Version* of the Bible (Good News Bible), the first thing said about love in *1 Corinthians 13:4* is that *love is patient*. The New King James Version of the same chapter and verse says *love suffers long*, the Amplified Version says *love endures long, and is patient*. In other words, true love endures or waits—patiently.

I am very impressed with Jacob's patience for Rachel. He suffered or endured fourteen long years of hard work for Laban, Rachel's father, because of Rachel. He even worked another six years for her father's flock. He suffered long, endured long, or waited patiently to marry Rachel. And why did he do this? Because he loved her.[18]

Don't Misconstrue Love for Lust
Now that we know that love is unconditional, a decision made, an attitude portrayed, a sacrifice, an investment and a fruit. And know what it

does: it forgives, gives, communicates and waits—patiently, we can understand love even further by knowing what it is not and what it doesn't do. Often, lust is misconstrued for love, and love is also misappropriated to be expressed in "any" sexual activity. Well, this is not true. Love is not lust, and it does not do premarital sex.

Sex is not a part of love, when it is the expression of lust.[19]

God made everything, sex inclusive. Therefore, God authored sex; and like everything else He made, He made it good—in fact very good. Did I hear an Amen! If God didn't make sex good, most of us, if not all of us, would never been in existence. In order to facilitate the procreation and multiplication of mankind, I believe God made sex passionate. Considering the work involved in raising children, if sex was not exciting, although some people are circumventing having kids but having sex thanks to modern biotechnology, I don't think anyone would have children.

I believe that God made sex feel good as an extra incentive coupled with the desire to have children for us to procreate. Since we procreate through sex, culminate intimacy through sex, and consummate the marriage vows through sex—which should take place in a marriage between two people who truly love each other; who will equate, merge or become one; and who'll be partners, agree and live together; then sex was made for love.

It's interesting that sometimes sex is referred to as lovemaking. This implies to me that in having sex you are building and expressing love. However, let's not misconstrue lovemaking for "lust-making." Lovemaking is having sex with love. Lust-making is having sex without love. You are expressing love when having sex with the person you love and should be married to. You are expressing lust when you have sex with a person you do not love.

In discussing sex, marriage, and differentiating between love and lust, I couldn't have said it better than the founder of the Christian Men's Network, Dr. Edwin Louis Cole:

Sex is also an external evidence of an internal work. When two people are joined together in marriage, they become 'one flesh.' Their spirits become united, and they enter into a relationship with each other through faith. The exchange of their vows is a confession of faith that they have entered into a covenant relationship in marriage, and sex is the physical evidence of it. Marriage is a covenant relationship.... Sex is the sign of a covenant relationship between a man and a woman. The covenant is why God gave sex only to those who are married. Sex wasn't made for lusting and getting. It was made for loving and giving.... Sex was given as an act of love, not lust. Lust is perverted love. Love desires to satisfy others, even at the expense of self. Lust desires to gratify self, even at the expense of others. Sex was made for giving. Love gives, lust gets.[20]

Expounding further from that frame of reference, let's look at God and the devil. God is the way, the truth, and the life and He is love. In contrast the devil is a murderer, a liar, a wolf in sheep's clothing who disguises himself as an angel of light. He is the prince of darkness. He represents lust (See John 8:44, 2 Corinthians 11:14, Matthew 7:15). As Dr. Cole pointed out, love gives while lust gets. Jesus said:

The thief comes only in order to kill, steal and destroy. I came that they might have and enjoy life, and have it in abundance, to the full, till it overflows. (John 10:10 AMP)

Knowing that God gives life while the devil's modus operandi is to kill, steal and destroy, then love gives life while lust takes life. Love gives you vitality and fulfillment while lust steals your dignity and lives you with disillusionment. Since Jesus is the truth, Love expresses truth. In contrast, the devil is a liar. Lust expresses a lie. Lust disguising itself as love just as the prince of darkness, the devil, disguises himself as an angel of light, is a lie, a perversion, a counterfeit.

Love is patient, but lust is impatient. Love is selfless, but lust is selfish. Love has self-control, but lust lacks self-control. Love is benevolent, but lust is malevolent and violent. Since love gives life, then love invigorates. But since lust steals dignity, virginity and also kills and destroys life, then lust violates.

Moreover, love communicates while lust excommunicates. As mentioned before, love communicates in giving or investing of itself, sacrificially and unselfishly, which prompts a similar response of love in return. However, lust excommunicates like someone is excommunicated after being exploited by being used to gratify someone else's sexual desire. In addition, bearing the brunt of somebody's lust tends to make you excommunicate or isolate yourself from everybody else. In some cases, the lives of victims of lust have been permanently excommunicated or taken.

The words of Psychologist Dr. Robin Smith, vividly reinforce the character of love, which is in sharp contrast to lust:

Love doesn't batter. Love doesn't demean. Love doesn't send you to the emergency room. Love doesn't huddle with you in a corner, crying your eyes out. Love doesn't scare the wits out of you. Love doesn't make you wish you were dead. If you believe it does, then you're living a lie. Love is gentle, it is kind, it doesn't keep score of wrongdoings. Love forgives, it repents and shows remorse, it changes its way when it has gone down the wrong path. Love affirms and makes room for differences; it makes safety and honor its backbone, and a sense of aliveness its gift.[21]

Having deliberated on love thus far, I hope that you have a better understanding of love. There is so much more about love that I might not have even scratched its surface. Nonetheless, while you are single, understand that love is unconditional, a decision you make, an attitude, a sacrifice, an investment and a fruit that forgives, gives, communicates and waits patiently. This might explain why some say that, love is as love does.

CHAPTER FOUR

Practice "Save" Sex

Irecall passing by the student commons situated in the heart of the urban arrangement of my alma mater, Virginia Commonwealth University, over a decade ago. While maneuvering myself through student traffic, two words from sentences displayed on a banner set up by a student organization, Inter-Varsity Christian Fellowship, caught my attention. Those words have been implanted in my memory ever since. The words were "save sex."

I cracked a smile as the meaning of those words began to unfold in my thoughts. In this chapter the relevance and significance of those words cannot be overemphasized. In essence, sex was to be saved—for marriage. While you are single, save sex for the person you are going to marry—the right mate for you. This will save you from the heartache of giving yourself to the wrong person, at the wrong time, and in a wrong way, all of which cannot be protected by "safe sex."

True love waits patiently. If you truly love someone you'd wait patiently for the person to be ready to marry you while God prepares you to be a suitable spouse for the individual, too. You've probably heard this before, but allow me to recapitulate. Sex is for marriage and having it outside marriage is sexual immorality.

...It's good for a man to have a wife, and for a woman to have a husband. Sexual drives are strong, but marriage is strong enough to contain

them and provide for a balanced and fulfilling sexual life in a world of
sexual disorder.... (1 Corinthians 7:2-6 MSG)

"What is the big deal about having sex before marriage?" you might ask.
"After all, I'm not hurting anybody," you might say. Gentleman or lady, you
are displeasing God. You are inadvertently hurting yourself and the person
you're sleeping with. You're hurting your chances of finding the right mate
for your life—God's best for you. God's best is the best person God desires
to give you as a mate. A helpmeet for you; a spouse most suitable for you.
For this individual to be God's best, the person must be submitted to God.
God won't give you someone who chooses to obey Him when you choose
not to do likewise. If God did this He would perjure Himself, because He
said:

Do not try to work together as equals with unbelievers, for it cannot be
done. How can right and wrong be partners? How can light and darkness
live together? How can Christ and the Devil agree? What does a Believer
have in common with an unbeliever? (2 Corinthians 6:14-15 GNB)

That passage is not necessarily saying that you should not work at your
job with people who do not believe in Christ. Notice it said "as equals," notice the term "partners," notice "live together" and the word, "agree." When
you get married to someone, you two become one. You become equal or
equate each other. You become partners with each other. And you both
should live together. Basically you two should be in agreement with each
other. However, this will not work if one believes in Christ and the other
does not.

Perhaps you're aware of sexual relations that ensued between a believer
and an unbeliever; even, between Christians outside of marriage. Make
no mistake about this. God did not endorse it. God had nothing to do with
it. The parties of their own free will indulged in the act; either, presump-
tuously or ignorantly. If you have transgressed against God by practicing
sexual immorality, acknowledge your wrongdoing to God. Ask Him to for-

give you, repent, and He will clean your slate completely. Having done this, stick your chest out, square your shoulders, keep your head up and move on, as you are back on track with Him.

God's instruction to us to refrain from premarital sex is not designed to restrict us from having fun; rather, to protect us from getting conned.

I believe sex in marriage is somewhat equivalent to receiving an excellent benefits package from a company you work for. In most cases, people don't look for employment in a particular company based on how hard they would work for that company. Rather, they look for a good benefits package. They look for how much money they will be paid, how much paid vacation they will get, and how many sick days they'll get off. They also look for dental, vision, and other health care benefits. All these perks motivate them to work for the company, and perhaps, ease the stress they will deal with in working for them. Though you should not get married solely because you want to have sex, making love to your mate is an excellent benefit that comes with the company that demands some work. The company is made up of you two. It's made up of your companionship and partnership in holy matrimony.

In addition, just like we eat to live and not live to eat, sex is for marriage but marriage is not—just for sex. God only permits sex to take place in a marriage. Even so, marriage is way more than just having sex. If everybody waited to get married before being physically intimate, making love to your spouse would be something enthusiastic to look forward to. Prior to getting married you should have a general idea about your prospect's personality, not the individual's sexuality. Your anticipation of fulfilling your desire to know the person sexually motivates you toward your marriage. However, if you had sex before marriage what is there "exclusively" to really look forward to when you get married? Having children? Yes, them too—that's if you don't have them already. Is there anything else? Whatever else, it couldn't be sex because you've already explored and exhausted that romantic surprise. More sex? Gentleman or lady, how good could it get? If you or both of you had previous partners, and then find out that intimacy with your spouse was not as good as the ones you had in your previous relationships, what then? Divorce?

I might be wrong. You might be looking forward to unveiling premarital masks, negotiating who washes dishes and takes out the trash. You might be looking forward to fighting over squeezing the top of the toothpaste tube instead of the bottom and not putting the toilet seat down. You might be eagerly relishing the opportunity to take your bath while your nose receptors are tap-dancing to the smell of the doodle forced out by your spouse's contracting abdominal muscles, grunts, and off-pitch singing of the song, *I've got the power*—while your mate is doing his or her number two on the commode.

I don't mean to overemphasize sex in marriage because many experts (married people) imply that you can only have but so much sex. Regardless, I've heard people say "you need to test the waters. You need to know what you're getting first." I suspect people say this so that they can end up marrying someone who's very good in bed.

Such statements are fabricated by the devil to lure people to live in sin. Let's take for instance a man and a woman, both of whom choose to be obedient to God. In doing so, they both abstain from having sex before marriage. As a result they maintain their virginity. They get married and become physically intimate for the first time. Since each of them did not have sex before marriage how would they know if their lovemaking was ecstatic or boring? On what criteria would they judge their intimacy? None. So what did they miss by not having sex before marriage? Nothing!

Another lie the enemy promotes is the claim that everybody is doing it. Nope! Everybody is not having premarital sex. I thank God that in the twenty first century, at 37 years old, having lived in the United States for close to nineteen years to the time of this writing, and been exposed to all kinds of temptations that compelled me to do the contrary, I have not been intimate with any woman in my life.

I was a virgin before I got married. I was more virgin than a virgin strawberry daiquiri with the whip cream and cherry on top! As far as sleeping with a woman was concerned, I was not just wet behind the ears, I was trying to stay afloat the water, which was neck deep. I thank God that He sent me my wife who became the "lifeguard" that took me out of the ocean of celibacy. She too was a virgin before we got married. We take no credit for our abstinence. All the credit goes to the Lord. Thanks to prayers from our parents, sisters, brothers, other family members, friends and other well-wishers. All their intercession allowed God to orchestrate some divine preventive measures for us.

Please don't get me wrong. Prior to getting married, I wanted to do the *do*—and I ain't talking about drinking mountain dew! Before I yielded myself to God and His purpose for my life, I wanted to have sex. Nevertheless, I chose to wait for my wife. I thank God that He didn't allow me to go past knowing the names of some of the women I contemplated on sleeping with. The ladies I liked didn't like me; and the one's that did, I didn't like them enough to have sex with them.

Despite my very questionable morality, I declined pursuing the ladies I desired to have sexual relations with. This was because they claimed that they had boyfriends. Though, they might have lied about this. Eventually, I came to my senses. What was the point in not enjoying life on earth as most people see it and still face the potential of living eternity apart from God? With that in mind, while I was single, I rededicated my life back to God and told Him that He had to do something about my raging desire to sin with, and against women. Guess what? He did.

Through God's help I was able to abstain from premarital sex. I'll share later how He helped me maintain myself. If you are not a virgin, please don't feel condemned. My intention is not to make you feel worthless. You are not. God does not love me anymore than He loves you. I just wanted to inform you that in this day and age there are people—men and women alike— who choose to do things God's way, despite the opposition.

Just because you're not a virgin "physically," doesn't mean that God won't bless you with His best for you. As long as you connect or stay connected with Him and yield to His will, I'm not better off than you are. Though I was a virgin, I had messed up foolishly in other areas of my life as well. God forgave me of everything I did wrong when I asked Him to. He'll do the same for you when you ask for His forgiveness. [22] Confess your sins to Him and forsake them. Take comfort in this:

Therefore if any person is (ingrafted) in Christ (the Messiah) he is a new creation (a new creature altogether); the old (previous moral and spiritual condition) has passed away. Behold, the fresh and new has come! (2 Corinthians 5:17AMP)

Although you still have the same physical body, you have a new spirit courtesy of your relationship with Jesus. The old way of sexual immorality is gone and the new way of sexual purity is formed. Therefore, you can see yourself as a virgin, "spiritually."

Continuing on potential reasons why we shouldn't have premarital sex, imagine that you are about to get married to someone. You are so excited about introducing this individual to your best friend. To your utter dismay you discover that your best friend has been physically intimate with your fiancé or fiancée. How would you feel faced with such information about the person you're about to marry?

Without God's intervention, how would you feel or how did it feel seeing previous sex partners while married to someone else? How would you feel or how did it feel knowing that somebody knows and perhaps told your intimate story, and that person was never your spouse? This would've never happened to anybody had individuals saved sex for marriage.

You might acknowledge and understand that sexual relations before marriage is wrong. Knowing this, you probably have the desire to obey God. Unfortunately, the temptation of premarital sex is strong and often causes people to err by yielding to it. How do you deal with this?I empathized with this situation. I also dealt with this struggle almost every day.

Television, music, and our society in general, does not make things easier. Understand, however, that with the devil all *sins* are possible. But most importantly, with God all things are possible. With the devil you will sin; with God you can overcome sin. Jesus already conquered it on your behalf. It's up to you to know this. Believe it and act like it is so—because—so it is:

For whatever is born of God is victorious over the world; and this is the victory that conquers the world, even our faith. Who is it that is victorious over (that conquers) the world but he who believes that Jesus is the Son of God (who adheres to, trusts in, and relies on that fact)? (1 John 5:4-5 AMP)

There is a struggle in resisting the temptation to sin. Notwithstanding, the aftermath of yielding to sin is worse than the struggle itself. Dr. Cole put it this way:

The torment of the temptation to sin is nothing to compare with the torment of the consequence of that sin.[23]

If you disagree with this, ask that person who contracted a sexually transmitted disease or diseases, or that single father, but mostly mother, who went through hell on earth in raising that child conceived out of wedlock, or the other mother who aborted the child and still has nightmares about it. Ask the lady who is unable to bear children now that she's married—due to complications from a previous abortion, or the baby who was left in the trash. Now think about the families of these victims. I understand that some of these situations have occurred without sexual immorality. But some others have.

In his comments about Samson and his indulgence in sexual immorality, Pastor and Author Jentezen Franklin reinforces the repercussions and deception of sexual misconducts:

Samson learned that sin has a binding effect, a blinding effect, and a grinding effect.... Sexual sin only shows you the excitement and immediate gratification; it never shows you the sexually transmitted diseases that ravage the body. Satan only shows you the prodigal son's hotel suite, never his pig pen. Satan only shows you his entrance, never the exit.[24]

Dr. Cole reinforced his point when he said:

Sin always promises to serve and please, but only desires to enslave and dominate.[25]

Do you want God's best or do you want the world's worst? With God's help you can abstain from sexual sin. If you are going to be resisting it with God's help, then you're going to be doing it with His words in the scriptures. His words are the instructions that will help you prevail against premarital sex and guide you to the right mate, whom you'll eventually have unrestricted sex with. Before you can resist anything, you have to be obedient and submitted to God first, as mentioned below:

Therefore submit to God. Resist the devil and he will flee from you. (James 4:7 NKJV)

Although we stumble sometimes, God understands that we desire to do right, obey Him, and adhere to His words. He acknowledged this and gave a way out of this situation when he made this statement:

All of you must keep awake (give strict attention, be cautious and active) and watch and pray, that you might not come into temptation. The spirit indeed is willing but the flesh is weak. (Matthew 26:41 AMP)

Your spirit is willing to do the right thing, but the natural desires of your flesh are willing to do wrong. Your heart and spirit is to obey God; but your flesh says "No!!!" With this in mind, it's best for you to feed your spirit and starve your flesh. The revelation from the following text recommends this mode of action.

For he who sows to his own flesh (lower nature, sensuality) will from the flesh reap decay and ruin and destruction, but he who sows to the spirit will from the spirit reap eternal life. (Galatians 6:8 AMP)

In addition to praying so that you will not enter into temptation, there are four things that you can do to help yourself refrain from sexual immorality. These are the guidelines I followed to save myself for my wife. I still follow them to *keep* myself with my wife. Let's explore them in the next chapter.

CHAPTER 5
Avoid, Resist, Flee…

1. Avoid every appearance of evil

Take control of your feelings. If you don't, the devil will exploit them to get you to transgress. Watch your emotions. Don't allow the enemy to use them to your detriment. Don't put yourself in a position where satan exploits your sensibility and causes you to sin.

Leave no (such) room or foothold for the devil (give no opportunity to him). (Ephesians 4:27 AMP)

If you are trying to stay away from chocolate chip cookies, you should not be holding the chocolate chip cookie jar. If you are trying to stay away from ice cream, you should not be chitchatting in Baskin Robbins. If you're trying to avoid premarital sex, living with the person of the opposite sex that you're not related or married to is usually not a good idea.

You shouldn't be alone with the individual on a huge, soft, richly cushioned black leather love seat, with your head laid on the person's thighs—in a room dimly lit with a tint of red, thanks to the red candles also responsible for the air smelling like strawberries and cream—while a soft ballad by Norah Jones, India Arie, Musiq, Jill Scott, Celine Dion, Luther Vandross or even Barry White is playing in the background. Giving such a scenario, the devil will have a field day in pushing your sensuous buttons to exude and exchange fluids with the person in the "lust boat" with you, thanks to your raging hormones, which are now acting like pheromones.

Don't give the devil a chance or a foothold to exploit your emotions. If you give him an inch, he won't ask, but he'll demand and might get more than a yard of you. Give him a crack in your frame and he'll try to make a canyon of you. Avoid being in a situation like that. The scripture reads:

Abstain from all appearance of evil. (1 Thessalonians 5:22 KJV)

If you're faced with a situation that looks evil or can cause you to displease God, avoid it. I hope you remember Jesus saying that you should pray not to enter into temptation. He does not want you to put yourself in a compromising position. I heard Dr. Joyce Meyer say something like this some time ago, "Temptation will come to you but don't go to it." When temptation comes to you then you apply the next point.

2. Resist the devil

You should not give the devil a chance; even so, there are some things that you are just going to have to withstand from him. It's only God who can help you stand against any temptation the devil brings your way. It's in your best interest that you're submitted to Him. Besides, you're going to need God's words to remind the devil that he's a liar. He's been defeated. He should take his whopping like a man as he writhes in pain under your feet.[26]

Jesus demonstrated to us how to resist temptation when the devil came to tempt him. He was first submitted to God, considering the fact that He left heaven and came to earth to embark on his world rescue mission. The Spirit of God directed Him to a place, the wilderness, where the devil came to deceive Him. He resisted satan by using His words in scripture.

The devil started his deception by trying to get the Lord to prove His identity when he asked Him to turn stone to bread. But Christ used His words in the scriptures to tell him that man shall not live by bread alone but by every word of God. The devil stepped it up a notch when he offered Jesus the world and in exchange, he asked Jesus to worship him. But Jesus resisted him by telling him to buzz off as the scriptures said that God was the only one to be worshipped and served. The devil was relentless. He is with you too. He tried to lure Christ to commit suicide by asking him to jump off the highest point of a temple. He even quoted a verse from the scriptures that assured Jesus that God would send His angels to catch Him so that He wouldn't injure Himself from His descent. But Jesus basically told him that the scriptures also said that God should not be tempted.

After Jesus rebuffed all his deceptive advances, satan flew away until another opportunity made itself available. Jesus was submitted to God. He resisted the devil with His Father's words or His words, since He is God, and the devil departed.[27] This is a very good and practical example of how the devil comes at you, and how you should resist him and cause him to take flight. He'll come again, but just give him a recap of what you did to him before. It's very important that you know the Word for yourself. It's in your best interest that you read the Bible and ask God to give you understanding of the scriptures you read, and apply them to your life.

Even the devil knows scripture. He used it against Jesus. He must have forgotten that Jesus authored the words he used. It's advantageous for you to know the Author of the words that you should use against the devil. This is why you submit to Him first, and He trains you on how to use them to resist the enemy. If satan had the animal boldness to use God's words against God, what do you think he'll do against you? Are you going to let the enemy use your weapon against you? It's like a roach using raid against a human. How preposterous!

The devil has been successful in using this tactic, and he continues to employ this means to deceive mankind. Just for reminders, he used God's instruction—His words to Adam and Eve against them and succeeded. As a result, you and I have to take that exam over and over again. He might have won that battle, but he lost the war. Thanks to Christ for what He did on the cross.

There are times, especially in the case of resistance to sex, that you don't just resist but drastically exempt yourself out of a compromising situation. Perhaps you might have tried to avoid being in such a quandary, but you found yourself in it anyway. Then you resisted but the opposing temptation kept on fighting back more seductively and vehemently. In this case, which is the next point, you *run for your life*!

3. Flee youthful lust

Run away from the temptation. Get yourself out as fast as you can. It might cost you, but it'll cost you more if you yield to the temptation. Thus, this text reads:

Shun youthful lust and flee from them, and aim at and pursue righteousness (all that is virtuous and good, right living, conformity to the will of God, in thought, word, and deed); (and aim at and pursue) faith, love, (and) peace (harmony and concord with others) in fellowship with all (Christians), who call upon the Lord out of a pure heart. (2 Timothy 2:22 AMP)

Joseph is one of the best examples of an individual who ran from a lustful situation. The Bible infers that this dude was hot! I guess that explains why his boss's wife was infatuated with him. She must have felt his heat which ignited the fire that flamed her passion for him. She was feeling him sensually. She was mesmerized by his looks. She wanted to *give it up* to him. I am not talking about a hand clap. But Joseph resisted her advances toward him. He did not want to sin against God. I hope you see that he was submitted to God. Although he had a lot of clout in his master's affairs, being a God-fearing man, he let her know that she was a no-go-zone to him.

Despite his attempts in resisting her, she kept on pressuring him. This went on for a few days. One day, in her state of nymphomania, she grabbed him. Did you notice his response? He didn't indulge in foreplay then retreat saying "you know...I...I...I sh...I...sh...I...shou...shouldn't b...b...be...

be doing this." He didn't pray to God to ask if it was okay to bite into the Egyptian pie. He split!

He took off running! He ran from her, but in doing so, he ran toward God's will. He left his garment in her hands, which she used against him. She falsely reported him to her husband saying that he tried to violate her. Her husband put him in prison.

It cost Joseph about two years for doing the right thing. It will cost you to obey God. You will pay a price to flee youthful lust. But your reward for doing the right thing far exceeds your sacrifice. He might have been in prison for about two years, but he was governor of Egypt for about 80 years.[28] Go figure.

4. Feed your spirit and starve your flesh

If you have not asked Jesus into your life, I encourage you to. These guidelines cannot work for you as effectively as they can if you don't know the Lord. It's beneficial for you to know the Author of the words that will help you overcome sin. It's to your advantage to have faith in the person who gave you victory over the world. That person is Jesus Christ.

We humans are triune beings. We have a physical body, the house in which our spirits, our *true self*—the other aspect of our being, resides. We also have a soul or a mind that is connected to our true self. When you become a Christian, your human nature or flesh is still the same, but you have a new spirit fashioned after the Spirit of God that takes up residence in you.[29] As you develop your relationship with God, let your mind be renewed by what He says to you through his words in the Bible.[30]

I mentioned previously that feeding the sinful desires of the flesh results in decay, ruin and destruction. It results in sinfulness and its consequences. Whereas feeding your spirit, the *real you*, the born again person who is now fashioned after God's Spirit, will lead to eternal life. Feeding your spirit helps you emanate Christ-like attributes. It results in you living Godly and therefore overcoming temptations that come your way.

Bearing that in mind, it's advantageous for you to have your spirit be in control over your flesh. It's beneficial for you to let your spirit dominate your natural fleshly desires so that you do the right thing. The following scripture alludes to this conclusion.

What I say is this: let the spirit direct your lives, and you will not satisfy the desires of the human nature. (Galatians 5:16 GNB)

In order to let your born again spirit direct your life, you need to empower it while you curtail your flesh. In addition to avoiding, resisting, and fleeing from sexual immorality, what kind of things can you expect to begin to manifest in your character when your spirit is in control?

But the fruit of the (Holy) Spirit (the work which His presence within accomplishes) is love, joy (gladness), peace, patience (an even temper, forbearance), kindness, goodness (benevolence), faithfulness, gentleness (meekness, humility), self-control (self-restraint, continence), against such things there is no law (that can bring a charge). (Galatians 5:22-23 AMP)

On the other hand, what kind of things manifest when your flesh is in control?

Now the doings (practices) of the flesh are clear (obvious); they are immorality, impurity, indecency, idolatry, sorcery, enmity, strife, jealousy, anger (ill temper), selfishness, divisions (dissensions), party spirit (factions, sects with peculiar opinions, heresies), envy, drunkenness, carousing, and the like. I warn you beforehand, just as I did previously, that those who do such things shall not inherit the kingdom of God. (Galatians 5:19-21AMP)

The result of being directed by your spirit is Godliness while that of yielding to your flesh is sinfulness. Therefore, strengthen your spirit and weaken your flesh. Before exhibiting the nature of fleshly desires, your flesh has to be aroused by a source which serves as the root cause that stimulates it to go berserk. It's to your benefit that you cut off that source. It's in your best interest that you unplug the power supply to your flesh. In order to kill something efficiently, it's to be killed from its roots. Thus:

And if your eye causes you to sin, pluck it out. It is better for you to enter the kingdom of God with one eye, rather than having two eyes, to be cast into hell fire. (Mark 9:47 NKJV)

I don't think that text is telling us to cut out our eyes literally if they cause us to sin. I believe there is an underlying principle here. Amongst other authentic applications of the verse, I believe it's applicable to what you allow your eye to see consistently. If what you see with your eyes causes you to transgress, cut it off! For example, pornography.

Sometimes what the eye sees somewhat determines how the body responds to it. If your eye sees the right thing, your body will be inclined to follow suite. Conversely, if your eye majors on the wrong thing, it will instigate your body to act accordingly.

What is submitted to in life grows stronger, what is resisted grows weaker.[31]

That is why one should abstain from pornography. This feeds your flesh through your eyes. Therefore, avoid, resist, and flee from pornography. When I said starve your flesh, I don't mean physical food, though this might be necessary when fasting. What I'm talking about is preventing your eyes from watching things like porn that stimulate your fleshly desires to practice sexual lewdness.

Excess alcohol and drugs feed one's flesh too. They make you act in a way that you would not normally act when in your right mind. You feed your flesh and starve your spirit when you indulge in such. Furthermore, what are you hearing? What are you listening to? The music you listen to seeps into your being. Music laced with vulgar, seductive, and sadistic lyrics stimulate your flesh through your ears to respond accordingly. Conversely, song lyrics that have no profanity and are gloriously inspirational edify you.

Also, who are you hanging with? And what is the nature of their conversation with you? Are they feeding your flesh or are they feeding your spirit? The character and habits of your friends, buddies, girls, boys, posse, road dawgs or clique can affect yours, positively or negatively. Their lyrics also infiltrate your being. This passage authenticates this:

Do not be misled: "Bad company corrupts good character."(1 Corinthians 15:33)

The Amplified Bible puts it this way:

Do not be deceived and misled! Evil companionships (communion, associations) corrupt, and deprave good manners and morals and character.

Knowing this, it's necessary for you to take inventory of what you're watching, what and who you're listening to and hanging around, and ascertain whether they build you up or bring you down. Then make the necessary adjustments. It's advantageous for you to avoid, resist and refrain from associations that hinder you from fulfilling God's purpose for your life. Instead, you should embrace those that lead you to God and keep you with Him.

Part of God's plan for your life is to give you the right mate. Are you going to allow the wrong friends to prevent you from finding the right person for your life? Do you want a counterfeit or do you want the real deal?

Do you want what the world recommends or do you want what the Word recommends? The world's worst or God's best, you choose.

The following are examples of those who yielded to their natural fleshly desires and reaped the repercussions of yielding to them. I'll start with Lot, Abraham's nephew. Thanks to uncle Abraham's intercession on their behalf, Lot and his two daughters were the only survivors after God destroyed Sodom and Gomorrah, the cities where they lived. Lot's daughters thought that there were no men in the world to marry. In order to bear children and preserve their father's lineage, Lot's daughters connived to get their father to have sex with them. How did they do this? They fed his flesh—with alcohol.

They got him drunk. They both slept with him while he was intoxicated. As a result they were impregnated by him. Which father in his right mind would have sex with his daughters? Notice I said right mind. Lot wasn't in his right state of mind. Why? Because his flesh was in control, thanks to the excess wine his daughters pumped into his system.[32]

Dear reader, what more can I say that you do not already know about alcohol intake and its ramifications? If this is applicable to you, perhaps you might argue that you only drink sociably. You drink once in a blue moon. Maybe a few brewskis here and there. A couple of tequilas won't hurt, would they? What is it with anyone if you down a few long island iced teas or vodka martinis? After all, they are "shaken, not stirred" like James Bond's. Friend, you might make it today; however, if you keep on with your indulgence you might end up with negative consequences.

A little leaven, leavens the whole lump.[33]

Give the devil a crack, and he'll make a canyon of you. A little bit here and there might lead to a whole lot here and there—that's if you're even alive spiritually and physically to even get there. I know the Bible usually talks about drinking alcohol in *excess*; even so, it's in your best interest that you avoid, resist, flee, and starve your flesh from *liquor.* Instead, feed your spirit with the *Savior* through His words to you and for you.

Let's revisit the story of Adam and Eve. Their disobedience started with evil company. The serpent communicated lies, which corrupted Adam and Eve. A little leaven of evil uttered into the ears of Eve leavened the whole lump of herself, her husband and mankind. This includes you and I.

The serpent fed Eve's flesh with his deception. Her natural desires were further aroused when she looked at the tree and contemplated the alleged benefit from eating its fruit. Her eyes might have saturated with water. Her throat might have run dry as she longed for the forbidden fruit. The image of the fruit in all its lusciousness on her retina—the moisture dripping very slowly and mellifluously from its glistening exterior, accentuated by its bright rich color—the thought of sinking her canine in its meat—and the feel of its juice snaking down her esophagus may have proved a temptation too irresistible to reckon with.

And what was Adam doing? Instead of head-butting the serpent for flirting with his woman, and repudiating his comments to her which was feeding her flesh, he should have been feeding her spirit with God's words to him, for them. Rather, just like she was checking out the tree's fruit, knowing how some of us men are, it stands to reason that he was checking out Eve's body's fruits. You know what I mean? In other words, he was feeding his flesh too.

Please don't get too sacrilegious on me. This is just my take, okay? You can refute my implication that Adam was checking out Eve because the Bible did say that they were naked and not ashamed. Yeah, I bet Adam was not ashamed seeing his wife naked. Perhaps that explains why he lost his focus.

Whichever case, the moral of this account is that their flesh was fed by what they *heard,* and *saw,* courtesy of the devil's bad company. This resulted in the destruction of the integrity of their relationship with God, and compromised God's perfect will for mankind. Since God is always ahead of satan, He repaired the breach through Christ. Through Him, *whosoever wills* is able to be reconciled to God.

Last but not the least, is David. The greatest king Israel ever had. He was considered a man of war. Even so, what is a man of war, Israel's commander-in-chief, doing on the roof of his house peeping like Tom at a woman taking her bath, while his men were at war probably dodging sharp steel blades of spears and swords aimed at their throats—getting dragged around and trampled on by horses—on dirt mixed with horse poop and mostly Ammonite cadavers? He was feeding his flesh.

The sight of the naked and very beautiful woman, Bathsheba, who might have possessed a voluptuous body etched with more curves than a *Lamborghini Countach,* sparked the natural desires of his flesh. This drove him to inquire about her and give her a bootie call.

He fulfilled his lust for her by having sex with her. And what was the result of yielding to his flesh?

1. Adultery, since she had her own husband Uriah, who was one of David's men in battle. 2. A child out of wedlock, since he impregnated her. 3. Deception, as he brought Uriah back from the battle and tried to cajole him by wining and dining him until he got drunk. Furthermore, he asked him to go home to his wife, probably believing he'll sleep with her and it'll look like David's child was really Uriah's. 4. Murder, since David's deception did not work, he sent Uriah back to the war, and got him killed by instructing the captain of his troops to place him right in the heat of the battle. 5. Death. The death of the child was another consequence of David's sin. There were more deaths in David's family, and subsequent generations, because of his iniquity.[34]

With these examples in mind, it is best for you to avoid, resist, and flee anything that incites your natural evil desires so that you can keep your flesh in control. I encourage you to embrace God's guidelines, which inspire your Christ-like spirit to hearken unto His voice. God's Word is the food for your spirit, gasoline that fuels your spirit, and the oxygen your spirit breathes. It is the life line on which your spirit thrives, and the Viagra that drives your spirit. It's His sayings in the Bible that inspire Godly attitudes, invigorates Godly character, which results in Godly actions.

Feast your eyes on His words by reading your Bible. Vibrate your ear drums with His sayings by speaking them to yourself, listening to messages from your Pastor, and other dedicated Christians you know of—either personally, or through television, radio and the internet. Also confirm if their messages are true by cross-checking them in your Bible. You can also be edified by listening to good inspirational music like gospel. Be it Praise & Worship, Classical, Jazz, Rock, Contemporary, Pop, R&B, Hip Hop, and Country just to mention a few.

At all times carry faith as a shield; for with it you will be able to put out all the burning arrows shot by the evil one. And accept salvation as a helmet, and the Word of God as the sword which the Spirit gives you. (Ephesians 6:16-17 GNB)

God has given you His Word as your offensive weapon. It's your spiritual baseball bat or 2 by 2 for the devil's head. When the devil comes to tempt you through premarital sex and the like, you withdraw from your being, which should have been fed with God's words, your nourishment and strength, and use it to *Jet Li* him like Jesus exemplified for us when He was tempted in the wilderness.

If the devil tempts you through your emotions and natural desires to sleep with someone to whom you're not married, don't give in. Resist him and speak against him by telling him that the scriptures say that you should abstain from sexual immorality. God is your new roommate in your new self—your born again spirit. The enemy was your old roommate in your old self. Remind him how he kept your house filthy and left you with all the bills of condemnation, which you could never pay. But you came to your senses and kicked him out with all his belongings when you asked Jesus to be your new roommate.

Remind the enemy that he tried not to move out, but when Jesus moved in, Jesus kicked him out through your window of obedience. Laugh out loud as you recall how he got tossed out of your life. Replay the scene in which Christ thrust him out of your spirit more violently than DJ Jazzy Jeff often got tossed out of Phillip Banks' house in the popular sitcom, *Fresh Prince of Bel Air.*

Tell him how much you love your new roommate who is peaceful, loving and not rowdy. Unlike your old roommate, your new roommate doesn't frustrate you but elevates you. Unlike your old roommate's parties that left you with shame, a hangover, and caused you to throw up— your new roommates parties left you with His "Name," made you an over comer, and caused you to grow up.

Tell him that your new roommate like the *godfather*, since He's your *God* and your *Father*, made you a deal which you could not refuse. He paid off *all* the rent and bills of sin you owed, with His blood. He cleaned out your house, and you're not trying to offend your heaven-sent roommate by having premarital sex. Actually, it is God's house now, since He bought it with a price, repaired all the damages the satan caused and protects it.[35] Tell him you'll be breaching your contract with your new land-*Lord* by giving the enemy access back into yourself through the sinful act. Tell the devil that you are obeying God's words; therefore, you are saving sex for marriage.

If the enemy continues to bug you through your friends or acquaintances by asking you why it is a big deal to you now, since you've had premarital sex before, tell him that you're not that person that erred before.

You're a different person now. If he tells you that you're lying and that you're the same person since you still feel those same old desires, then, tell him that unlike him who's still the same and a liar, you're a new person in Christ. The old *you* has been done away with. Tell him you walk by faith and not by sight.[36] Tell him you go by God's Word which is the source of your faith.[37]

You do not go by the devil's words, like the ones he said to Eve, which exploited her sight to disobey God. In essence, you don't conduct yourself strictly by how you feel or what comes naturally. You conduct yourself by what God said, which comes spiritually. While you are at it, ask the devil how the sole of your timberland whose embedded logo is the Tree of Life—Christ, feels on his head, which is writhing in excruciating pain as he flees from you.

That was just a brief dramatization of how you can apply God's Word against the devil when He speaks to you through your *mind* and emotions. You need to know the scriptures to be able to do this. It's the source of your faith, your strength, your support, and your courage against the devil's attacks. Your spirit needs them to keep your flesh under. With you in control over your flesh, then you're in a better position to save sex for marriage. Saving sex for marriage is truly the one and only ideal way to really practice safe sex; because, in all honesty, the answer to safe sex is not the condom but the *kingdom*—of God.

If we dissect the word "kingdom," we get, "king-dom." Definitions of the word "kingdom" include: "the territory or country subject to a king or queen; the dominion of a monarch; and the sphere in which one is king or has control."[38] Looking at these definitions and the word itself, we can conclude that a kingdom means an area under the dominion of a king. Therefore, according to my reasoning subscribed and substantiated by scriptures I referred to previously, the answer to safe sex is a King having dominion over when you have sex (marriage), and who you have it with (your spouse). That king is Jesus.

To have more clarity about what I'm saying, you might need to redefine what safe sex means to you. If safe sex only means having sexual activity at anytime, with anybody, in anyway and anywhere—while you're being protected from diseases and unwanted babies—then the condom and other devices designed to achieve that definition of safe sex are sufficient. All the same, are they sufficient to protect you from the loss of a sense of dignity as a result of sharing yourself with different men or women that you were never married to? Do they protect you from being conned, exploited, and the heartache that goes along with it?

You will be protected from those repercussions if you do things God's way. If you let The King—dom—inate or direct you while you are single, you would not have to worry about unwanted babies, STDs, and other consequences that accompany pre—or extramarital sex. More so, the King guides you to the right mate for your life. When you get married to this individual, with both of you still adhering to God's directives, you wouldn't have to be concerned about infidelity.

The idea of the condom and its affiliates as a means of practicing safe sex are a complete mismatch to God's method of truly practicing safe sex. God's method is save sex for marriage. The condom can never protect the wounds of a broken heart. God can heal those wounds. Therefore, while you are single, practice save sex for marriage.

CHAPTER SIX

Date God First

In our society dating is commonplace. Usually when couples date they are attempting to get to know each other better. The dating scene is also an avenue through which individuals try to find their soul mates, ascertain their compatibility, and build their relationships. I'm not one to overemphasize dating since the Bible doesn't say anything about it as a means of finding a mate. Although some good relationships have evolved from couples who started out dating each other, you don't have to date *forty* different people, call singles' lines, sign-on with online dating services, or enroll as a member of dating clubs in your area in order to find the right person for you.

You don't need to consult Miss Cleo to find your God-sent. You don't need to browse the horoscope section of your local newspaper via your alleged zodiac sign to figure out who is best for you. You don't need to be a guest in a day time talk show to hook up with your childhood sweetheart. It's not necessary for you to audition for a spot in reality dating shows in order to get hitched. And you certainly don't need to interview various individuals under the guise of a date, and check *right* or *wrong* on your mental notepad as a stamp of approval or disapproval—and a means of screening out your prospects and narrowing them down to the right person for you.

You might argue that although the good book doesn't say anything about dating, it doesn't say that it is wrong, either. I concur. Dating is *not* wrong; sometimes, it might just be a waste of time—except, if you date the right person first. This will help you save some sleep, gas mileage, cell phone minutes, dollars, and maybe even your sanity. You'll probably also save yourself from unnecessary disappointments, time for project deadlines or school assignments, professions of love, and of course—your pick up lines, if you date the right person the first time out.

The only way you can accomplish that, though, is to make God your first date. It's best that you date God first because He's the guide to finding the right mate for your life. Not only is He your guide, He's also the best lover. He is love. As you date Him and allow Him to woo you with His love, He shows you true love which enlightens you on what to look for in a prospect, what to expect from him or her, and how to radiate this same love to the person. Besides, if you're into blind dates, you couldn't have a better blind date. He puts a new meaning to the concept of a blind date—since you can't see God when on a date with Him. Also, God is a "hot" date. You can't get any date hotter than God because He's a consuming fire.[39]

By dating God I mean seeking Him, getting to know Him, and spending time with Him. You build your relationship with Him by reading and adhering to His words in His book. Dating God includes attending and committing yourself to a good Bible-based local church where you listen to and learn from your Pastor and peers in Bible study or other "extra-churchicular" functions. And perhaps, other ministries on radio, television and internet broadcasts. You also date God by communicating and complimenting Him through prayers and songs of praise and worship. This is somewhat similar to how couples often communicate and compliment each other during a date.

Although people are encouraged to come out of the closet, I suggest that you go into yours, and pray, cultivating your date with God.[40] Your prayer closet could be your walk-in closet. It could be your room, a quiet spot under the shade of a tree in your favorite park, or your car if you have one. It could also be a rich, green, neatly, mowed lawn juxtaposed to a lake, where you feel God's breeze blow softly through your Jerry curls, greasy fade, corn rows, wig, weave, dreadlocks, receding hairline or afro, which might still have a comb in it. Or blow through braided, blonde, black, red, or brunette hair that may or may not need a touch of Vidal Sassoon.

God is the best date and lover that you can ever have. He is never late for a date. He never stands you up. He always knows what's on your mind, even before you tell Him, if you tell Him. You don't have to wear a special attire to impress Him. He accepts you just as you are. But after dating Him, He won't leave you as you are. He never embarrasses you by being unmannerly or obnoxious during your date with Him. He never ignores you, neither does he disrespect and demean you by blatantly checking out others while on a date with you. This is the best part: He always picks up the tab. Actually, He already picked up the tab on the cross.

He is always available to talk to you. You can call Him anytime, any day and anywhere. Sixty seconds a minute, sixty minutes an hour, twenty-four hours a day, seven days a week, fifty-two weeks a year. He never puts you on hold although you might feel like He does, especially when you're waiting for your mate amongst other "seemingly" unanswered prayers. He's the only lover that does not mind you having an affair with someone else. As long as that someone else is the mate He gave you in marriage. He's the only lover that allows you to express the love He lavished on you to the person He gave you. He even instructs you on how to treat the mate He brought to you. If you have any problem with your mate, He's the only one that can help you solve it. He said:

Therefore I say to you, do not worry about your life, what you will eat or what you will drink; nor about your body, what you will put on. Is not life more than food and the body more than clothing? (Matthew 6:25 NKJV)

Jesus tells us not to worry about basic necessities like clothes to wear and food to eat. He acknowledges that life is more than these things. Life has to do with everything that concerns you. Everything that has to do with your total existence, which must also include the person that you'll be living the rest of your life with. In addition to concerns about those basic needs of life, He's also saying that you should not worry about your mate. He knows you need somebody, but don't worry about who that person is, where that person is, and when you would meet and establish your relationship with that person. Thus, the scriptures read:

> ...*If God gives such attention to the appearance of wildflowers—most of which are never even seen—don't you think he'll attend to you, take pride in you, do his best for you? What I'm trying to do here is to get you to relax, to not be so preoccupied with getting, so you can respond to God's giving. People who don't know God and the way he works fuss over these things, but you know both God and how he works. Steep your life in God-reality, God-initiative, God-provisions. Don't worry about missing out. You'll find all your everyday human concerns will be met. (Matthew 6:30-33 MSG)*

God already knows what you need, but what does He tell you to do? Seek Him first, or should I say date Him first. After doing this then everything else, which must also include your mate would be added to you. He knows you need somebody in your life, but seek Him first, date Him first, get to know Him first, and He'll add that person to you. Always keep in mind that He's your guide to your mate.

When you seek God's kingdom, you allow God the King to have dominion over you. In doing so, He calls the shots. You yield to His proficiency in directing you according to His will, and offer him the liberty to have control of your life. When you let Him direct you in line with His purpose, He's able to lead you to the right person courtesy of your full cooperation with Him. During your date with Him He reveals more of Himself to you. He gives you guidelines that'll help you identify the person He reserved for you. He implores you not to get involved with someone who does not believe in Him. If you're a man He commends you to look out for a woman who's virtuous, not promiscuous, hardworking and reverences Him. A woman who's gracious, excellent, wise, and expresses an attitude of servant hood. A woman who has good understanding and is beautiful to you.[41]

If you're a woman He advises you to look for a man after His own heart. Since you dated God you should know His heart and desire for you. You utilize this information to discern any man that comes your way. God admonishes you to look out for a man that is Christ-like, valorous and faithful. He instructs you to look out for a *just* man, not just a man. A man of wisdom, understanding, vision and integrity. A man who's prayerful, you're attracted to, and of course, employed.[42]

And my God shall supply all your need according to His riches in glory by Christ Jesus. (Philippians 4:19 NKJV)

God already knows your needs. He also supplies them. These needs include having someone to love you and be loved by you. They include having someone to be married to. Someone who's open to your thoughts, soothes your hurts, protects your heart, and encourages your desires. Someone who does not berate you for your failures, celebrates your triumphs, appreciates your time, dime and feelings. Someone who beams at your smile, empathizes with your tears, and embraces your idiosyncrasies.

Trust in the Lord with all your heart; do not depend on your own understanding. Seek his will in all you do, and he will show you which path to take. (Proverbs 3:5-6 NLT)

As you spend time with God and get to know Him you learn to trust Him. You learn not to depend on your understanding of the ideal person for you, but acknowledge Him in everything you do. You completely depend on Him to direct your path to the person He intends for you. You should let Him be responsible for finding the right person for you because anybody can claim, perpetrate to be, and look like the right person for you.

Lots of people claim to be loyal and loving, but where on earth can you find one? (Proverbs 20:6 MSG)

It is only through God that you can find a faithful person. The text below further shows God as the best Person for the marital setup job.

House and riches are the inheritance from fathers, but a wise, understanding, and prudent wife is from the Lord. (Proverbs 19:14 AMP)

The Good News Version of this same scripture simplifies this statement even further:

A man can inherit a house and money from his parents, but only the Lord can give him a sensible wife.

The Message version puts it this way:

House and land are handed down from parents, but a congenial spouse comes straight from God.

If you don't know God, you cannot benefit from this exclusive service. More so:

Whoever does not love does not know God, because God is love. (1 John 4:8)

How can you truly love the person God is going to give you, if you don't know God? You can't truly express and operate in love which is birthed from God if you don't know Him. I presented some information about love, but applying them to yourself would be futile without God in your life. Trying to love without God is like having knowledge without understanding such knowledge. It's like undergoing surgery without a surgeon, taking a prescribed drug without its prescription, or building a house without an architect. Given these situations, you're heading for disaster.

If the Lord does not build the house, the work of the builders is useless.... (Psalm 127:1 GNB)

Unless God builds your marriage by finding the right person for you and directing you on how to build and maintain your relationship with that person, your efforts in building your marriage by yourself will be in vain. It's to your advantage that you have God in your life first, and through your relationship with Him, He serves as an unshakable foundation for your marriage.

For who is God, except the Lord? And who is a rock, except our God? (Psalm 18:31 NKJV)

Anyone who comes to me and listens to my words and obeys them, I will show you what he is like. He is like a man who, in building his house, dug deep and laid the foundation on rock. The river flooded over and hit that house but could not shake it, because it was well built. But anyone who hears my words and does not obey them is like a man who built his house without laying a foundation; when the flood hit that house it fell at once, and what a terrible crash that was! (Luke 6:47-49 GNB)

Without God in your life prior to marriage you stand a reasonable chance of finding the wrong person. And if you marry this individual and you still don't allow God's say-so in your marital affairs, the storms of life will rage and flood your marriage toward the rocks. On the other hand, knowing and trusting God as your Rock and obeying Him regarding your relationship with your spouse amongst other things, helps prevent your marriage from hitting the rocks—since it was built on *The Rock* in the first place. Understand? You're standing on what you could have collided with.

The good book says that men should love their wives like Jesus loves the church and gave His life for her. But a man cannot love his wife like Jesus loves the church if he does not know Jesus. If he does not know the Lord then he does not know how to love like Him. The only way he can love his wife like God loves the church is by knowing God in the first place. This is why you date Him first. In addition, since the church is the body of Christ, a man is supposed to love his wife like he loves his body or himself.[43] This is applicable to a woman as well.

If you don't love yourself how can you love someone else? Why would you not love yourself? Maybe you feel condemnation due to things you've done in the past and even the present. Perhaps you feel you're not physically attractive enough, smart enough, good enough and so forth. Thanks to labels that you've allowed others to place on you—and perhaps, you also placed on yourself. Possibly because you've been abused and abandoned by people who should have loved you, but their actions said otherwise and likely contributed to a low self-esteem. If these apply to you and Jesus is your Lord, you must not know who you really are—and you must not know how special you are.

Whether you know Jesus as your Lord or not, it's imperative that you know that you're somebody because He loves you. Since the Absolute Person of Love loves you, you must be very valuable to Him. He died for you. You must mean something to Him. This is what you should use to measure your value. Whatever you might have done wrong in the past—and even the present, irrespective of its magnitude, He took care of it—all of it—or all of them. You can only benefit from this if you acknowledge, believe and accept Christ and all that His done for you. If you haven't, please do. If you have, know that you're His child, His beloved and very precious to Him.

Since you're worthy of God's love, you're worthy of your love. This should motivate you to view and carry yourself with the dignity and prestige that Jesus placed in you by loving and laying down His life for you. Begin to know who you are by beginning to know the Person who truly loves you. As you begin to know Him, He helps you to know and love yourself. This is God's standard platform from which you launch off to love whomever He brings to you. So take the label off and unwrap your real self. God is love. Spending time with Him offers you the privilege of knowing true love and knowing Him intimately.

While you are single, endeavor to date God first before dating anybody else. Have a relationship with God before embarking on any other relationship. Your relationship with Him helps you understand and know love. It serves as a blueprint that defines, outlines and qualifies how you interact with your mate. Having a relationship with God first, teaches the man who did not know God, how to love his wife like Jesus loved the church and gave His life for her.

CHAPTER SEVEN

Find Out What Makes Relationships Successful

I had just finished watching the movie *Fire Proof* with a group of friends. As I walked out of the theater pondering on some of the lessons that I planned to apply in my life, I was surprised by a comment made by one of the ladies in our entourage. She was disappointed with the movie. Her disappointment was not because the movie was bad. It was because she felt that she watched the wrong movie. The lady had been informed that we were all going to watch a movie, but she did not know that *Fire Proof* was the movie we intended to see. She was disappointed because she was a single lady and she felt that the film was geared toward married people.

You know, I was somewhat taking aback by that comment. At the same time, what the well-meaning lady said only reinforced what I believe is part of the cause of a lot of bad relationships. There are a lot of single people doing things that married people should be doing, while they are single. And there are a lot of married people doing or *dealing* with things that they should have dealt with when they were singles, while they are married. Scores of single adults are dating. Nothing particularly wrong with this. Some are professing love to their significant others, which is awesome. Some are also having sex, which should be for marriage.

"Okay, cool, so what's your point?" you might ask. Well, while some singles are doing things that should be done in marriage, they are *not* doing things that they should be doing while they are single. Consequently, some of such singles end up in marriages where they now have to deal with the things that they should have dealt with as singles. This in turn discourages and distracts them from doing what they should be doing in marriage.

While they were single, dating, hanging out, having physical intimacy often took precedence over really knowing the person that they intended to marry. Therefore, when they get married and begin to discover that the person they married is a live example of their worst pet peeves, all hell breaks loose. Once married, they now discover that their spouse was bringing grand ma, grand pa, and the rest of the family whom they dislike, to live with them, the relationship heads south. Once married, couples begin to find out things that are not only deal breakers, but things that would have caused them not to have had a "deal" in the first place.

The issues they now have to deal with, whether it's their partner's true personality, religious beliefs, family, quirks, or bad habits—some of which could have been discerned or discovered by careful study and asking the right questions while they were single—now takes precedence over the things they should be doing in marriage. The married couple, out of resentment, don't date anymore. They don't profess love to each other anymore. They don't make love to each other anymore. The married couple now refuses to hangout, compliment and care for each other like they did when they were single. The things the couple are supposed to do in their marriage are now hindered by the things that they did not do while they were single.

Things they should have done include learning about each other's medical histories, finances, relationships with their families and their families' backgrounds, past experiences, relationship goals, how they can make their relationship successful, their respective needs in the relationship, their purposes, dreams or aspirations in life, what kind of person they really want in their life, and their belief in God, just to mention a few.

It was with those things in mind that I wondered why the lady who was disappointed in the movie did not realize the tremendous advantage she had. She could learn some things that would prepare her to not only meet and marry the right man for her life, but also help her keep the man in her life. While the movie did help her recognize areas were she could improve in her relationships, her overall feeling for the movies' relevance to marriage appeared to have overshadowed the fact she had an advantage to learn certain things about marriage before she ventured into one.

This book is about knowing fundamental things about relationships. Knowing these things while you are single will help you have success when you get married because, according to pastor and author, Dr. Myles Munroe:

A successful marriage is only a product of two people being successfully single.[44]

One of those fundamental things that we need to know about relationships is: *what makes relationships successful.*

While you are single, it's beneficial for you to find out what makes relationships successful. Once you discover this you'll have a good head start in ensuring that you end up in a great relationship. So, what makes relationships successful? How can we assure ourselves that once we say *I do*, we and our respective partners will also say *I'll stay...* happily ever after?

Christ gives us a clue. Some Pharisees approached Jesus and asked Him if it was okay to have a divorce.

Some Pharisees came and tested him by asking, "Is it lawful for a man to divorce his wife?" "What did Moses command you?" he replied. They said, "Moses permitted a man to write a certificate of divorce and send her away." "It was because your hearts were hard that Moses wrote you this law," Jesus replied. "But at the beginning of creation God made them male and female. For this reason a man will leave his father and mother and be united to his wife, and the two will become one flesh. So they are no longer two, but one. Therefore what God has joined together, let man not separate." (Mark 10:2-9)

They asked the Lord if it was lawful for a man to divorce his wife and Jesus responded by asking them what Moses said in their law. They said that Moses permitted them to divorce. But Jesus said that Moses permitted them because of the hardness of their hearts. This informs us that *one of* the reasons why people divorce is because of the hardness of their hearts. Nonetheless, Jesus went on to tell them that *at* the "beginning" God made male and female and they were to become one flesh. Reflecting on what Jesus meant I gathered that there are guidelines which we can find in the beginning that will make relationships work.

While the religious leaders were interested in *testing* him about legal separation, Jesus was interested in legal unification. The Pharisees emphasized divorce; the Lord emphasized unity. The fact that Jesus referred to the beginning speaks volumes. While divorce signifies the end of an unsuccessful relationship, Jesus' response reveals that a successful relationship can be achieved from its beginning. This is why I believe He referred to the beginning of creation. It is there that we find out God's intent for a relationship. Once we discover God's design and *adhere* to it, we will be successful in our relationships.

The Success of a Relationship is *In the Beginning...*

A phrase that sums up what it takes to make a relationship between a man and a woman successful, is found in the beginning sentence of the beginning chapter of the beginning book of the Bible (See Genesis 1:1 NKJV). It simply says, "In the beginning God...."

The success or failure of a relationship can be determined from its beginning. Is God in the beginning of a relationship? Or are we in the beginning of a relationship? Did He start the relationship? Or did you or I start the relationship? Did He begin it? Or did you begin it? Did He initiate it? Is

God a *part* of it or *apart* from it? If He did not begin it, it's likely that that relationship will not work.

Relationships will not *head south* if the couples involved in the relationship *headed* and *stayed* north, first. How a relationship starts determines how it continues ... or ceases. If the goal is to continue, it's in the best interest of the parties involved to have God in the beginning of their union. He will give their relationship longevity because He is everlasting.

"In the beginning God..." denotes, at least, two things. First, God was in the beginning. The second can be deduced by focusing on the words "beginn-ing-God" in the phrase "In the beginning God...." This leaves us with "beginn-ing-God"; *begin in God*. So, the guidelines are that relationships should be begun by God and begin in God. A relationship will be successful if it is started, initiated or inspired by God. God has to be in the beginning of it. Hence, this is one of the reasons why we are encouraged to seek first the kingdom of God and His righteousness and everything else that we need will be added to us (See Matthew 6:33 NKJV).

Furthermore, not only should a relationship be *started by* God but it should also be *started with* God. In other words the relationship should *begin in God*. Before we embark on a relationship with anyone, it's to our advantage that we begin a relationship with God, first. It's through our interaction with Him that we'll learn how to love and live peacefully and harmoniously with someone else. How God treats us exemplifies how we should treat our prospective mates. In addition, the ideal person for us is someone *in* God. By beginning in God we position ourselves to find the person *in* Him. Just as much as the right person for you is in relationship with God, you should *be in* God, too. At God's timing He'll guide you to each other.

It was God's idea, not Adam's, that it was not good for man to be alone (See Genesis 2:18). While Adam was in la-la land, God decided to make Adam a helper *suitable* for him. God *began* Adam's relationship with Eve. God inspired and initiated it. God started it. Abraham's servant must have understood the importance of this principle so much so that he went to God for help to find a wife for Isaac (See Genesis 24:1-15). In a sense the man prayed to God to initiate the relationship. He must have known that for a marriage to be successful God had to be consulted first about it. He has to find it and be behind it. He has to be the founder and the foundation of it.

Furthermore, Isaac, like Adam, already had a relationship with God. It was while he was on the way to meditate, that he saw his wife coming toward him (See Genesis 24:62-24). These men's marriages were started by God. And before they got married, they had a relationship with God first. Both men's relationships began by God and began in God.

Having a relationship start by God and start with God is one side of the coin of successful relationships. This is the spiritual part; there is also a practical part. The former is God's part; the later is our part. One side deals with finding the right person; the other deals with keeping the person right. One hand deals with the obtaining a spouse; the other deals with maintaining the relationship. To have a successful relationship, there is a part where God guides us in finding the right person and the part where we follow His guide in keeping the person.

According to Dr. Edwin Louis Cole, it is easier to obtain than to maintain. Therefore let's go back to the beginning to find out how to maintain a relationship that only God can help us obtain.

"In the beginning God created...." Similarly, in a relationship we are to *create* with each other not *cremate* each other. We are to build our relationships not destroy them. We are to build with each other and build each other, not knock each other down.

"In the beginning God created the heavens and the earth." The best we can do in the beginning of our relationships is to create a heavenly atmosphere for our union here on earth. Just like heaven is saturated with harmony, peace, love, praise and worship, we should also cultivate an atmosphere of peace and harmony with our mates. We should love and express affection to our spouses. We should also shower them with praise, adoration and affirmation. This way we'll be creating a heavenly atmosphere in our relationships.

Furthermore, when God decided to make man He made a profound statement in Genesis 1:26. He said, "Let *Us* make man...." He did not say, "Let *Me* make man." Drawing from this, the building of a relationship should be a collaborative effort not an independent one. In order to ensure a successful union it's to our benefit that we collaborate, cooperate, and communicate with our mates. If we don't *integrate* our efforts in building a relationship, the relationship will *disintegrate*. Perhaps this explains why it takes *two* to have a marriage but *one* to have a divorce. In essence we need to be in *agreement* for our relationships to flourish. Amos begs the question: Can two walk together, unless they are agreed (See Amos 3:3 NKJV)?

God also said, "Let Us make man in Our image...." Before anything can be created in a relationship, the couples involved in the building process must have an *image* that serves as the template to build the relationship. And the image should be a reflection of them *both*. The image should be *our* image; not *my* image or *your* image. If a couple does not have a mutual image that depicts how they want to develop their relationship, they'll head for disaster because Proverbs 29:18 says "where there is no vision, the people perish...."

Vision is also a synonym for image. So, if a couple does not have an image or a vision for their relationship, their relationship is on its way to its demise. Sometimes couples in a relationship do have a vision for their relationship. But their vision for the marriage is different. Consequently they have two visions. This leads to *di* vision—division. Hence, *die* vision. The vision dies. And so does the relationship. To avoid this from happening, it's to their advantage that they have a *mutual* image for the relationship. This is provided if God is in the beginning of their relationship and if they began their relationship with God. The image is provided through Christ since He's the image of God (See Colossians 1:15 NKJV).

A psychologist once said that when people come in contact there is friction. In the mechanical industry lubricants are used to reduce the friction between mechanical parts that are in contact with each other. This further explains why we need Jesus to be in the center of our relationships. The Lord is the Christ, which means He is The Anointed One. This also means that He has an anointing, and oil represents the anointing. Therefore Jesus serves as the lubricant in a relationship. He reduces and removes the friction between couples. His anointing removes the burdens and destroys yokes that might result from two people being in constant *contact* with each other. He prevents us from wearing and tearing each other apart.

God told Adam and Eve to be fruitful and multiply (See Genesis 1:28). From the beginning this is how God wanted relationships to function. He wants us to be fruitful and multiply. He does not want us to be brutal and crucify each other. Before God brought Eve to Adam, He placed Adam in the Garden of Eden and took a rib out from Adam to form Eve. In the same way, before God can bring someone into your life, He has to do at least two moves. He has to move you out of an environment: circumstances, people that hinder you, or the wrongs of your past. He also has to move things out of you: unforgiveness, bitterness, and scars of your past. God will accomplish all that for your benefit and the success of your relationship if you let Him.

The Bible also mentioned that Adam and Eve were naked and not ashamed. In the beginning of our relationships we should be naked or *open* to our respective prospects, and them to us. We should be *transparent* about who we are, where we're from and what we've been through. And we should not be ashamed. Simply put, we should be *honest*. Tell the truth about who you are, where you are, and what you want in the relationship. I like the way Dr. Robin Smith states the importance of truth, which is also applicable to men as well:

Truth is what holds my life together now. It is not an accessory. It is a necessity. As with a credit card, I never leave home without it. But I walked through the darkness of lies to get there. I would like to spare the pain of every woman who fears that she can have love only if she erases her needs and makes herself small. I would like to shout it from the rooftops and mountain peaks that truth is better, warmer, stronger. It is the only way to have a great marriage or a great relationship.[45]

While you are single, if the person with whom you're involved is ashamed of you, this is not someone you should be in relationship with. Unfortunately, some of us hide our real selves and put on a facade. We put on MASK-aras. Some of us do this because we fear rejection. We fear that if our prospects get to see the real *us*, they will be discouraged from getting involved with us. If this is how we operate in relationships, no wonder the divorce rate. In the beginning that is not how God wanted things to be. He wants us to be naked and not ashamed. He desires that we operate in honesty and integrity.

Author and Pastor Joshua Harris put it this way:

You can't love what you don't know. You can't be truly loved if you're not truly known. And the only way to know and be known by another person is to communicate—openly, honestly, sincerely, humbly.[46]

This way, right from the start, before we go any further, we'll know where we stand in our relationships with others. We'll know if we're ready for commitment or heading for disappointment. What's the worst that could happen if you get rejected for being honest? You will be protected from getting involved with a lie while you preserve your honesty, your integrity and

your dignity. I suggest that you bear Hugh Prather's words in mind when
you are at the crossroads of choosing to cover up or expose your true self:

*Some people are going to like me and some people aren't; so I might
as well be me. Then, at least, I will know that the people who like me, like
me.*[47]

Besides, if someone is ashamed of who you are, then that person does
not love you. 1 John 4:18 says that there is no fear in love. If someone
loves you like you deserve, the individual would not fear and would not
be ashamed of being involved with you despite your past. Likewise, you
should not fear rejection because of who you are. If you do, then your love
for yourself is not as mature as it can be because perfect love or love that is
mature, casts out fear. If you're not mature in love, you can be. Simply have
a relationship with God who is the epitome of love.

Through your relationship with God, you'll realize that you're special.
He loves you, and He'll help you know the person you really are. Acts 17:28
says that it is in God that we live, we move, and have our being. It is in Him
that we have life. It's also in Him that we find ourselves, our identities and
our personalities. It's in Him that we find out who we are and through Him
that we find our respective life partners. It was through God that Adam
found Eve—who was actually a part of Adam—a part of himself—a part
of his "being."

The success of any relationship lies on the foundation of that relationship. If a relationship is built on rock, when the flood, torrential rain and
hurricane of life beat on that relationship, it will not crumble because it was
built on rock solid ground. Conversely, if a relationship is built on sand, the
torrential rain and hurricane of life will flood that relationship toward the
rocks.

That is why relationships should be begun by God and begin in or with
God. He is the Rock. When the trials of life come against your relationship

founded on the Rock it will not collapse. If your relationship did not start in the beginning by God and in God, or if you've experienced a broken relationship, this does not mean that you cannot have a successful union. You can. All you have to do is have what is called "a new beginning" —began by God and in God. You can start today.

CHAPTER EIGHT

Find Out the Purpose of Relationships

There is a popular saying that I've often heard from Dr. Myles Munroe. He usually says that if you do not know the purpose of something, abuse is inevitable. If you don't know what something is used for and why it exists, you are likely to misuse it. You are likely to use it the wrong way and use it to do the wrong thing. You're going to abuse it.

I believe this is one of the reasons why some relationships don't work. Some individuals are clueless about the purpose of relationships. As a result, if they get into a relationship they are likely to abuse it. If you don't know what a relationship is designed for, you're going to have wrong expectations of the relationship, and you're going to have conflicts with your mate because the person is likely not going to meet your expectations.

The best way to find out the purpose of relationships is to find out about it from the designer of relationships. God established relationships. First, with Christ and the Holy Spirit. Hence, we have the Trinity or what the Bible describes as the Godhead. Second, following His relationship design, he established relationships with Adam and Eve. It only makes sense that we look to Him for guidance in having a successful relationship. Once we find out the purpose of relationships and adhere to them, then we can have REAL-ationships.

Before I present some of the reasons why God wants us to be in relationships, I need to let you know that these reasons are by no means all there is to know about relationships. There are probably other reasons for relationships. Notwithstanding, I hope the purposes of relationships that I'll be sharing with you will help you make better relationship decisions and assist you to find someone with whom to share a wholesome relationship.

I've learned that there are at least eight purposes of relationships. And these purposes are not only applicable to marital relationships. They are also applicable to all other kinds of relationships. The reasons for which God designed relationships are as follows:

1. Companionship – To have someone to connect with (Genesis 2:18)

God said, "It's not good for the Man to be alone; I'll make him a helper, a companion."…. (Genesis 2:18 MSG)

God established relationships for companionship. He gave us a way that we can connect with someone. While we don't have to be married to have companionship, friendship is relevant to making a relationship successful. Therefore, before you get into a relationship, it's important for you to know that part of what you're supposed to contribute and receive from a relationship is companionship. So if you or your prospect is not cool with the friendship thing, then perhaps you might reconsider being in a relationship.

2. Identity - To have someone to be affiliated with (2 Corinthians 5:17, Acts 11:28, Genesis 2:23)

God established relationships as a way for us to derive our identity. We've been made according to God's image, therefore it's beneficial for us to have a relationship with God first. In addition, our relationship with someone else should emulate our relationship with God.

Therefore, if anyone is in Christ, he is a new creation; old things have passed away; behold, all things have become new. (2 Corinthians 5:17 NKJV)

for in Him we live move and have our being…. (Acts 17:28)

We can conclude from the above verses that we carve our identity from our relationship with Christ. If you are in relationship with Him you are a new person. You have a new identity based on your relationship with Him. It's through your relationship with Him that you exist. Who you are is in Him. It's through Him that you have your being. Your being … "be in" God.

Any relationship that you embark on should reflect your relationship with God and the character of God. Are you going out with someone now? If you are, do people say "praise the Lord" when they see you both together, or do they say "Lord have mercy" when you're together? Are you seeing someone that you can take home to your parents? Or are you keeping the relationship on a "DL"; on a *down low* from your parents? Before you go out with anyone you should ask yourself this question: What kind of identity does this person give me? Is it a wholesome identity or a troublesome one?

3. Help - To have someone to assist and be assisted by (Genesis 2:18, Exodus 2:15-17, Genesis 29:1-10, 18)

God designed relationships for help. We are supposed to be in relationships to have someone to assist and to be assisted by. The help you get in a relationship is essentially to help you fulfill your purpose. I like the way Matthew Kelly articulated this premise:

The first purpose of every relationship is to help each other become the-best-version-of ourselves…. The first purpose, obligation, and responsibility of a relationship is to help each other achieve our essential purpose.[48]

Getting help was basically the principal reason why God created Eve for Adam. Notice the scripture below:

The LORD God said, "It is not good for the man to be alone. I will make a helper suitable for him." (Genesis 2:18)

What kind of person was God planning to make for Adam? A helper. This also suggests that God is in the business of setting up *helpers*; not *help mes*. God sets up people who are willing to serve people. Individuals who have a heart to support and help others, not people who have a "what's in it for me mentality." God did not decide to make just a woman for Adam. God did not decide to make just a companion for him. God decided to make him a woman, companion, and spouse that was going to *help* him. If you want God to help you find the right mate for your life, become the right mate for someone else's life. Be a helper. Have a "what can I do for him or her" mentality.

Furthermore, I know it's been said that the woman was created to serve the man. The following passage is notorious for validating this:

> *And man was not made for the woman, but woman for man. (1 Corinthians 11:9 NLT)*

While that passage reveals that woman was made for man, it is actually referring to a wife helping her husband like Eve was created to help Adam. Generally speaking, that verse is not saying that a woman is supposed to help out just *any* man. She is supposed to help her husband. Even so, just because a woman is made for her husband, this does not mean that he is to treat her like a slave. In fact, common sense should let us know that women need help, too. Their husbands are supposed to provide that help. This is an essential purpose for any marital relationship.

Do you recall that God created Adam a helper comparable to him? If God created a helper comparable to Adam, if God made a wife similar to Adam, if God made a companion like Adam, then Adam must have been a helper, too. If Eve was designed to be a helper to her husband and God created her with the rib he took from Adam, then Eve constituted of parts of Adam. My point is that Adam was a helper, too. This means that men are supposed to help their wives. In fact they are to out-serve their wives. I also believe that the word "helper," is a contraction of the words, "*help her.*" In essence, helper means a person to help her or help a woman. The first *human* helper was male. Adam. So a helper is someone like Adam.

Jesus is the head of the church, and the church is the body of Christ. He is also known as the last *Adam*. Jesus is the bride groom, and the church is His bride.[49] Let me ask you a question. Who out-served whom? Jesus or the church? The Head or His body? Christ of course! Therefore, who's supposed to serve whom more? The man or his wife? While women are to serve their husbands, husbands are to serve their wives, too; if not more. The way a married couple serve each other will differ because men and women are wired differently. They have different strengths. By serving each other they should meet each other's needs, complement their strengths and cancel their weaknesses.

Thankfully some men are already serving their wives and vise versa. Some men serve their wives by providing a house for them. Some women serve their husbands by making the house a home. Some men serve their wives by providing groceries. Some women serve their husbands by transforming those groceries into food. Some women serve by providing the house, making it a home, and working to support their husbands. Some husbands return the favor by maintaining the house and supporting their wives wherever they need help. How a husband and a wife serve themselves is relative to them. But the bottom line is that they are to help each other out.

Either way, before you embark on a relationship, be mindful that you're supposed to help your spouse. If you don't want to help anyone but only want someone to help you, then being in a relationship might not be something you should have as a priority. God designed relationships so that we can have someone to assist and be assisted by.

4. Agreement – To have someone to agree with (Deuteronomy 32:30; Amos 3:3; Matthew 18:19)

Another purpose for relationships is agreement. God established relationships so that we can have someone to agree with. There is a popular saying that goes something like this:

One can put a thousand to flight and two can put ten thousand to flight.

Well, without the proper context, that statement is often quoted inaccurately. That verse was derived from Deutoronomy 32:30. And it actually reads this way from the NKJV:

How could one chase a thousand, And two put ten thousand to flight, unless their Rock had sold them, unless the LORD had surrendered them?

That verse starts as a question. A lot of people quote it as a statement, and this does not do justice to the passage. The verse is a question that is eventually answered. We can't conclude on the outcome of what one person and two people can do respectively, until we answer the question of *how* they can accomplish their objective.

The scripture asks how one can put a thousand to flight and how *two* can put ten thousand to flight. Ultimately the victory can be achieved with God surrendering the chased into the hand of the chaser(s). However, in order for two people to accomplish that feat they have to be in *agreement* first; and, God has to help them achieve the victory, second.

Can two people walk together without agreeing on the direction? (Amos 3:3 NLT)

Agreement precedes God's help in anything. This is the case because God is in the midst of agreement. And when God is present in any situation, His power is also available in the situation.

For where two or three are gathered together in My name, I am there in the midst of them. (Matthew 18:20 NKJV)

God is *not* in the midst of people who are just *gathered*. He is in the midst of people who are gathered *together*. In *His* name. In order for two people in a relationship to walk *together*, they have to be in agreement. *Can two people walk together without agreeing?* In order for a relationship to succeed there has to be agreement. God designed relationships for agreement. If you want to be in a successful union with someone else, while you are single, make your mind up to be in agreement with whomever God has for you. This does not mean that you will never disagree with your partner. If you choose to disagree with your spouse-to-be, it means that when you disagree with your mate you will agree to disagree. You will disagree without being disagreeable.

You and your partner should agree in prayer. To prevent your prayers from being hindered, you and your mate should be in agreement before, during and after prayer. (See Matthew 18:19; 1 Peter 3:7) Whether it's a decision you have to make, or a course of action you have to take, it's in your best interest to be in agreement with your spouse regarding the issue. Have the mentality that relationships are not about *me* but about *we*. They are not about me, myself, and I. They are about us, ourselves, and we.

5. To learn authority - To have someone to be accountable to (Ephesians 5:21; 6:1-9, 1 Peter 3:1-7)

God designed relationships so that we can learn authority. Relationships serve as avenues for us to be accountable to our partners. They offer us checks and balances to ensure that we make informed decisions. Unfortunately Adam and Eve went against this purpose of relationships. They did not keep themselves accountable regarding the fruit on the tree God told them not to eat from. Adam did not protect and keep his wife accountable. And together they did not submit to God's authority. They resorted to placing the blame of their misconduct on others. Adam blamed Eve, and Eve blamed the serpent. Consequently, they lost their bond with God and their position in the Garden of Eden.

Relationships are not occasions for us to blame our mates. They are opportunities for us to take responsibility for them. They are not places for us to throw our partners under the bus. They serve as opportunities for us to prevent them from getting hit by the bus.

Submit to one another out of reverence for Christ. (Ephesians 5:21)

In a relationship, we are to submit to, and be responsible for one another. We are to keep ourselves accountable to each other and to God. If we don't do this, God will keep us accountable. And this is not always fun. Being under authority is not synonymous with being inferior or less significant to the authority figure over you. The Father, Son and Holy Spirit are one. Yet, the Holy Spirit is under Christ's authority, Christ is under the Father's authority, and interestingly, the Father is under the authority of His Word, whom is Jesus. (See Psalm 138:2; John 16:13; 1 John 5:7)

In the same vein, though a husband and wife are one, according to God's design, the wife is under the authority of her husband who in turn is under God's authority. That does not mean that his wife is inferior or a doormat to him, nor should she think it's acceptable for her husband to treat her as such. If you're a lady, the issue of the husband being the head and having authority over his wife might be difficult to accept. I don't think I can explain the importance and significance of this better than author and speaker, Staci Eldredge:

Issues of headship and authority are intended for the benefit of women, not their suppression....God desires that wherever and however you offer yourself to the body of Christ, you'll have the protection of good men over you. Not to hold you back, but to set you free as a woman. Christ has made man as his warrior, to offer his strength on behalf of Eve so that she might flourish. If that's not the context you've found yourself in, find one that is.[50]

Having these things in mind, if you don't like anyone telling you anything, if you have a problem with authority or with someone keeping you accountable, being in a relationship might not be something you should be involved with. God established relationships for us to protect and account for each other. It was designed for us to look out for one another. It is a forum for us to learn and exercise submission to our partners. It's for us to learn and practice being under authority.

6. Production and Dominion - To have someone to produce and manage with (Genesis 1:28)

So God created human beings in his own image. In the image of God he created them; male and female he created them. Then God blessed them and said, "Be fruitful and multiply. Fill the earth and govern it…. (Genesis 1:26-27 NLT)

God designed relationships for production and dominion. Adam and Eve were the first human beings. God blessed them and instructed them to be fruitful, multiply, fill the earth and govern it. Together they were to produce, expand and manage their production. This brings me back to the scripture that asked the question of how one can put a thousand to flight and then two put ten thousand to flight. Like I said previously, in order for two people to accomplish more than either of them can do by themselves, they need to be in agreement and God has to help them with their objective.

It's obvious that God was behind the mandate for Adam and Eve to be fruitful and multiply. Similarly, we are supposed to be productive in our relationships. What you can do by yourself should be enhanced and multiplied when you hook up with someone else. This is a very important point to remember before you embark in a relationship with anyone. If your productivity is diminishing after you've gotten involved with someone, and that someone is responsible for the regression, this might be a red flag that you need to pay attention to. Your mate is supposed to help you be more fruitful.

While I believe that God's will for us to be fruitful includes having kids, I believe being fruitful is also applicable to things we do. Whether it's working in a job, starting a business, contributing to the welfare and well-being of your mate, relationship, family, community, or society. This also includes making an impact in the lives of people. Once you are in agreement and you've got help in a relationship, both will enable you and your mate be fruitful and multiply. God established relationships so that we can have someone to produce and manage with.

7. Independence and Unity - To have someone to unite with (Genesis 2:24)

"At last!" the man exclaimed. "This one is bone from my bone, and flesh from my flesh! She will be called 'woman,' because she was taken from 'man.'" This explains why a man leaves his father and mother and is joined to his wife, and the two are united into one. (Genesis 2:23-24 NLT)

God designed relationships for us to find someone to unite with. Relationships enable us to be *independent* of our parents and *unite* with our mates and start a family of our own. Uniting with our mates is the reason we become independent of our parents. This obviously doesn't mean that we abandon our parents or have nothing to do with them. However, once you get into a relationship with someone, your priority shifts from your parents to your spouse. Too many people do not understand this, and as a result have contributed to unnecessary frictions in marriages.

You are to be married to your spouse; not to your momma or poppa. If you love your parents so much so that you are thinking of subordinating your prospect to the whims of your parents, then you might rethink being in a relationship with that person. Conversely, if you sense that you are going to be treated as second fiddle to your prospect's parents, this might be an alert for you to know that you're heading for disaster.

A popular saying used to describe being independent of your parents to unite with your spouse is, *leave to cleave*. You are to leave your parents to cleave with your spouse. You are not to *bring* your parents to *grieve* your spouse. God created relationships so that we can have someone to unite with, not someone to fight with.

8. To demonstrate love - To have someone to love and to be loved by (Ephesians 5:25)

Finally, God designed relationships for us to love one another. Like I discussed previously in chapter two, a man's love for his wife should mimic Jesus's love for His church. Christ's love for His church also emulates God, the father's love for his son, Jesus. A relationship between a man and his wife should reflect the love connection that exists in the Godhead, or what most of us know as the Trinity: The Father, The Son, and The Holy Spirit. In their love dynamic there is love, there is the object of love, and there is the spirit of love.

God the Father is love, Jesus is the object of His love, and the Holy Spirit is the spirit, power or ability to love. Likewise, it's beneficial for us to know beforehand that relationships offer us that kind of opportunity to love and be loved. In a sense we play all those roles. We are the lovers loving our mates, the objects of our love. The Holy Spirit in us empowers us through the love He deposited in us to love our mates. Simultaneously we are also the object of our mates' love. And the Holy Spirit enables them to love us, too.

Love is a two-way street. We are to love and be loved. God designed relationships for this. Have this in mind before you hitch with anyone. If you are a man, you are supposed to love your wife, and she is supposed to return the favor.

CHAPTER NINE

Find Out How to Find the Right Person

You might be one of those who skipped the introduction and the first eight chapters of this book to get to this chapter. If you are, I have two words for you: "Got ya!" Notwithstanding, don't feel bad. It's ok. I know that feeling of wanting to find someone like yesterday. I'm not going to waste your time. I'll just go straight to the point. However, after you've finished reading this chapter, I highly encourage you to go back to the beginning of this book and read to the end of it. It will give you a better perspective on how to find the right person for your life. Having said that, let's find out how to find the right mate for your life.

In order to find the right person, there are at least three things you should be mindful of.

It is hard to find something if you don't know what you are looking for. And if you do not know what you are looking for, then you will not be aware of it when you come across it. With this in mind, the first thing that will help you find the right person is to:

1. Find out what makes a person right

Once you discover what makes a person right, then you can use this information to find the right person.

The second thing you need to be mindful of is that:

2. There is a difference between the right person and the right person *for* you

The "right person" is usually an abstract image of someone who is supposedly right for you. That image often stems from whomever or whatever you subscribe to. If you are into chick flicks, soap operas, magazines and other media that project images of suitable mates, whatever they project as the right person is what lots of people assume is the ideal mate for them. Unfortunately, this is usually not the case. What your favorite show, magazine, or friend depicts as the right person might be right for *them*, but not necessarily right for you.

Don't fall into the trap like some women who end up with a guy who might be tall, dark and handsome, but *brawls*, *barks*, and is *troublesome* to you. If you're a man, don't give in to ending up with a lady who might be blonde, blue eyed and a bombshell, but is *disrespectfully blunt*, *blacks eyes*, and *burns well* your clothes when she's upset. She might be "da bomb," but you don't want to be "da shell" when she explodes. What might be right for someone else might be wrong for you. Look for someone who is right for you.

A scene toward the end of the movie, *Made of Honor*, adequately reinforces this point. Michelle Monaghan's character, *Hannah*, was about to make the biggest mistake of her life by marrying the wrong guy who *appeared* to be the right guy. Fortunately for her, thanks to the help of the right guy for her life, she was able to say *I don't* just in time before she tied the knot with the wrong guy. This crunch time decision enabled her to eventually marry the right guy *for* her. A comment within her parting words to the wrong guy explains her reason for not marrying him, and reiterates the notion that there is a difference between the right person and the right person for you. She said thus:

...You are the perfect guy...just not the perfect guy for me.

The third thing that you should be mindful of is that, since the ideal is to find someone who is right for you, then before you can find someone right for you:

3. You need to find *you*, first

If you are oblivious of who you are, your purpose, your personality, your preferences, you are likely to end up with someone who is right for someone else and not for you. Once you find out who you are, you are in a better position to find the person who suits you. In order to find yourself you need to seek God who created you and knows all about you. Incidentally, it is Him who also makes people right. Jesus made *us right*. He *righted us* thereby making us *righteous.*

Being aware of what makes a person right, what kind of person is right for you, and finding yourself, will help you find the right mate for your life. If you think about it, you are the common denominator in all of these three points. It is in your best interest to know yourself before you can find someone who will blend with you for the rest of your life. Knowing yourself will help you find someone who will coincide with you and complement you.

Let me tell you a story that came to me a while ago. There was a guy who wanted to find a Godly woman to marry. He asked himself where he could find such a woman. He concluded that church was the best place to find such a lady. So, he proceeded to go to church. He didn't go to church to have a relationship with God. He didn't go to church to develop his character. He only went to church to find a woman.

Guess what? He found a woman. They began a relationship. But it was a disaster. He was disappointed and disgusted with the woman he ended up with. Consequently, he concluded that church women were fake. There was also another woman who was interested in finding a Godly man. She asked herself where she could find such a man. She also arrived at the conclusion that church was the best place for her to snag a decent man. So, she went to church.

She didn't go to church to cultivate a relationship with Jesus. She didn't go to church to develop her character. She simply went to church to find a man. Guess what? She found a man and they began a relationship. Unfortunately for her, the relationship went south fast. She was disappointed and devastated by the relationship. She could not believe that she found a man like that in church. Consequently, she concluded that church men were hypocrites. Well, it turned out that the man whom she found and had a terrible relationship with, was the other man who was also looking for a woman in church. This story reminds me of what author and leadership expert, Dr. John Maxwell, describes as the law of magnetism:

Who you attract is not determined by what you want. It's determined by who you are.[51]

In the movie, *Runaway Bride*, not knowing herself was the main reason why Julia Robert's character, *Maggie Carpenter*, kept running away from the altar. It was after she found herself that she ended up with the right mate for her life. In the same vein, before you can run into the love of your life, you need to run into yourself first. The fastest way for you to find the right person is to look in the mirror. If you don't know yourself, not only are you susceptible to ending up with the wrong person, you are also susceptible to *missing* out on the right person.

If you know what is right, this will help you know *who* is right. If you don't know what is right, then you won't know who is right for you. Having a relationship with God will not only help you know what is right and know who is right for you, but it will also help you be right. And this is really what helps you find the right mate for your life.

I can't say this enough: to find the right person you have to be the right person. You are the template for the right person. Just like it takes a good doctor to know a good doctor, it takes being the right person to find the right person. Before God made Eve for Adam, the Bible said that God would make him a helper comparable to him. God did not decide to make

Adam a helper; He decided to make Adam a helper *comparable* to him. He decided to create someone *suitable* for him. Someone who *suited* him. This corroborates my point that the ideal spouse for you is someone who is not just right, but right for you. Someone suitable for you. Someone who suits you.

That means if God is to bring you someone who is suitable for you, someone who suits you, someone "tailor-made" for you, then God needs to take *your* measurements. In order for God to give you someone who fits you, He needs to *fit* you. I've been to the tailor's before. When the tailor takes my measurements, he cuts my fabric to align with the measurements for the final product. You are the fabric for your final product—the right spouse for your life.

God needs to "cut" you. If you disagree with me, then let's take another look at how Adam ended up with Eve.

After God decided to make Adam a *helpmeet*, God did not speak Eve into being. He did not wave a magic wand and chant *abracadabra*. He did not form her from the dust of the ground. He worked *on* Adam. He cut a rib out and used it to form Eve. This is a picture of how God brings you the right person. He needs to work on you. Jesus is the bride groom, and the church is His bride. How did Jesus get his woman? Well, He worked on Himself; ultimately on the cross. Because of His sacrifice, we now have the church; those that believe in Him, His resurrection and what He did on Calvary.

Before a building is built, architects and engineers go to the site on which the building will be built. They prepare the location, take measurements, make demarcations on the site and sometimes drive pegs on the plot to prepare it for its building. Likewise, you are the site for the "building" God desires for you. My friend you need to be the right person to find the right person. You are the raw material for your spouse-to-be. God utilizes *you*, to guide you to the right mate for your life.

Find out what Kind of Person God Blesses with a Spouse

Ok. So, you have to be the right person. Being right for someone else will help you find and receive someone who is right for you. So, what does being right look like? If you are not already, what kind of person do you have to become for God to bless you with your "missing rib"? What does the right person look like? What are the traits of the right woman for you? What are the characteristics of the right man for you? Whatever they are, like I said previously, it's to your advantage that you learn these traits and apply them to your life. The key to finding the right person is to be the right person. You need to sow yourself as a seed to reap your harvest of the right spouse.

When I talked about the purpose of relationships, I mentioned that God is in the business of setting up helpers. Obviously being a person of help is an attribute of a good spouse. In addition to this trait, there are other things about some individuals that enable God to bless them with wholesome spouses. There is something peculiar about individuals that God blesses with mates. Let's explore some characteristics of a person that God hooks up with a life partner. Once you know these attributes, and if you are lacking in these traits, I encourage you to learn them, and live them out in your life. By doing this you'll be positioning yourself to be set up by God when He deems that you're ready.

Ever so often I've heard relationship experts and preachers encourage singles seeking life partners to write down the attributes of the person they want. The idea is to have a vision and also have something tangible to look at to evaluate people that cross their paths. Writing down what you want in a mate serves as something you can use to validate that you've found who you want when you come across him or her.

I understand the concept behind that advice. I believe it's a good idea. Notwithstanding, before I married my wife, Dana, I never really had a "list." I did not write down anything to use as a reference of who I wanted her to be, or what I wanted her to look like. Do you know why? Because her attributes were already written. They were documented in the Bible. I figured that I didn't need to come up with a list when God already had His list. Unless your list lines up with God's, He is not obligated to grant the requests on your list. He is only obligated to grant requests from His list, the Bible. Yes it takes time and effort to piece together the profile of a good mate from passages in scripture. But this profile is recorded in the Word. It is from it that I'm presenting you with the lifestyle of the kind of person that God blesses with a spouse.

I'll be using some female characters in the Bible as a reference for the ladies, and male characters for the guys. The attributes, however, of these biblical characters are applicable to everyone regardless of their gender. While I'll highlight certain traits from various women and men in the Bible, I'm mainly using Rebecca for the ladies and Moses for the guys. I'm using Rebecca and Moses because they both exemplify Godly character, they were both found beside a "well" before they got hitched, and we have some information on the circumstances that led them to get married. Let's begin with the ladies first. To do this, join me in looking at some verses in Genesis 24.

Abraham was now a very old man, and the LORD had blessed him in every way. One day Abraham said to his oldest servant, the man in charge of his household, "Take an oath by putting your hand under my thigh. Swear by the LORD, the God of heaven and earth, that you will not allow my son to marry one of these local Canaanite women. Go instead to my homeland, to my relatives, and find a wife there for my son Isaac." (Genesis 24:1-4 MSG)

Genesis 24 basically is a chapter that shows us how God set up Isaac with Rebecca. Regardless of our gender, we can learn from this narration what kind of person we need to look out for, and what kind of person we need to be for God to get us hitched. The passage starts out by showing us how Abraham was making arrangements through his head-servant to get Isaac a wife. Bearing this in mind, I am for arranged marriages. But it depends on *who* is doing the arranging. As long as God is doing the arranging, I'm for it. And this is the way it is supposed to be for you too. I believe parents should arrange their children's marriages. Before you tell me off, relax, and let me finish what I'm saying. I believe parents can and should arrange for the espousal of their children by *praying* to God to find a spouse for their children. This is essentially what happened for Isaac.

While at face value, it looked like Abraham was the one trying to arrange a wife for his son Isaac, the fact that he asked his servant to carry out this task speaks volumes. The nickel dropped for me when I read a commentary made by Dr. Fuschia Picket about the wedding arrangement. She said that Abraham represented the Father God, Isaac represented the Son Jesus, and the servant, whose name is Eliezer represents the Holy Spirit. Eliezer means *God of help* or *mighty divine helper.*[52] Here goes that word "helper" again. The Holy Spirit is described by Christ as a helper, comforter or counselor (See John 16:7 & 13). The anology was that the Holy Spirit, Eliezer, was to fetch a bride, Rebecca, who represents the church, the body of Christ, for Isaac, the Son of Abraham, who signified the Son of God, Jesus.[53]

Similarly, in order for you to end up with the right spouse, it's to your advantage that you ask the Holy Spirit to bring your spouse to you just like Eliezer brought Isaac to Rebecca. I know that I'm getting ahead of myself in deciphering this passage. But after we've finished analyzing the process it took for Isaac to get Rebecca, you'll have at your disposal the information you need in order to position yourself for your Rebecca or Isaac. Let's read on.

The servant asked, "But what if I can't find a young woman who is willing to travel so far from home? Should I then take Isaac there to live among your relatives in the land you came from?" "No!" Abraham responded. "Be careful never to take my son there. For the LORD, the God of heaven, who took me from my father's house and my native land, solemnly promised to give this land to my descendants. He will send his angel ahead of you, and he will see to it that you find a wife there for my son. (Genesis 24:5-7 MSG)

After Abraham asked his servant to find a wife for Isaac, the servant was concerned that the lady he might find would not be willing to come back with him. He asked if Abraham would let him take Isaac back to where he came from. But Abraham refused. Abraham assured him that God would send an angel before him to help him find a bride for Isaac.

My friend, guess what? There is an angel that is supposed to help you find your spouse. You have your own personal angel that is supposed to help you hook up with your sweetheart. However, I have a question for you: Are you frustrating your angel? Is your angel going before you or is your angel *chasing* after you? Is your angel losing his wings? Is your angel asking God to have him reassigned? Since God is not granting this request, is your angel going behind God's back and asking the other angels if they want to switch assignments with him? Is your angel considering quitting his job because of you? Is the angel Michael, the *war* angel, tired of your angel asking him for backup because of you (See Daniel 12:1)? Am sure you know the answer to those rhetorical questions.

Let's skip some verses and look at verses 10 to 23 of Genesis 24.

The servant took ten of his master's camels and, loaded with gifts from his master, traveled to Aram Naharaim and the city of Nahor. Outside the city, he made the camels kneel at a well. It was evening, the time when the women came to draw water. He prayed, "O GOD, God of my master Abraham, make things go smoothly this day; treat my master Abraham well! As I stand here by the spring while the young women of the town come out to get water, let the girl to whom I say, 'Lower your jug and give me a drink,' and who answers, 'Drink, and let me also water your camels'—let her be the woman you have picked out for your servant Isaac. Then I'll know that you're working graciously behind the scenes for my master." It so happened that the words were barely out of his mouth when Rebekah,

the daughter of Bethuel whose mother was Milcah the wife of Nahor, Abra-
ham's brother, came out with a water jug on her shoulder. The girl was
stunningly beautiful, a pure virgin. She went down to the spring, filled her
jug, and came back up. The servant ran to meet her and said, "Please, can
I have a sip of water from your jug?" She said, "Certainly, drink!" And
she held the jug so that he could drink. When he had satisfied his thirst she
said, "I'll get water for your camels, too, until they've drunk their fill." She
promptly emptied her jug into the trough and ran back to the well to fill it,
and she kept at it until she had watered all the camels. The man watched,
silent. Was this GOD's answer? Had GOD made his trip a success or not?
When the camels had finished drinking, the man brought out gifts, a gold
nose ring weighing a little over a quarter of an ounce and two arm brace-
lets weighing about four ounces, and gave them to her. He asked her, "Tell
me about your family? Whose daughter are you? Is there room in your
father's house for us to stay the night?" (Genesis 24:10-23 MSG)

If you noticed, the servant prayed to God to get a wife for Isaac. This
cannot be overemphasized enough. Prayer is necessary for you to find the
right mate. It's fundamental. Furthermore, from the above passage I'll present five attributes that are prevalent in the life of a person that God blesses
with a mate ... and any other thing for that matter.

The person that God blesses with a spouse is:

1. Faithful

The passage said that Abraham's servant came to the well at evening
time, the time that women usually come to the well. At a time that women
were to come to the well, it appeared that only a *woman* showed up at the
well. In other words, at the time that a bunch of ladies were supposed to
show up, only one lady showed up. And she got the blessing. Rebecca represents a faithful person.

A faithful person is someone who does what they are supposed to do,
when they are supposed to do it, how they are supposed to do it, whether

anybody else does it or not. A faithful person is not a no-show. He or she shows up. A faithful person is consistent, diligent and reliable. It makes sense that God will set up someone who's faithful because a successful marriage is one that constitutes faithful spouses. Fidelity in marriage is synonymous with faithfulness to the marriage vows. Rebecca was a faithful woman. She showed up when others didn't. The Bible says that when you are faithful with what is another man's, God will give you your own (See Luke 16:12 NKJV). In a sense, Rebecca was faithful with *another* man, and God gave her, *her own* man.

2. Holy

Rebecca was described as a virgin. And it meant that she had not been physically intimate with any man. Notwithstanding, my emphasis on her holiness is not because of her sexual inexperience. My emphasis is more on what virginity represents. Let me reiterate that just because you've had premarital sex does not mean that God cannot bless your socks off. Ruth was not a virgin but she ended up with Boaz. I'll be talking about both of them later. Your past is your past. We've all made mistakes. God is not going to hold it against you. Once you've confessed your indiscretions to Him and turned a new leaf, you're still a prime candidate for His best.

Rebecca's virginity represents her purity. As you will find out in my discussion of being set apart in chapter 13, synonyms for the word *holy*, include "set apart," "consecrate," "wash," "cleanse," and "purify." The bottom line is that a person who is holy separates himself or herself from things that can hinder them. Rebecca was holy. This premise is reinforced by the fact that she set herself apart literally, from other potential suitors for Isaac by showing up while others didn't; at least, at that point in time. A holy person is distinguished and stands out and above the crowd. This person's peculiarity is more character-based than intellectual. This person does not do what everybody does just to fit in with the crowd. This person is a prime suspect for a Godly spouse.

3. Obedient

Rebecca was obedient. She really didn't have to help the man out. But when the man asked her for a drink she obliged. She did not have any qualms assisting him. She simply gave him a drink. My friend, obedience is a prerequisite for the blessings of God. The Bible says that when we are willing and obedient we will eat the good of the land (See Isaiah 1:19).

4. *Submissive*

Not only was she obedient, she was submissive. She was willing to help the man out. This is evident by the fact that she not only gave him a drink but she also volunteered to water his camels, too. Do you remember that he brought ten camels? Can you picture her running back and forth with a jug on her shoulders trying to accommodate a stranger and ten camels? Yeah, she was running. Not walking. Read the passage again. This sweetheart was running.

I'm not asking you to run for any man or woman. But judging from the narration I'll be surprised if you miss the heart of this woman. She was doing this for a total stranger. This is deep. If you've been to church or been around people that talk about the role of submission in helping one to get hitched and maintaining a good relationship, a tendency for some bachelorettes and bachelors in church is to appear submissive in church to impress people they are trying to hook up with. This was not the case with Rebecca. She did not know who this man was. She had no ulterior motive. She was simply helping him out from the bottom of her heart. Now, that is the kind of heart that God blesses.

In the church I attend, I used to be one of the leaders of a ministry that ministered to adults in their late 20s to 30-somethings. More often than not, about an hour and half before service, I would go to the room in which our services were held to setup chairs for the room. One day I had just parked my car on one of the church's parking lots. I got out of my car and approached the church's building. That's when I noticed Dana leaving the building. At the time she was just a friend who served alongside me in the same ministry. We exchanged pleasantries. She got in her car and went home. I got into the building to go prepare the room for service.

When I got into the room, the chairs were already set. All 120 of them. I thanked another young lady who was the administrative assistant of the ministry for setting up the chairs. She had done this quite a few times in the past. The lady told me that she didn't set the chairs. She told me that Dana did it. Dana's action reminded me of what Rebecca did. Her sacrifice was a significant seed that was planted in my heart that she would make some man an outstanding wife. I am forever grateful to God for His grace that ensured that that man turned out to be me.

5. *Humble*

Rebecca was humble. A humble person esteems others better than him or herself. This person puts others first. They make themselves of no reputation to help others (See Philippians 2:3-9; 1 Peter 5:5-6). The passage mentioned that she was beautiful and a virgin. She had beauty and character. She was a standout. Even so, she did not let her looks make her haughty. Despite her physical appeal, she still made herself of no reputation to serve the man. In our time, physical attractiveness and humility don't always go hand in hand. But Rebecca didn't let her looks and reputation make her too big to help someone out. In a nutshell, she wasn't too cute to help a brother out.

If you're a lady, you might be wondering how come the ladies do all the work. What do the guys ever do? I'm glad you asked. The attributes you look out for in a guy is no different than Rebecca's above. With this in mind, let's look at Moses. He is kind of the male equivalent of Rebecca. Just like Rebecca watered Abraham's camels, Moses also watered Zipporah, his eventual wife's father's flock.

We first discover Moses' meeting with Zipporah in Exodus 2:15-21. Moses killed an Egyptian and Pharaoh had gotten wind of what Moses did. So, he was out for Moses' throat. Moses fled Egypt and went to Midian, where he found a well and sat beside it. Later on, seven women who were Jethro, the priest of Midian's daughters, came to the well to water their father's flock. Unfortunately, some shepherds drove them away. Moses stood up for them and watered their flock for them.

The daughters then went home, and on arriving home their father was surprised that they came home earlier than usual. The ladies told their father that the reason they were home early was because Moses *helped* them out. From the story and Moses' role in getting the Israelites out of Egypt, we can reach the following conclusions about Moses:

1. He was holy

He basically set himself apart from Egypt to discover and fulfill his purpose (See Hebrews 11:24-28).

2. He was obedient

With regard to getting the Israelites out of Egypt, for the most part he did the things God told him to do.

3. He was faithful (See Numbers 12:7, Hebrews 3:2 & 5)

4. He was humble

In fact Moses was the most humble man on the earth in his time (See Numbers 12:3).

5. He was submissive (See Exodus 3:17)

Though he escaped from Egypt as a *prince*, he humbled and made himself of no reputation to help fetch water for Jethro's daughters and watered their flocks. Prior to doing this, he protected the women from the shepherds who drove them away from watering their father's flock. He also watered *all* their flock. Can you imagine how many flock of sheep the women brought?

There were seven women. Talk less of the number of sheep they each brought with them. Moses watered all of their flock. This is a demonstration of his submissive heart. And he did not do this with strings attached. In short, despite Moses' reputation, he wasn't too cool to help a sister out. With these in mind, is it any wonder that the women's father, Jethro, gave Zipporah to Moses as a wife (See Exodus 2:21).

Being faithful, holy, obedient, humble and submissive are character traits of a Godly spouse. Male or female. These are character traits that we should develop in our lives to become the right ones for others. These are attributes that we need to sow by living them out, in order for us to reap the harvest of ending up with the right life-partners who'll also emanate similar characteristics.

Furthermore, if you're a lady, there are at least three other things that you should also look out for in a man. These attributes were also exemplified by Moses and Boaz, who I will be talking more about later. A Godly man will:

1. Provide for you

Moses provided for Jethro's daughters by watering their flock. Boaz provided for Ruth by giving her wheat for her and Naomi (See Ruth 2:14-16; 3:15).

2. Protect you

Moses protected Jethro's daughters from the shepherds. Boaz protected Ruth from the people working for him by instructing them not to harass her. He also instructed her to work within his field and not wander to someone else's property, where, perhaps, he would not have enough latitude to protect her (See Ruth 2:8).

3. Propel you

They will speed things up for you. In other words, things that were difficult for you to accomplish and as a result took a lot of your time and effort, will be accomplished faster when God's man for you comes to your assistance. Did you notice that Zipporah and her sisters came home earlier than usual when Moses came to their aid? This happened because they were able to water their flocks on time thanks to Moses keeping their detractors at bay. Ruth became pregnant after she married Boaz. She was unable to do this in her previous marriage with Mahlon whom the scripture suggests she was married to for *ten* years (See Ruth 1:4). Not too long after hooking up with Boaz, Obed their son, *popped* out (See Ruth 4:13). She got propelled.

And for the guys, there are also things that you can look out for in women.

1. Wisdom

The Bible said that Abigail had a good understanding (1 Samuel 25:3).

2. A good attitude

While I do not dispute that Abigail was physically attractive, the wording that she had a beautiful countenance suggests that her beauty was more about her attitude than her looks. Even so, a beautiful attitude facilitates a beautiful person. A meek and quiet spirit is very precious in the sight of God and the average man (See 1 Peter 3:1-4). Look out for a woman with a wholesome demeanor.

3. A reverent woman *(A woman that will show you respect)*

Deborah exemplifies this well. Despite being the head honcho of Israel, she had no qualms in esteeming Barak as the man God chose to deliver Israel. She didn't let her prominent position as the leader of Israel prevent her from appreciating and encouraging a man to be the man God created him to be. This is evident when he asked her for help. She had told him that he was to proceed in a battle to deliver Israel from their oppressors. But Barak said that he would not proceed unless she followed him. She responded that if she did, a woman would take the credit that was supposed to go to him (See Judges 4:4-10). This shows the heart of a woman who understands and was sensitive to the heart of men, despite the fact that she had the credentials to ignore him.

Barak also represents a *real* man who has no problem asking a woman for help. Real men and women don't focus on their positions but their purposes. Their mentality is "what's best for us" rather than "what's best for me." Similarly, the right mate thinks of what's best for the marriage and not what's best for him or her. And, truth be told, what's best for the marriage is what's best for either of the individuals in the marriage. Conversely, what's best for either of them is not necessarily what's best for the union.

CHAPTER TEN
Get a Job

Now the LORD God had planted a garden in the east, in Eden; and there he put the man he had formed. (Genesis 2:8)

Despite the number of times I've heard the story of Adam and Eve, for some reason or the other I always thought that Adam was created in the garden. He wasn't. He was created outside the garden and brought in the garden by God to tend and keep it.

Then the lord God took the man and put him in the Garden of Eden to tend and keep it. (Genesis 2:15 NKJV)

In reference to that verse, especially if you're a man, while you are single—get a job. The first thing that God entrusted to Adam was a job. Adam got a job while he was single—before he got Eve. God delegated Adam to manage and run His garden. He specified exactly what he wanted Adam to do. In the same token, while you're single, find out from God what He wants you to do. This goes beyond just having a regular job, but having a purpose that God wants you to fulfill.

In giving Adam a job, God put him in the garden. This means that God led him into the garden. God guided him into the garden where he eventually discovered Eve—the right person for Adam. I believe we can perceive God's garden as God's special environment or His will per se. Adam was created outside the garden but Eve was created in the garden. Therefore, in the quest of fulfilling God's mandate, Adam found his wife. In your quest for the job God has for you, or while you are on the job, somewhere along the line, your mate is around the corner. If you're fulfilling the task God has entrusted you, and positioned where He wants you placed, you're being set up for your mate who is relevant to your purpose in life.

If there is a generic title for the job God has for you, I'll like to call it, "God's servant." It doesn't matter your field of expertise, be it technological, theological, medical, analytical, agricultural, architectural, managerial, judicial, educational or what have you, do your job as best as you can like God is your boss. He is really your Boss.

Whatever you do, work at it with all your heart, as though you were working for the Lord and not for men. (Colossians 3:23 GNB)

With that kind of mindset you're truly undertaking your job as God's servant. Besides, no one pays like God does. Adam served in God's garden and got blessed with Eve amongst other things such as having control over God's botanical edifice. Before Adam got his mate, he got a job. He was relocated from outside the garden into the garden because that was where God had a job and a woman for him. Before Adam got his beloved he got a job. And before he got a job he was relocated.

Relocate

While you are single, you might need to relocate to get a job, which in turn is relevant to finding your mate. The job in question is God's purpose for your life. In addition, relocation for you might not necessarily be regional migration but spiritual and relational migration. Relocation for you might mean that you need to change the way you're living if it's not in line with God's ways.

The right person for you is living a life that is in accordance with God's ways and therefore, in His will—His garden. If you're outside God's will, before you can get espoused to that individual, it's in your best interest that you *step up* and *step out* from where you are, and *step in* to where you need to be. Change your ways. Change your lifestyle by crying out to God to take hold of you, rescue you, and guide you into His compassionate and affectionate embrace where your beloved is also *waiting patiently* for you.

Relocation for you might mean moving out of your comfort zone into a zone where God calls you to *come forth*. That is, moving out from a substandard lifestyle that you might have grown accustomed to, thanks to society's approval, and moving into a place that thrives on a higher standard of living—a place where your true love resides.

If you're single but involved, relocation for you might also mean changing dates. It might mean *breaking up* with Lucifer who hooked you up with some *misfit*, and *making up* with Christ who'll blow your mind with someone who *is fit* for you. It's to your benefit that you relocate from him or her who's bringing and keeping you down or mediocre, to seeking God's direction for your life—your job, which in turn guides you to finding the right mate that will bring you up and keep you up.

In addition to spiritual and relational migration, relocation for you might also mean regional migration as exemplified by the lovely damsel Ruth. In a sense, this young lady got a job before she got her mate. She and her eventual marriage to the man, Boaz, is one of the best examples of how God places people together. Ruth, through her conduct, suitably depicts the kind of person we should emulate in order for us to be portrayed as the right ones to be sought. Here is part of her story:

Naomi had a relative named Boaz, a rich and influential man who belonged to the family of her husband Elimelech. One day Ruth said to Naomi, "Let me go to the fields to gather the grain that the harvest workers leave. I am sure to find someone who will let me work with him." Naomi answered, "Go ahead, daughter." So Ruth went out to the fields and walked behind the workers, picking up the heads of grain which they left. It so happened that she was in a field that belonged to Boaz. Some time later Boaz himself arrived from Bethlehem and greeted the workers. "The Lord be with you!" he said. "The Lord bless you!" they answered. Boaz asked the man in charge, "Who is that young woman?" The man answered, "She is the foreign girl who came back from Moab with Naomi. She asked me to let her follow the workers and gather grain. She has been working since early morning and has just now stopped to rest for a while under the shelter." Then Boaz said to Ruth, "Let me give you some advice. Don't gather grain anywhere except in this field. Work with the women here; watch them to see where they are reaping and stay with them. I have ordered my men not to molest you. And whenever you are thirsty, go and drink from the water jars that they have filled." (Ruth 2:1-9 GNB)

Jesus is my ultimate role model; however, Ruth is up there on my top role model list. It has taken me years to understand some of God's ways of doing things and accept his plan for my life. I am still learning since I haven't arrived, and God has so much more to teach me. The little I know has been and continues to be based on, and linked to, the inexhaustible resource called the Bible. I don't think Ruth had this privilege. Yet, this woman of substance, through her conduct, is demonstrating to us, inadvertently, how to be rewarded with a Godly mate.

She started out looking for a job and started out from the bottom! Did you notice that she was *behind* the workers? She pleaded for a job and when she got it, she did not demand to be a manager or a supervisor. She started out below entry level, if you ask me. She humbled herself, probably without having this scripture that I am still learning to obey:

Humble yourselves before the Lord and He will lift you up. (James 4:10 GNB)

Did you also notice that Ruth happened to end up in her eventual husband's field? Kind of sounds like a setup. Kind of sounds like God had something to do with this. Sounds like how Adam happened to end up in the garden from which Eve emerged. When Boaz showed up he noticed

Ruth. He must have noticed that she did her job heartily and with humility. If you do your job heartily and with humility unto *The Lord*, and not unto *reward*, your beloved will notice you and inquire about you from The Lord and will be your reward.

Her work ethic could be deduced from the fact that she had been working all day except for the period she rested. Her humility was further evident when she listened to Boaz and went along with his advice. Goodness! Do you know any woman that has a problem with taking directions from a man—and vice versa? If as a single, you have a serious problem adhering to instructions from a man or woman, how much more would it be when you get married … if you get married? Then, you'll be taking instructions from your spouse.

Boaz' instruction to Ruth was for her benefit. He offered her relief from her hard work by restricting her to work only in his field and perhaps, check her out a little more. He also asked her to learn from the other women, and she submitted to his request with no questions whatsoever. Ruth did not throw a fit about working with the other women. She did not lash out at Boaz saying "what they got that I ain't got?" She did not hiss, roll her eyes, twitch her eyelashes, or cock her head to one side of her shoulders. She did not purse and protrude her lips to a side of her face, with one of her hands akimbo on her hips, while the other's fingers are spread out navigating which part of Boaz' face was going to get it. She simply submitted to his request.

Do you spontaneously respond like Ruth when asked to do something or do you act otherwise? Even if you submit to the task at hand, do you need Dr. Phil to convince you why you have to obey the instruction? Or do you have to show some drama worthy of a golden globe before you do what you were asked to do? While you are single, it's beneficial that you learn to be humble and submissive. If you want to be promoted or lifted up, humility is a character trait necessary to be developed in you while you are working heartily as God's servant. Ruth got lifted up after she humbled and submitted herself, first to God which I'll talk more about later, and then to Boaz. Boaz instructed the people who she was supposed to learn from to take good care of her and give her water that they fetched, when she was thirsty.

On a side note, I'm not saying you have to apply for a less prestigious job, quit your well-paying job, or step down from your managerial position as a gesture of humility. I believe humility and submission are attitudes, not acts. Perhaps you're aware of people who have no job or earn minimum wage and still express contemptuous attitudes. Regardless of your income bracket, if you express a selfish, haughty, antagonistic personality, please stop. It's in your best interest to step down from that high horse so that God can put you on His horse—beside your knight-in-shining armor or princess charming—whose radiance represents God's presence on him or her.

Oftentimes, in requesting for a mate we ask for someone who looks good. And sometimes we end up with someone who does look good, but not necessarily good, or good for us. Judging from Ruth and Boaz's character, you should be asking God, first, to help you possess an attitude of servanthood, humility and submission and give you someone who is likewise. Since God does more than we ask, not only will He give you someone with a Christ-like personality, but He'll give you someone who'll make Matthew McConaughey, Halle Berry, Morris Chesnut, Charlize Therone, Brad Pitt, Angelina Jolie, Taye Diggs, Eva Mendez, Shemar Moore, Catherine Zeta Jones, Dewayne "the Rock" Johnson, Roselyn Sanchez, Boris Kodjoe, Kerry Washington, Jude Law, Sanaa Latham, Leonardo Decaprio, Gabrielle Union, Denzel Washington, Salma Hayek, Laz Alonzo and Megan Fox look very average.

Okay, I admit, I'm pushing it. But, you catch my drift. For instance, take a look at beautiful Rebecca. This babe was so *muy bonita* (very beautiful) that Isaac her husband, told the men that inquired about her that she was his sister, lest they kill him because of her. However, the king of the place where Isaac lived protected Isaac and his wife by warning the men sternly not to mess with Isaac's woman.[54] The king must have learned from a similar episode that took place before Isaac was born, when God nearly busted his chops for trying to mess with Isaac's mother, Sarah, Abraham's wife.[55]

Even the lovely Rebecca was sort of on the job before she got her man. She was on the job of fetching water for her household when she kind of stumbled into her destiny. There was a well outside the city where she lived from which the women drew water. As mentioned in the previous chapter, Abraham's servant, who was charged with the responsibility of finding Isaac a wife, was by the well praying to God to guide him to the right mate for Isaac. Notice his request again and God's response to it:

He prayed, "Lord, God of my master Abraham, give me success today and keep your promise to my master. Here I am at the well where the young women of the city will be coming to get water. I will say to one of them, 'Please, lower your jar and let me have a drink.' If she says, 'Drink, and I will also bring water for your camels,' may she be the one that you have chosen for your servant Isaac. If this happens, I will know that you have kept your promise to my master." Before he had finished praying, Rebecca arrived with a water jar on her shoulder. She was the daughter of Bethuel, who was the son of Abraham's brother Nahor and his wife Milcah. She was a very beautiful young girl and still a virgin. She went down to the well, filled her jar, and came back. The servant ran to meet her and said, "Please give me a drink of water from your jar." She said, "Drink, sir," and quickly lowered her jar from her shoulder and held it while he drank. When he had finished, she said, "I will also bring water for your camels and let them have all they want." She quickly emptied her jar into the animals drinking trough and ran to the well to get more water, until she had watered all his camels. (Genesis 24:12-20 GNB)

I conclude that the servant asked God for a woman who was humble and had an attitude of servant hood. It takes such spiritual fortitude to do what she did for him and the *ten* camels he brought. Her humility was evident in not only serving a stranger but the animals as well—*as much as they wanted.* Finally, the fact that she was a virgin and *very* beautiful, sealed her irresistible package.

Abraham's servant did not ask for a beautiful woman. He asked for a woman of Godly character and got a *fine* woman in addition to his request. See what I mean? I was serious when I implied that when you ask God for someone with His kind of personality, not only will He give you someone like Him, but also someone who possesses *wholesome* attributes. By the way, when I prayed for my mate, I asked for both character and looks. God blessed me with Dana who has character, looks and then some.

Do you see a pattern here? While on the job in God's field Adam received Eve. While on the job in Boaz' field, Ruth got set up with her man who had a job first, and through it, found his woman. While Rebecca was on the job of drawing water from the well, she met the man that eventually brought her to her husband. Even Rachel, Jacob's main-squeeze, followed that pattern. She was a shepherdess before she met her husband.[56] It was while on the job of trying to water her father's flock with her father's servants that she met Jacob. Adam was in the garden, Ruth in the field, Rebecca and Rachel beside the well, and in the process of doing their respective jobs they got hitched.

And Jacob? He chose to serve seven years for Rachel.[57] What do you think he was doing all that time? He was working. Jacob got a job before he got Rachel. The smart man must have known the importance of having a job before being married. His love for Rachel prompted him to humble himself and render his services to her father. He agreed to work for his daughter for seven years, but his father exploited his love for his daughter and made him work twenty years instead. Notwithstanding, he didn't let this faze him but submitted himself to the task. He was inspired by his love for Rachel. He must have felt she was worth every drop of his sweat.

If you're a man, having a job is not an option, it's an obligation. The woman God has given or is going to give you is worth the sacrifice. Besides, you have to provide for your impending family. You're supposed to treat her like Jesus treats His church. Jesus gives His church, believers, houses, like the place you worship or should worship. He also feeds His church with Himself, His Word, since He's the bread of life.[58] In other words, He gives of His substance to His woman—the church. He even got a job.

Since Christ got a job before he got married, what makes you think you'll do any different? "Got a job?" You might wonder. Yes, He got a job, and I'm not talking about carpentry work, either. Despite being God the Son, Jesus humbled and submitted himself to His Father's will by coming to His Garden, Earth, to undertake the job as His Servant. Jesus embraced the job of salvation.

Jesus left heaven, came down to earth, and did His job excellently, completely and heartily unto His Father. While on the job He wore different hats. As The Deliverer, He cast out demons from people they oppressed. As The Great Physician, he healed people. As the Anointed One or The Christ or The Messiah, he removed people's burdens and destroyed their yokes. As The Provider He fed people with food and also supplied all their other needs. As The Teacher, He taught people His Word. As The last Adam, He made us righteous, thereby making up for the first Adam who made us sinners. As The Redeemer, He paid the price, His Blood, to redeem us from our sins. And He sealed the deal as Savior when He went on the cross, died, was buried, and then resurrected after the third day. Now He's seated on the right hand of God The Father as King and He rules and reigns forever. As Judge, He'll judge everybody.[59]

You might be wondering what I meant by Jesus being married. In a sense He's married to those who have invited Him into their hearts—Believers—all of whom comprise the church. As a result, He's one with them, just like a man and woman become one when they marry. He's the Lamb and Bridegroom, and the church is His bride. The official wedding ceremony will take place sometime in the future as mentioned below:

Let us rejoice and be glad; let us praise his greatness! For the time has come for the wedding of the Lamb, and His bride has prepared herself for it. She has been given clean shining linen to wear. (The linen is the good deeds of God's people.)Then the angel said to me, "Write this: Happy are those who have been invited to the wedding feast of the Lamb." And the angel added, "These are the true words of God." (Revelations 19:7-9 GNB)

Christ got a job before He got His bride. In fact, it was through His purpose that He found or birthed His woman. The church exists because of Christ's finished work on the cross. By fulfilling His purpose, Jesus gave rise to the church. This is a picture of the correlation between God's mandate and mate for your life.

My purpose helped me find Dana. Just like Boaz's field ended up being the environment where he found Ruth, a class where I taught Bible study in the church I attend was the field where I first met my lovely wife. For a while, I didn't really notice her. Eventually my eyes were opened, and I discovered how captivating she was. Her love for God, compassion for people, her Licensed Master Social Work degree or LMSW, coupled with her passion for justice and counseling, complemented my call to ministry. It was these attributes of hers that led her to the classes that I taught. She loves helping and mingling with people. Don't let my writing fool you, I've been labeled anti-social. I am more reserved and have a preference to hibernate. When necessary, I reach out and chat with people, but that's outside my comfort zone. Her people-first attitude cancels what others might perceive as my weakness. Dana complements me. Our purposes brought us together.

Your field (God-given career) is often an area where you discover your spouse. Granted that you're in the right field—God's job for your life, God brings your spouse to your *field* of view.

The LORD God said, "It is not good for the man to be alone. I will make a helper suitable for him." (Genesis 2:18)

When I discussed the purpose of relationships, I disclosed that this verse revealed that God intended to give Adam a helper. Likewise, God wants to give you someone who'll help you, too. With that in mind, it's pertinent to ask this question: "Help you with what?" This is a question for you to answer. When that helper comes, it's your duty to enlighten the person on what you need help with. This is why you find out what job God wants you to undertake. Your helper should help you accomplish your mission. Your helper should support and encourage you by being your cheerleader in this game of life in which you both participate. Your mate should be your teammate with whom you score points by giving assists to each other. Your mate should help you be *you*, by bringing out the best in you.

Knowing that you're supposed to have someone who's to help you do your job efficiently will help you screen out anyone who does not conform to your God-given task. Knowing your prospect's goal in life will help you determine if that person is the right one for you, too. This is why you need to get a job first and communicate your task to whomever you are thinking of betrothing. Likewise, find out the other person's plans as well.

Your helper will be part of a series of triggers that will propel you further toward your purpose in life. That helper might be a lawyer that God brings to you. Someone you should help with integrity issues. You should have enough of God's substance in yourself to help the person contend in cases with such fervor that will bring about the God-kind of justice. When your lawyer spouse comes home, the person will want you to be his wife or her husband, not the judge, client, opposing lawyer, jury, news press or paparazzi. God might bring a doctor to you who you should help to be an outstanding medical practitioner. When your doctor spouse comes home, the person would like to be treated like your special patient so that when the person returns to work the next day, your spouse can treat his or her assigned patient with the care and tenderness you bestowed upon him or her in your mutual intensive care unit (MICU)—your house—excluding the intimacy of course. God might pair you up with someone in church ministry. Somewhere along the line, you'd be equipped to help with the person's calling. Now you'll understand why you spent so much time involved with church activities such as counseling, Sunday school, picnics, singles groups, discussion groups, youth groups, etc.

God wants to give you a helpmate not a cellmate. He does not want to give you someone who will make you feel like you are in prison, but someone who will help you out of prison if you get yourself in one. Mind you, you should be complete in Christ before you get married. You should be content in who you are and where you are in your relationship with God before marriage. The person you're going to marry is not the answer to any insecurity you might have as a single. Jesus is. This is why you should hook up with HIM before you hook up with "him" or "her." Please don't think that getting married to someone will be the answer to any discontentment you might have now, because that is not the case.

In the words of Matthew Kelly:

Before you can learn to be with someone else, you need to be alone. Until you are comfortable being with yourself, you will always be afraid of being alone. If you are not comfortable alone, if you are not comfortable in your own company, there is a great danger you will end up hanging out with the wrong friends because you are scared to be alone...and, worse than that, if you don't learn to enjoy your own company, there's a good chance you will end up dating the wrong guys and marrying the wrong man because you will act out of fear of being alone.[60]

How could one chase a thousand and two put ten thousand to flight, unless their Rock had sold them and the Lord had surrendered them? (Deuteronomy 32:30 NKJV)

With God's help, one can put a thousand to flight, but two can put ten thousand to flight. This implies that what one person can do is greatly increased with two people. But guess what? This cannot take place without God's help. Two people cannot put ten thousand to flight if they are not willing to work together, and if they do not know how to put a thousand to flight. They might just put themselves to fight. Before each of these individuals become a team—while they are single, each must seek God's help and must be willing and able to work together. Each needs to understand the goal of the team and their individual roles on how to accomplish that objective. Each must know how to put a thousand to flight so that when they both come together, their collaborative efforts can result in putting ten thousand to flight.

While you are single, if you are not content with who you are and where you are in your relationship with God, who is perfect, you will not be content in marriage with somebody else who is imperfect. If you have unresolved issues while you are single, getting married will not solve your problem. It will exacerbate it.

Whoever is faithful in small matters will be faithful in large ones; but whoever is dishonest in small matters will be dishonest in large ones. (Luke 16:10 GNB)

Considering that the demands of the single life are less than that of marriage, if you're faithful, secure, pleased, and can handle yourself while you're single, then you'll be faithful, secure, pleased, and will be able to handle yourself in a more demanding responsibility in a relationship with your spouse, as a couple. This will be possible because Jesus is your security. It's in Him you live, you move and have your being. You are strong in the Him and the power of His might. His joy is your strength. This same Lord who is with you while you're single will still be with you in marital bliss, and as your foundation, will help you and *yours* have a great marriage.

I believe a piece of wisdom I learned from Dr. Myles Munroe best describes the connection between singleness and marriage:

...an omelet is only as good as the eggs that are in it.[61]

If marriage is an omelet made up of two eggs, then the eggs are the two single individuals that make the omelet. Can you see the picture now? The success or failure of that marriage is determined by the singles that "yoked" to form the marriage. To have a good marriage you have to have two good singles. This reinforces Dr. Munroe's notion that a successful marriage is only a byproduct of two people being successfully single. If you can't handle yourself while you are single, without God's intervention you won't be able to handle yourself as part of a couple. An accident about to happen, meeting another accident that may or may not happen, ends up being an accident that happens.

To better illustrate this point of view, consider a pound cake. It's complete, good by itself, and ready to be eaten. However, when you put icing on the cake, *bon appetite*! This enhances it even more. You need to be a pound cake before God can put icing on you. The icing is the person God has for you. Some singles are in the flour stage of the pound cake. Some of them just got placed in the oven, yet want God to put icing on them. How would you like to eat a pound cake, which is in the flour stage and not even out of the bag, mixed with icing? Yuck!

CHAPTER ELEVEN

Find out God's Will for Your Life

There is a correlation between your purpose and your life-partner. The right mate for your life is linked to God's plan for your life. Therefore, it makes sense that finding your purpose in life will help you find your life-partner *for* life. Despite this connection, I'm in no way saying that your motivation for discovering your destiny should be because you're trying to get married. On the contrary. Whether you get hitched or not, finding God's plan for your life will help you live a fulfilled life. Finding your spouse in the process is, I believe, an added benefit.

There are a plethora of books that guide us on how to discover our purposes. Notwithstanding, I believe that God's purpose for your life can be placed in two categories. God has a generic plan and a specific plan for your life. God's generic plan for our lives applies to us all. For example, it's God's will for us to obey His commandments, have a relationship with Him, worship Him, love Him and love our fellow man and woman as we love ourselves. These are things that God desires all of us to do. They are generic to us all.

Furthermore, God's generic plan for our lives is more character based. Whereas, God's specific plan for our lives is more performance based. His specific purpose for you deals with you specifically, and it usually involves you doing something or some things. God's specific plan for you differs from His specific plan for me. I do believe, however, that we will find fulfillment and be more successful in God's specific purposes for our lives, when they are preceded by us living out God's generic purposes for our lives.

Having said this, I will like to share seven pointers that will help you discover your purpose; by this, I mean your specific purpose.

1. It is through God that you will find it

Before you can find God's will for your life you would need to find God first. If someone wanted to give you some money, you would need to find the person in order to get the money. After you've found the person, the individual would either give you the money or direct you to where you would find it. Similarly, you have to find God in order to find His will for your life. This will in turn assist you in finding your spouse who is also part of God's plan for your life. It is through God that you will discover your purpose. He knows all about you because He created you and placed in you all that you need to fulfill His call on your life.

You made all the delicate, inner parts of my body and knit me together in my mother's womb. You watched me as I was being formed in utter seclusion, as I was woven together in the dark of the womb. You saw me before I was born. Every day of my life was recorded in your book. Every moment was laid out before a single day had passed. (Psalm 139:13, 15-16 NLT)

The LORD gave me this message: "I knew you before I formed you in your mother's womb. Before you were born I set you apart...." (Jeremiah 1:4-5 NLT)

It was through God that Abraham found his purpose. The same holds true for Moses who found God at the burning bush. Similarly, Paul's encounter with God on His way to Damascus forever changed him and helped him discover his destiny. Finding God will help you discover His plan for your life.

Even so, how can you begin to recognize what God has assigned you to do? How can you decipher His purpose for your life? Well, the first step is to begin to know God. Get acquainted with Him. Seek Him. You can know Him based on what He reveals about Himself, which is in the Bible. It is through the scriptures that He primarily talks to us. It's also through them that I'm presenting you with the remaining six points that will help you in figuring out the job He wants you to undertake.

2. You will have a heart for it

There will be a desire in your heart to undertake the job God has for you. You might not have it now, but it will come eventually like it did for Moses.

"Now when he was forty years old, it came into his heart to visit his brethren, the children of Israel. (Acts 7:23)

When Moses was forty years old…*it came into his heart.* What came into his heart? A desire to visit his fellow Israelites whom he was to deliver from Egypt. Similarly, God's plan for your life *will come* to your heart. You will have a passion, desire, longing, or heart for it. Perhaps you might argue that you don't know His plan for your life. You might say that you don't have a passion. You might feel like you don't have a clue of what you're supposed to be doing with your life. Relax. Don't stress yourself.

Chances are that there are things in your heart that you've overlooked, or considered not important. If this is not the case, then it's likely that your mission has not come into your heart *yet.* If you revisit the previous passage again you would realize that Moses's purpose *came* to his heart. This means that there was a time that it was not in his heart. This brings me to the third point that will help you discover your purpose.

3. There is a time for it

Before I proceed further I want to comment on something I've observed regarding the discovery process of God's will for our lives. Without taking away from the intrigue and quest for our callings, perhaps the frustration that some of us encounter in finding our purpose stems from the possibility that we are going about it the wrong way. I don't think we are supposed to find our purpose. I think it finds us. We are to stay put and wait to receive it. This verse comes to mind:

Then the LORD answered me and said: "Write the vision And make it plain on tablets, That he might run who reads it. For the vision is yet for an appointed time; But at the end it will speak, and it will not lie. Though it tarries, wait for it; Because it will surely come, It will not tarry. (Habakkuk 2:3-4 NKJV)

In the text above, God asked Habakkuk to write the vision and make it plain so that the person that reads it will run with it. This suggests that the person that was going to read the vision was different from the person who wrote it. This also suggests that someone else was going to receive this vision. In addition, the person(s) who was to read the vision hadn't read it yet. Furthermore, the vision was for an appointed time. And when the time came for it to be fulfilled, it would speak, it would come. Until that time the individual(s) to whom the vision was written was to *wait* for it.

There is a time for you to discover your purpose. God already has it written. When the time comes, it will come to you and it will speak to you. This is why I don't think we necessarily find our callings. Our callings find us. They speak to us. Perhaps this explains why your purpose is referred to as *your* calling. It calls you. It comes to you. But it does so at a certain time. Moses was called from the burning bush. Through circumstances beyond his control Joseph was sold to Egypt where he fulfilled his call. Paul was swept off his feet and called to ministry on his way to Damascus (See Acts 9:1-30). Virgin Mary had a visitation to birth Christ.

In the same vein God has a calling for you too. If you don't know or have a desire for it, it might be because it hasn't been revealed to you yet. Wait for it. Expect it. It will come to you at a certain time. Like it did for Moses, it will come into your heart. Like it did for Paul, it might come like a life-changing event. Like it did for Mary, it might come in a spiritual encounter and visitation from God. Like it did for Joseph, which most of us don't like, it might come as an unwanted circumstance that grabs you and forces you to go somewhere and/or do something that you never planned to do. Little do a lot of people who find themselves in such predicaments know that God had a purpose for allowing them to go through such experiences. The purpose was to help them find and fulfill their callings.

There is a time for you to fulfill your purpose. God's plan for Moses did not only come to Moses' heart, it came when he was forty years old. Moses was eighty years old when he went to Pharaoh to demand the release of his people. He died when he was one-hundred-and-twenty years old.[62] Therefore, the desire to fulfill his mandate—at least part of it, came to him at the third of his life.

There is always a timing factor. You might not know God's will for your life yet, but at the right time—at the set time, it will come into your heart. And when it does, that does not mean that you should launch out immediately and do your job. You're probably untrained in the task. Don't jump the gun. Moses was forty when he desired to visit his brethren. He proceeded to unofficially begin to deliver his brethren when he murdered an Egyptian. In a sense, he went ahead of himself and this transformed him from a prince to a fugitive.

You are not to start something before God's appointed time even though that's what you're supposed to do. God is going to do it—through you. You are the messenger; He is the sender. He's your Boss; He calls the shots. You're to wait on Him to train you on how to undertake the task, and give you the green light to execute the task.

You see, friend, I've always used the words *time* and *seasons* interchangeably; but, on closer look at those words, I've come to the conclusion that seasons are basically divisions of time. For example, the year 2009 is a time period. The fall season is a division within the year 2009 time period. My point is that, while there is a time for you to fulfill your purpose, there are different seasons within that time that God will prepare you to fulfill the task at hand. I believe that there are at least four seasons within the time period that you discover your purpose. There is a season for you to discover your purpose, the next is to train you for the task, the next is for you to carry out the task, and the last is to see the fruit of the task.

Moses was forty when he discovered his purpose. The next season, between forty and eighty years of age, he was being prepared for the task. In his third season he went to Egypt to begin the task, which pretty much took forty more years of his life. At 120, his fourth season, he saw the fruit of his labor from afar. He did not get into the Promised Land, but saw it from afar.

I am not saying that you will be forty before you begin to ascertain God's will for your life. Neither am I saying that you'll be eighty before you get to do the job. At eighty you should be enjoying the fruits of your labor, the fruit(s) of your loins, and perhaps getting ready to meet God and hear Him congratulate you for a job well done.

I am saying, however, that there is a time to find your purpose, a time for you to be trained for it, a time for you to do it, and a time to see the fruit of it. This is necessary because God needs to ensure that you are *seasoned* for your season. Joseph was seventeen years old when he dreamt about his job, which he began to actualize thirteen years later. I hope you noted the time factor again. He was seventeen when he discovered his purpose. Between seventeen and thirty, unbeknownst to Joseph, as a slave in Potiphar's house and prison, he was being trained for his job. This was his second season. His third season started when he was made the governor of Egypt. By this time he was thirty years old. I guess we can say that the next eighty years of his life gave him the opportunity to see the fruit of his labor, which included having a clearer understanding of why he ended up in Egypt. Joseph ended up in Egypt to save his Israelite brethren from the famine that

God foresaw was going to happen, and also help the Egyptians and other nations as well, to have food despite the famine.

4. There is a place for it

Another important point to be considered in the quest for your destiny is that there is a place for it. Until you get to that place, you're likely not going to find and fulfill God's plan for your life. This place can be a physical place or a spiritual place. By physical place, I mean a physical location. It can even be a person. Until you get to that place or bump into that person, your purpose might not happen. For example, Moses's place was the burning bush. Joseph's place was Egypt. Paul's place was near Damascus. Once these guys got to those places, bingo! They discovered God's plan for their lives. Furthermore, Joseph connected with the butler who eventually referred him to Pharaoh. Paul connected with Ananias who restored his sight. Paul also connected with Barnabas, who was the main person that endorsed his credibility as a bonafide convert to Christianity (See Acts 9:10-17, 26-27).

The spiritual place necessary for you to discover your purpose is your relationship with God. In other words, where are you with God? What's your relationship with Him like? Are you yielded to Him? Some call this spiritual place *brokenness*. This probably explains why so many people undergo a "life-changing event," which breaks or humbles them, and then alters their course in life. Paul was broken in Damascus. Joseph was broken in Egypt. Moses was broken in the desert. In a state of humility and total dependence on God, God can now flood you with grace to do what He wants you to do in life.

Sometimes, the reason why some people have not found their purpose is because they are not in the right place—whether physical or spiritual. Until they get to that place, they won't find their destiny. At times the key is to get to that spiritual place by seeking God, then that physical place by going to the location and/or person who is a connector to your calling, and then it will be time to know what you're supposed to do.

You might wonder if you are in that place, and if you are not, how can you get there? This is a good question. This also causes me to refer you to the second point about discovering God's call on your life. It will be in your heart to move to a certain place. Fundamentally, that's one of the better ways that God prods you to go somewhere, where you'll meet someone or some people, to do something(s). Usually being in that spiritual place or having a relationship with God through prayer, Bible reading, and spending time with Him will help you with this quest.

However, sometimes some people don't have and don't want a relationship with God. Some are disobedient, and some are fearful. As a result they don't go where they are supposed to go. Sometimes, despite a relationship with God, some people are not clear if God is telling them to do something. So, if you're supposed to go somewhere and you don't know it, what do you do?

Well, God has numerous ways to get you where He wants you to go. Unfortunately that might mean heartbreak, rejection, or something not working out to the point where it drives you to your knees, and/or causes you to move to another location—be it another job, residence, city, state or country. If you would like to find out more about the alternate way that God uses to lead you to a certain place, you might consider getting my other book *Rejected for a Purpose*, which was dedicated to elaborate on how God uses rejection to help you find and fulfill your destiny. This destiny also includes the right person for your life.

5. You will have the ability for it

There is a saying that goes something like this: *wherever God guides, he provides*. God will equip you with the knowledge and ability to accomplish your mission. You will possess the skills to do the job. You will have the ability, skills, gifts or talent for it. Looking at Moses again:

Moses was educated in all the wisdom of the Egyptians and was power-ful in speech and action. (Acts 7:22)

Moses possessed all the wisdom of the Egyptians. This makes sense since he contended for his people's release from their hands. He possessed the knowledge and skills necessary to relate and communicate with the Egyptians. Furthermore, when Moses encountered God at the burning bush...

Then the LORD said to him, "What is that in your hand?" "A staff," he replied. The LORD said, "Throw it on the ground." Moses threw it on the ground and it became a snake, and he ran from it. Then the LORD said to him, "Reach out your hand and take it by the tail." So Moses reached out and took hold of the snake and it turned back into a staff in his hand. (Exodus 4:2-4)

The instrument that God used mightily in delivering His people was in Moses's hand. Moses already possessed the means to the end—the skills to the task—the ability to fulfill God's purpose for his life. It was in his hand. However, he had to find God first to draw his attention to the rod in his hand, and reveal to him what he could do with it—and how he could handle it.

I found it funny and profound that Moses ran away from the serpent. Perhaps you've been running away from God's will for your life. Perhaps you've been shying away from an ability that God has given you to fulfill His call on your life. This, in itself can be another clue to help you find your calling. What are you running from? If this applies to you, you might be doing this out of fear that you will fail, fear of criticism, or fear that you will not be able to handle the responsibility that comes with your calling. Don't be perturbed. Brace yourself. Handle that gift by the tail. Through God's help you will be able to control and utilize your gift to accomplish your mission in life.

6. You have expressed it.

Now Moses was tending the flock of Jethro his father-in-law, the priest of Midian, and he led the flock to the far side of the desert and came to Horeb, the mountain of God. (Exodus 3:1)

Why do you think Moses had a rod in his hand in the first place? He needed it for the flock. The staff that God used to deliver the Israelites was in Moses's hands. He was already using it to shepherd the animals. Unbeknownst to him, he had in his hands a life-changing instrument, which he used to tend the flock of sheep. In a sense, Moses tending the sheep was a metaphor for Moses's purpose of tending God's sheep—the Israelites. God refers to his children as sheep. Moses was expressing with the animals, the ability he would be using in a broader scale to guide God's people.

Just like Moses, you have probably experienced the ability relevant to your purpose. You might be currently expressing your purpose, in a lesser scale, in some endeavor or the other. Maybe you have an ability to influence a lot of people, which comes in handy in sales and overseeing companies. God can use your gifting to lead people to Him. Maybe you're a financial guru, good with numbers, and savvy with a variety of investment and money management strategies. God can use your financial acumen to deliver people from the land of debt.

When Moses first received the desire to visit his brethren, he went to check them out. Unfortunately he saw an Egyptian maltreating one of his countrymen. Well, the ability to deliver his people began to be used when he slew the Egyptian. The next day the guy he rescued got into an altercation with another Israelite and Moses inadvertently tried to utilize his gift as a judge to quench their strife. Also, when he fled Egypt to seek asylum in Midian, his ability as a deliverer came in handy again when he stood up for the priest of Midian's daughters from shepherds who were trying to drive them away from watering their father's flock. By the way, that's how Moses met his wife—en route to the full revelation of his job as the ruler and deliverer of Israel.[63] While relocating from Egypt to Midian, a *place* where he encountered God—at the burning bush—Moses met his wife. She was one of Jethro's daughters—Zipporah. Can you see the connection between Moses finding his purpose and finding his life-partner?

Joseph also utilized his gifts to some capacity before he became Governor of Egypt. As a slave, he utilized his administrative skills to take care of his master's house. While in prison, his gift as a dream interpreter came in handy when he interpreted the dreams of his fellow prisoners over whom he was placed in charge. Both gifts were instrumental in helping him land his job and do his job effectively and efficiently. Moses's and Joseph's gifts brought them before great men—the pharaohs of Egypt. Is it not interesting how both their skills were honed and enforced in Egypt?

7. People tell you about it

Finally, people will help you discover your purpose. They will tell you about it. And they will tell you about your purpose in at least three ways. They will reveal your purpose to you indirectly, positively and negatively.

Indirectly: They show you

By people helping you discover your purpose indirectly, I mean that they show you your purpose. This is where you discover your purpose by watching people do things that pique your interest. And as a result of seeing someone do something, this inspires you to emulate that person. After mimicking the individual you then discover that you are good, if not better, in doing the thing that the person you emulated, did. I guess discovering your purpose this way can be stated thus:

You don't know what you want to do until you see someone doing it.

Positively: They affirm you

Discovering your purpose by people telling you about it positively is when people affirm you. This is where someone sees you doing something and complements you on the task. This is when you get *positive* feedback and hear people tell you that you are very good in doing something. Usually someone acknowledges that you have a gift, talent, or expertise in a certain area and encourages you to develop your talent and apply it more in a larger scale.

Negatively: They Doubt You

Now, let me stay here a little bit. I want you to pay close attention to how you can discover your purpose through people telling you about it negatively. In this case, they doubt you. This is where people criticize, and belittle you about something that you're trying to do. If different people at different times in your life have discouraged you from doing something in particular, chances are that the thing you were trying to do is your purpose. By this, I mean that you can discover your calling by listening to what different people at different times in your life have told you that you *cannot* do. Those people, through their negativity, are inadvertently telling you what you are supposed to be doing.

Moses thought that his own people would realize that God was using him to rescue them, but they did not. The next day Moses came upon two Israelites who were fighting. He tried to reconcile them, by saying, 'Men, you are brothers; why do you want to hurt each other?'"But the man who was mistreating the other pushed Moses aside and said, 'Who made you ruler and judge over us? (Acts 7:25-27)

Moses thought his brethren would have understood that God would deliver them through him. I wonder where he got that idea from. It came from his heart. When he saw two of his brethren fighting, Moses tried to make peace between them, but the guy who caused the fight mocked him saying: *who made you ruler and judge over us?* God did! And Moses had to find God at the burning bush to confirm it. He found God and then found God's will for his life, which was the role his countryman sarcastically questioned him about. The very thing that the man mocked Moses about was the very thing Moses became.

The same happened to Joseph. He had a dream and told it to his brothers and this was their response:

His brothers said to him, "Do you intend to reign over us? Will you actually rule us?" And they hated him all the more because of his dream and what he had said. (Genesis 37:8)

Yes, Joseph ended up reigning over them. He also told another dream to them and his father, and this was their response:

When he told his father as well as his brothers, his father rebuked him and said, "What is this dream you had? Will your mother and I and your brothers actually come and bow down to the ground before you?"(Genesis 37:9)

Absolutely! Joseph ended up reigning over them as governor of Egypt. Did you note that in Moses and Joseph's cases, the negative attack and discouragement of their efforts revealed what they were supposed to be doing? Moses was questioned if he would be a judge and a ruler. He turned out to be a judge and a ruler. Joseph was mocked by his family members when they questioned if they were going to bow down before him. They ended up bowing down before him.

Did you also note that Joseph did not interpret his dreams to his family? Joseph told them his dreams, but his family members sarcastically interpreted them for him. Similarly, watch out for people who negatively give you hints about God's call on your life. Especially if you never told them what you were thinking of doing in the first place. When people attack and label you for something that is worthwhile, and something you might not have even been thinking about— this suggests that there is something about the way you conduct yourself that people see, which causes them to label you as such.

Even Jesus was taunted by being called, "King of the Jews."[64] Not only did He turn out as the King of the Jews, He's also the King of Kings.

I said all these to let you know that sometimes, unfortunately, those closest to you, like your family members and friends might not see your potential. In fact, they might tease you by questioning your qualification to handle certain tasks. Prop your ears open if they do this. They might just be giving you hints of exactly what you're going to be doing. Their lack of perception of your potential doesn't invalidate God's purpose for your life. If they don't support what you believe you're to be doing, don't be discouraged. God is the one who gave you the assignment and is the one that will see you through to fulfill it.

In finding God's specific will for your life, with "it" being your purpose, remember that it is through God that you will find it. You will have a heart for it. There is a time for it. There is a place for it. You will have the ability for it. You have expressed it. And people tell you about it. Mind you, all these points are connected to each other.

I do not want to leave you with the impression that just because you have a passion for something, it means that that thing is your purpose. Not at all. You might have a passion for something, but if you don't have the ability, gift or talent for it, that is not your purpose. Many people want to be on *American Idol*, but only end up with their *pants on the ground*. God's call on your life comes from Him and you will have the ability and passion for it. Perhaps you've already expressed and experienced some of this ability. There is also a time and an environment for you to bring this to fruition.

The main reason that I brought you on this journey on a way to discover God's specific purpose for your life is for you to see a connection between finding your purpose and finding your mate. Not only is your destiny and heavenly mate connected, but the way you find your call is similar to the way you find your mate. Just like your purpose finds you, so does your partner—either by a guy coming to you—or an opportunity presenting your spouse to you.

It is through God that you'll find your mate. You will have a heart, desire or passion for the person. There is a time for you to meet and marry the person. There is a place or environment for you to be in, where you will find the person. And you will have the ability or empowerment from God to handle and take care of the person.

The sixth point in discovering your purpose addresses the possibility that you have likely exercised the abilities relevant to your call already. The sixth point in discovering your spouse is that you might have met the person already. You might have experienced the person's presence. And you might have expressed the personality that appeals to the person but rebuffed by others to whom you expressed yourself. This was just one of God's ways to keep you from others and direct you to the best person for you.

Finally, people tell you about who your spouse is. This can be very tricky, and as a result, in subsequent chapters, particularly chapters 19 and 21, I dedicate some time to help you avoid ending up with the wrong person just because people recommend someone to you. The fact is, whether indirectly, positively, or negatively, people tell you who your spouse will be. You just have to be careful to discern with wisdom which recommendations you accept or reject.

All those tips helped me find Dana. First, God helped me find her. For years immemorial, I prayed for Dana. Of course, at the times I prayed for a spouse and *for* my spouse, I didn't know that I was praying for her. Second, I developed a desire for her. The desire was not there initially. Later on, a strong desire for her came into my heart. Third, there was a time this happened. I first met Dana in 2007. It was in one of the classes in which I taught Bible study that this took place.

Much to my chagrin, Dana said I came off as a snub when she first chatted with me (not exactly her words, but just being concise). I was about to teach a class, and I came to her to say "hi." Prior to teaching a class I usually went around greeting class attendees, especially new ones, to make them feel welcome. Dana noticed my name tag, and suspected I was of Nigerian heritage. So she asked if it was a Nigerian name. According to her, I confirmed her suspicions, but, I then walked *away.*

It was maybe close to a year after our first meeting, which unfortunately I don't recall, that *I* began to notice Dana. She began to be on my radar. The problem was, prior to really noticing her, there were a few other people already on my radar, too. After experiencing a few reality checks, by the end of 2010, everyone was cleared off my radar—except Dana. I asked her out on May 8, 2011. We married on August 10, 2013.

Fourth, there was a place we met. I was born in Inglewood, California in 1975. Barely six weeks old, my parents took me with them back to Nigeria, where they're from. I was raised there for 19 years. I came back to the states via Richmond, Virginia, in 1994. I moved to Houston, Texas in 2006. Dana, on the other hand was born and raised in Plymouth and Southbend, Indiana. Her desire to get her masters in social work (hint: purpose), brought her to the University of Houston, in 2007, where she received it. She decided to remain in Houston, Texas. We found ourselves not only in the same State and city, but in the same church. There was a place for our meeting.

Fifth, we had the ability for, or relevant knowledge about, each other. Just like Moses was educated with the wisdom of the Egyptians, I was somewhat Americanized, and she was, well, Africanized. Though Dana hails from a Hispanic Dad and a White Indiana mother, her best friends in her formative years included Nigerians. They were her friends in college, and roommates in Houston. Though I had predominantly African American friends when I lived in Richmond, Virginia, I underwent a seamless shift in choice of friends in Houston.

When I relocated to the Bayou City, most of the friends I made were Hispanic. For a long while, I was the only black person playing soccer with a number of Hispanics from Mexico, Honduras, Costa Rica, and El Salvador, just to mention a few. Interestingly enough, for about two years, I played soccer with those guys on a field right next to the school where Dana worked. I had no clue that she worked there until about another two years later when I started dating her.

Most of my Hispanic friends were from church. I did not plan it that way. That's how the chips fell. Prior to dating Dana, I had more Hispanic friends than friends that were African American, White, and from other ethnicities. Interestingly, after Dana and I hooked up, I made more Nigerian and other African friends. The point is, prior to seeing each other, Dana and I were equipped for each other and somewhat educated about our respective ethnicities.

Sixth, we were experienced with each other. By this, I mean that we were already around each other. Yeah, only for *four* years. We weren't just around each other, we served with each other and occasionally met in group functions when hanging out with our respective friends. Finally, we were told independently by others that we should see each other. My best man at my wedding was the second person to bring Dana to my attention (God was first, but I didn't get it). But much to my chagrin, *again*, I dismissed the idea. With my head between my tail, after I saw the light (soprano sings), I went back to him and admitted that he was right and I was dumb.

Prior to going out with me, Dana had not seriously dated for 10 years. Her family from Indiana and friends in Houston and Indiana often asked her if she was interested in anyone. She would tell them she wasn't, but there was a guy that she was impressed with. To date, her friends still tease her about her choice of word: impress. It turns out that the guy that impressed her was me. But after she felt I turned my back on her during our first meeting, she decided not to raise her hopes regarding me. The rest is history.

Though people might help you find your spouse, sometimes they can lead you to *lose* someone that God wants for you. While there were a few people that saw Dana and I being together, there were others who didn't. I will be discussing one of such people in the last chapter.

If you feel like people gave you wrong advice about someone and you turned them down, but you realized your mistake, but you're still single and the person has moved on, take courage. Don't despair. God will give you another chance.

CHAPTER TWELVE
Let God Do His Job

If God gives such attention to the appearance of wildflowers—most of which are never even seen—don't you think he'll attend to you, take pride in you, do his best for you? What I'm trying to do here is to get you to relax, to not be so preoccupied with getting, so you can respond to God's giving. People who don't know God and the way he works fuss over these things, but you know both God and how he works. Steep your life in God-reality, God-initiative, God-provisions. Don't worry about missing out. You'll find all your everyday human concerns will be met. (Matthew 6:30-33 MSG)

God is aware that you have needs, which must include a life partner. God acknowledges that you need someone in your life, and as a result, He'll make someone available for you—to help you. It's not your job to make someone available for yourself. You don't have the expertise to handle this task. Unfortunately, many people still try to get someone for themselves. And the result of their vain efforts is ending up with someone who gives them hell—instead of someone who'd have given them help had they allowed God to do His job.

If you let God do His job, not only will He make someone available for you, He'll also pair you up with someone who's comparable to you, compatible with you, and who also complements you. This sounds reasonable since He doesn't want us to be unequally yoked with our mates.[65] He desires balance, which allows for compatibility, facilitates partnership, efficiently functions on agreement, fosters oneness and brings peace.

I once heard that it's not the best for two people in a relationship to have *exactly* the same personality. If this was the case, it's likely that they had the same weaknesses. I believe that to avoid this from happening God gives you someone comparable to you. Someone who comes-pair-able to you. Someone who fits you and icings your cake. Someone who gravys your mash potato and efficiently scratches your itch.

That is necessary so that you end up with someone who is strong where you're weak and weak where you're strong. Together you cancel out each other's weaknesses. In light of this, don't be surprised when God brings someone to you whose personality is not exactly like yours. If you are re-served, don't be surprised in getting hitched with someone who is flamboy-ant. If you are soft-spoken, don't be surprised in getting someone who's outspoken.

So Adam gave names to all cattle, to the birds of the air, and to every beast of the field. But for Adam there was not found a helper comparable to him. (Genesis 2:20 NKJV)

God has said that it was not good for man to be alone and He would make him a helper comparable to him (See Genesis 2:18 NKJV). God already identified the fact that Adam needed someone in his life. Since God is omniscient, meaning that He knows everything, then He already knew that there was no one good enough for Adam at that point in time. Certainly not the animals.

That verse, however, says that there was no one found comparable to Adam. Saying that there was no one found implies that somebody was looking, since finding something means something is being looked for. I don't think God was looking for somebody for Adam since He already decided to make someone for him. God would not be making someone for Adam if the person already existed. But like the scripture said, there was no one *found* comparable to Adam. Bearing that in mind, I'm left to con-clude that Adam was looking.

Sometimes that is how we are, aren't we? Instead of letting God make someone available for us we make someone available for ourselves and get ourselves in a mess; and at times, blame God for our mistakes. Visualize Adam looking for someone to be a helper comparable to him. Imagine Adam checking out the animals for companionship. Considering that many men like women with long hair, Adam's hormones might have gone haywire when he saw the lion's hair. However, the animal's fangs probably kept things in perspective.

I know it sounds ludicrous thinking of Adam trying to get acquainted with the animals. Did it ever occur to you that this might be the same reason why some people end up with animals, too? Instead of allowing God to bring the right person to them, some people take matters into their own hands and end up with individuals who act like pigs, goats, monkeys or cats.

God is trying to pair you up with someone who would love you and treat you like a person. But because of ignorance, impatience, disobedience and sometimes unbelief, some folks end up with mates who behave like pets. What's a popular pet that people have? How about a dog?

Why do some settle for an animal outside the garden when God wants to give them someone like Him in His garden? God wants to give us mates that will make us shout, "Glory! Hallelujah! You Rock!"... since He is the Rock. Instead of God's best, sometimes, people settle for less and get spouses that make them shout, "Who let the dogs out, woof! Woof?" Or worst still, "Who let the devil out?"

Although Adam was created outside the garden, God brought him into the garden before he got Eve. Therefore, regardless of where Adam came from, Eve found her man in the garden, too. If you feel like you've acted like an animal, if you feel like you're outside God's will, if you feel like you're outside God's garden, even if you used to be in it, put your past behind, submit to God and let Him take or bring you back to His garden.

While there, let Him operate on you after He puts you to sleep, like he did below.

So the LORD God caused the man to fall into a deep sleep; and while he was sleeping, he took one of the man's ribs and closed up the place with flesh. (Genesis 2:21)

God caused Adam to fall into a deep sleep. Not just to sleep, but a *deep* sleep. It's like God is saying, "I'll handle this, while you relax." This is interesting because He allowed Adam to take care of the garden and its inhabitants but the making of the helper, God took upon Himself. Why? Because He is the only one that can do a thorough job of bringing you the right person. He is the guide to finding the right mate for your life.

"Be still, and know that I am God...." (Psalm 46:10)

I believe that part of what God is saying is that you need to relax and let Him be in control. You need to calm down and stop being agitated and anxious about whom your marriage partner will be. When you chill out and refrain from your anxiety which distracts you from perceiving God's move in your life, you'll be focused enough to trust God and allow Him to withdraw from His infinite repertoire as a means of bringing your heavenly mate to you.

Can you imagine Adam trying to direct God in making someone for him? Imagine Adam barely standing up and bent over beside God holding the side of his body from which the rib came out and which is now oozing out lots of blood. While writhing in pain, envisage Adam having the moxie to bark instructions at God. Imagine him telling our Maker that he wants her eye color to be a blend of green, brown, sky blue and grey. Although God is slow to anger, merciful and of great kindness, visualize Adam tap-dancing on God's nerves by insisting that Eve's hair be blonde, her face like Halle Berry's, her figure like J-Lo's, her busts like silicon, her accent like Nicole Kidman's, and please God don't forget the Cindy Crawford mole.

Of course God can give you someone who has testosterone-driving physical attributes; however, our tendency—especially men—to only focus on such, validates why we should let God bring someone to us. He's more interested in giving you someone with the proper and balanced combination of the spiritual, physical and emotional, than *just* the superficial.

Then the LORD God made a woman from the rib he had taken out of the man, and he brought her to the man. (Genesis 2:22)

I hope you noticed that God brought her to the man. She did not bring herself to him—God did. Adam woke up and alas! there was Eve. Rebecca wasn't thinking about Isaac, but when she went to fetch water for her household, she got the hookup. While meditating, Isaac looked up and Becky showed up (See Genesis 25:63-64). Isaac had nothing actively to do with finding Rebecca. God found and brought her to him, for them.

Let God bring him or her to you. Don't take matters into your own hands. Do you want to end up with a dog? If you do, make sure it's a *French poodle*, a *Dalmatian* or any other kind of dog that's a real animal. If not, make sure it's a *Frankfurter, Ball Park, Oscar Mayer* or any other brand of hot dog. Stay away from men and women who act like dogs. You can accomplish this by allowing God to bring the person to you without trying to help Him out.

Adam was in a deep sleep when God took his rib out and used it to form Eve. Do you feel like Adam in a deep sleep when you're wondering about your heavenly mate? Adam in a deep sleep could represent a very long interval of time in which it seems nothing is happening regarding you getting someone in your life. It's been said that when you think God is not doing anything that's when He's working the most. We know God is working hard on Adam; however, Adam in his dormant state, doesn't.

I know that it seems like God is not doing anything, but this is not true. He's working hard on your behalf. It's taking a while because God is trying to set you up with someone who's fearfully and wonderfully made for you. He's being meticulous in making the person he has for you. He is preparing the individual for you. Be patient. He is trying to give you someone special. He is trying to amaze you and make you react like Adam when he saw Eve.

On seeing Eve, Adam said, "She is bone of my bones, flesh of my flesh." God wants to give you someone that will make you say something similar. In other words someone that will make you acknowledge your overwhelming admiration by saying things like, "She da one! He da one! That's my baby mama! *Esta bonita!*"

Furthermore, God had to take Adam's rib out to form Eve. Another way you can look at this, I believe, is that God had to take the rib out from Adam before He could bring Eve to him. So, the question is: what kind of rib does God have to take out from you before He can bring your mate to you? What does God have to do in you, and out of you, before He can bring the right person to you? You want God to bless you with His best, don't you? Did you consider that the person God intends for you deserves His best, too? Would you like to go out with *you*? Would you like to marry *you*? Would you like to live the rest of your life, or lay down the rest of your life for *you*? If you can't put up with yourself, why should anybody else?

I encourage you to be like the person you're trying to attract. I encourage you to desire God's best. In order to receive God's best, it's imperative for you to undergo God's test or His spiritual and physical examination. Having done this, and allowed Him to make all the necessary adjustments in you, then He can present you as His best, to His best for you.

Since God is The Great Physician, allow Him to be the surgeon and let the Holy Spirit be the anesthesia that'll put you in a deep sleep. In addition, let God's Word which is quick or alive, active, powerful and sharper than any two edge sword, be the scalpel used to incise your flesh.[66] Let it go down through your spirit, thoughts, mind, will, emotions and attitude.

Let it expose and surgically remove the rib of being unsaved, impatience, unforgiveness and offence. Let Him remove the rib of disobedience, arrogance, noncompliance and pride. Let him eradicate the rib of rebellion, irreverence, selfishness and bitterness. Let Him get rid of the rib of laziness, joblessness, lust and prejudice. Allow Him to free you of the rib of holding grudges, condemnation and low or no self esteem. After they are removed, God can now bring you your spouse.

After God finishes His operation on you it's interesting to know that His Word is the only surgical instrument that He can leave in your body. Think about a real-life surgery going on in an operating room. Can you fathom the consequences if the patient undergoing surgery suddenly wakes up in the middle of the operation? And not only this, but becomes uncooperative and struggles to get off the operating table? This will be disastrous. The operating team will have to restrain that patient, get the patient back on the operating table, repair any new damage incurred, and complete the original operation. This results in the surgery taking longer than anticipated. Is this the case with you?

If you don't allow the Holy Spirit to work in you, perhaps because you think you have enough of God in you, and as a result you choose to do your own thing, God would have to restrain you and start the work you did not allow him to complete all over again. He would have to resolve any new challenges that befell you as a result of doing your own thing. Now it takes longer for you to wait.

God needs to clean you up completely; and, He requires you to pass His examination before he gives you your man or woman. Are you letting God do what he needs to do in you, with you, and for you, or are you moving from the operating table? Are we letting the Holy Spirit deal with what He needs to deal with in us? Are we letting God cut out those ribs that he needs to remove?

Sometimes we get up from the operating table before time. We are often impatient. We don't allow patience to have its perfect work in us. Consequently, we cause more damage to ourselves. God is then forced to restrain us, make up for the damage, and start all over again. He's not finished until he does what he needs to do.[67]

Abraham and Sarah come to mind. God promised them a child. Instead of continuing to wait on the Lord to fulfill His promise to them, Sarah suggested to her husband that he sleep with her maid, Hagar, so that perhaps, the promised child might come from her. Abraham complied with his wife's advice and slept with Hagar who, as a result, gave birth to Ishmael. I suppose they decided to assist God in doing His job by speeding things up, since His promise to them had not manifested after ten years.[68]

But God didn't tell them to do that. God promised them a child but He didn't give them details on how He was going to bring it to pass. They took matters into their own hands and it resulted in Ishmael, who turned out to be a wild man—a trouble maker.[69] In addition, after the incident it seemed like God did not talk to Abraham for thirteen years. I drew this conclusion because Abraham was 86 years old when Ishmael was born. The next time we hear of God talking to him was when he was 99 years old. Furthermore, the first thing God told him was that Abraham should walk before Him, be blameless, and God would fulfill His covenant with him.[70] Sounds like God was telling him that if he wanted God to fulfill His promise to him he had better trust God, be obedient and not take matters into his own hands.

It appears that Ishmael was not part of God's original plan but he came into play and cost Abraham and his wife about thirteen years of their life. Years they had to deal with their mistake. Years they had to raise and provide for Ishmael. Years that they might have gotten more details from God and proceeded in obtaining His promise to them. Years that they might have been using to raise and nurture Isaac, the promised child they were to receive. But thanks to their efforts in helping God out, perhaps, Isaac had to be put on hold because Ishmael had to be attended to.

Isn't this how some of us are sometimes? Instead of waiting on God to fulfill his promise to us by giving us helpmates comparable to us, we try to help Him out and bring people into our lives who turn out to be "hell mates unbearable to us." They and the situations they bring cost us precious years of our lives. Years we could have used to develop our relationships with God. Years we could have received more details from God that would have guided us to our promised mates. Years, that perhaps, we could have found, courted, married our mates and started a family.

Why do some of us go out of our way and out of God's will to settle for an Ishmael when God wants to give us an Isaac? Why do we end up with trouble (what Ishmael turned out to be, Genesis 16:12) instead of laughter (meaning of Isaac). Why do we end up with drama and chaos in the expense of joy and happiness? Oftentimes, it's because we're impatient, unbelieving, and fearful that we're getting too old. If these are the case, then it's in our best interest that we allow God the liberty to take out those ribs in us.

The children of Israel also come to mind. They were given the Promised Land, the land of Canaan.[71] They could have journeyed into the land in eleven days but it took them forty years.[72] This happened because the children of Israel were disobedient. They didn't trust God enough to give them the land He promised them. They complained that there were giants in the land. Except for Joshua and Caleb, they were afraid that the strong-looking inhabitants of the land would destroy them. Joshua and Caleb made it into the land eventually since they trusted God to deliver. But the other Israelites did not. Because of their unbelief and distrust of God, they lost their blessing. They were allowed to roam in the wilderness for 40 years until everyone in that generation from twenty years and older, capable of military service, died.[73]

To them, those giants were barriers that prevented them from obtaining God's promise. They should have relied on God completely to help them eradicate the giants from the land. But they didn't. They chose to do their own thing, and as a result, what they could have obtained in eleven days took 40 years. They didn't even make it into the land. They roamed about in the wilderness, and that generation (20 years and older and capable of military service) never received what God promised them.[74]

The giants in the land are analogous to the ribs in you that need eradication. If you harbor ribs of ungodliness and unbelief, they will act as barriers against God from bringing the right person to you. Submit to God and let Him extricate those ribs from you. Having done so, He can now lead you into your promised land—your promised life with your promised mate. If you don't allow God to cleanse you like He needs to, just like it took the Israelites 40 years to wander in the wilderness instead of eleven days to enter and besiege their promised land, it might take you forever or never to obtain the mate for your life. Someone you might have received, betrothed, and married in six months, a year or two, more or less.

Another important point that I like you to consider regarding the rib God took out from Adam, is that since our rib cages guard our hearts, then when God took the rib out of Adam He must have exposed his heart. How is this significant? I believe this signifies that God wants to give you someone close to your heart—not your head. God did not take a side of Adam's brain to form Eve. He took out his rib, the side that guards and is close to his heart. God is not trying to give you someone in your head but someone from your heart. He's not trying to give you someone your limited understanding creates but someone whose wholesome attributes are too good for your head to comprehend. God centers on the heart. Do you know why? Because:

For where your treasure is, there your heart will be also. (Matthew 6:21)

A Godly man and woman are treasures to behold and cherish—treasures close to our hearts. Having been put right with God, your heart might want him because he's a good man, but your head might say he's out of bounds because he's too old or too young. Your heart might want her because she fulfills all the Godly requirements and God put that desire in it, but your head says you can't marry her because—she's Catholic but you're Baptist, he's Charismatic but you're Methodist, she's white but you're black, he's African American but you're Hispanic, she's African but you're Asian, he's Greek but you're American, she's Latino but you're Spaniard or just simply a foreigner to you. God might place a desire in your heart for someone, but your head says that person is not the right person for you because the individual would not be accepted by your parents, and he or she does not fit your tradition. I guess this explains why Jesus said:

So for the sake of your tradition (the rules handed down by your fore-fathers), you have set aside the Word of God (depriving it of force and authority and making it of no effect). (Matthew 15:6 AMP)

It's sad to say that God's purpose for us can be hindered by our traditions, our opinions and our ideologies often adopted from the way we were raised, and things we learned during the course of our social development. Unfortunately attitudes that stem from such traditions can permeate our hearts and mess up our lives, since this text reads:

Guard your heart above all else, for it determines the course of your life. (Proverbs 4:23 NLT)

This course of your life must include the path to the wife or husband you end up with. God wants to give you your heart's desire. In addition to being mindful of how our traditions can negate God's plan for our lives, we should also be aware of the passage below:

For out of the heart come evil thoughts, murder, adultery, sexual immorality, theft, false testimony, slander. (Matthew 15:19)

It's in your best interest that you keep your heart right. This is why you need to date God first. He'll cleanse your heart. He'll cut out those ribs blocking your heart from obtaining His promise to you with His Word, and leave His Word in your heart so that He can give you His Word—His will, His desire, His best for you.

Delight yourself in the LORD and He will give you the desires of your heart. (Psalm 37:4)

People often say that "God will give you the desires of your heart." Many people are frustrated that this has happened for them. Usually they haven't received their heart's desire because they are only quoting part of that passage. The entire verse says that we should delight in the Lord *and* He will give us the desires of our hearts. The first part of the passage: delight in the Lord, is the prerequisite for the second part of the passage: He will give you the desires of your heart.

The desire of your heart is given to you after you *delight* in the Lord and not before. Why? Because before you delighted in God, your heart might have had junk in it; like, traditions that go against God's Word. Other junk include such that lead to evil thoughts, sexual immorality, disobedience, etc. It takes an encounter with the Lord to eradicate these wayward tendencies. That's why you date God first. He flushes out all the iniquities, which effuse from your heart with His blood. He takes up residence in you in The Person of His Word, Jesus, who helps maintain your cleansed heart. This is an example of how you guard your heart diligently—with God's Word.

Furthermore, the word translated as "delight," is the Hebrew word, *anag.* Anag means to be "soft and pliable."[75] Therefore, to delight in the Lord means to be soft and pliable in His hands. When we are potty in God's hands, then He can do what He wants with us—and for us. Are you soft and pliable in God's hands? If you are, He will give you the desires of your heart. If you aren't, you hold yourself back from receiving His best.

God placed Adam in the Garden of Eden. Eden also means "delight" or "pleasantness."[76] Therefore, Adam's placement in the Garden of Eden is a picture of what it means to delight in the Lord. God placed him in the garden of delight. He purposed him there, and then partnered him there. When you allow God to put you somewhere, and do what He tells you to do there, you are delighting in Him.

Let God place and purpose you. Surrender to Him. When you let Him place and purpose you, He will partner you. When you're where He wants you to be, and you're doing what He wants you to do, in due time He'll give you your mate. He will grant you the desires of your heart. As you delight in God, take pleasure in knowing Him and enjoy His company in dating Him, you allow Him to speak to you and radiate His Word into you. Since His words are His desires for you, you begin to long for the desires He wants you to have. With this in mind, while you are single, let God do His job in guiding you to the right mate for your life.

CHAPTER THIRTEEN

On Your Mark … Get Set … Get Ready and Go …

Frequently a lot of us desire the "pros" of God. By pros, I mean the beneficial things from God that start with "pro." Things like prosperity and promotion. Things like a product, prospect or project. They are blessings, rewards, or just plain good results. However some of us either don't realize or refuse to acknowledge that "tests" precede results.

There is another pro of God that we need to be mindful of. And this pro is one that a number of us shy away from. This pro is something that a lot of people like to skip all together. There are three things relevant to receiving blessings from God. Even so, too many of us only focus on two of the things. They are the subject and the project.

We are the subject. The project is the prospect. It's the product, promotion, or the prosperity. It's the favorable end-result of what we are expecting from God. The project, prospect, product or promotion is a desirable outcome or end that we want from God. It can be a job position, an increase in our finances, a house, a car, a business or ministry. In light of what this book is about, that prospect is a spouse. These are all good and well.

However, there is a pro that precedes the other pros. It is the third thing that is necessary for us to receive the blessings of God. It's called "process." We, the *subjects*, need to go through the *process* to get the *prospect*. In order for us to receive whatever we are seeking or praying to God for, in this case a Godly spouse, we need to go through at least a "screening" process per se. In the previous chapter I mentioned that we need to undergo God's physical and spiritual examination before He can bring someone into our lives. By this, I meant that it was in our best interest to go through and pass His tests of readiness so that we can receive the result of the right mate for our lives. These tests are checkups to ensure that we are prepared for whomever He has for us. There is a process for us to undergo in order for us to receive our prospect. That process is sanctification.

Are You Whole or Do You Have Holes?

Now may the God of peace Himself sanctify you completely; and may your whole spirit, soul, and body be preserved blameless at the coming of our Lord Jesus Christ. (1 Thessalonians 5:23 NKJV)

Some of the words that describe *sanctify* include: set apart, consecrate, purify, cleanse, and wash. Sanctify means to make holy. In essence when God sanctifies us He is making us holy. He is setting us apart. He is consecrating, purifying, or washing us for His use.

If you noticed, the passage said that we should let God sanctify us *completely.* The fact that the verse said that we should let God set us apart completely, suggests that it is possible for God to "separate" us for His use *incompletely.* It's possible for us to prevent God from finishing the sanctification process.

If you've been to college or any other level of formal education you'll agree with me that if you have an "incomplete" in a class, you are not going to graduate. You are not going to receive your diploma. You will shortchange yourself from receiving your certificate and going to the next level of education. Along the same line, when we do not let God sanctify us completely, we'll not be able to graduate into the next level of the things of God. In the case of a mate, we'll not be able to receive our *marriage* certificates. You might get one from Las Vegas; but not from *El Dios* (The God). It's to our advantage that we allow God to sanctify, separate, or set us apart completely for marriage and for other things that He has in store for us.

After the verse said that we should let God sanctify us completely, it also said that "may your *whole* spirit, soul, and body be preserved blameless until the day of Christ." The truth is that once we've been set apart completely, we'll be "whole." We'll be complete. We'll be ready for whatever God has in store for us. To be whole is to be healed. It's to be fully restored and refreshed. It's to be fully intact; it's to have integrity. When you're whole you're not missing anything in yourself. You're complete. Sanctification precedes and leads to wholeness. Complete holiness is synonymous with wholeness.

When we allow God to set us apart completely, we'll be whole. If we don't allow Him to sanctify us completely, we'll have *holes*. Therefore, the question I am posing to you is this: Are you whole or do you have holes? If you're whole, great! You're ready for the spouse God has for you. If you're not, then you might have holes. And it is to your benefit that you allow God to stop those holes to prepare you for your mate. If not, if someone comes to your life and comes in contact with your holes, you both might just have an "accident." If two people who have holes come together in a relationship, they'll only make a bigger hole. Is it any wonder that they cannot connect?

Perhaps you don't know whether you're whole or have holes. Not to worry. Let's look at a few things about the sanctification process. This will help you ascertain whether you are a person ready for a meaningful relationship. To do this we need to refresh ourselves on one of the meanings of sanctify. The word we'll focus on is "set apart."

Obviously the word separate comes to mind when we think of "set apart." In fact if you rearrange the words "set apart," and replace one of the "ts" with an "e," you will end up with "separate." Notwithstanding, let's look at that word more closely. Let's set apart *set apart*. When we do this, we are left with the words, "set," and, "apart." Obviously the word "apart," by itself reflects the word "separate," which is basically what "apart" means. On the other hand let's examine the word, "set."

"Set" means a number of things depending on how you use it. How we use the word is dependent on how we want to apply it. For the purpose of this discussion let's look at five different synonyms for the word. They are:

1. To *put, place, position,* or *move*

For example, if you take an object from a particular location and transfer it to another location, you've put, placed, positioned or moved that object to a new location—*apart* from it's original location.

2. To *cause to rest*

Going back to the example above, when you were moving the object, the item was in a state of motion. But after you placed it in its new location the object was now in a state of rest. Therefore you caused the object to *rest* at its new location.

3. To *prepare*

For example, if you set a table for dinner, you prepared the table for food to be served. Interestingly, before God can *pair* you with a mate He has to "pre-pair" you for the mate.

4. To *fix* or to *adjust*

For example, when an alarm clock is displaying the wrong time and we correct the time on it, we just fixed or adjusted the alarm clock. Another example can be derived from the field of orthopedics. If an individual fractured a leg, the individual is placed in a cast. The cast is in place around the bone so that the individual's bone that was fractured could fix or adjust itself. That process of the bone fixing or adjusting itself is called *setting.*

5. To *fill in* or *fill up*

For example, diamonds in engagement rings are *set* among stones. If the diamond is taken out of the ring, there will be a "hole" in the ring. By placing the diamond in that hole, the hole is being filled in or filled up. The diamond is *set* amongst stones. Similarly, in the construction industry, when bricks are stacked on each other to erect buildings, usually the bricks have holes. When the bricks are placed and aligned on each other, cement or hot sand, which is in liquid form is poured into the holes in the bricks. The cement solidifies and becomes hard and brittle in the holes, thereby acting as glue that holds the bricks together. That process of the cement solidifying and becoming hard and filling in or filling up the hole is also known as *setting.*

I'm going to use these five descriptions of *set* to illustrate to you a process that I believe God puts us through to set us apart for marriage. This process is not limited to marriage. It's also for any purpose that God wants us to fulfill. We all need God's grace to thrive in marriage and any other endeavor. Some have defined the word *grace* as an acronym that denotes:

God's
Riches
At
Christ's
Expense.

Furthermore, some scholars have deduced that the number *five* represents grace, which also is a five-letter word.

Interestingly the process that I'll be presenting to you is a five-step process, which coincides with the five synonyms. More so, we'll be going back to the "beginning" to look at five verses from which we can excavate and identify this process, and see how God uses it to make us the right person for someone else.

Join me and let's look at bits and pieces of Genesis chapter two. We'll be looking at verses 7, 8, 15, 21 and 22. These verses give us a glimpse of a five-step process that God uses to sanctify or set us apart for the right mate.

Verse 7: *And the LORD God formed man of the dust of the ground....*

Verse 8: The LORD God planted a garden eastward in Eden, and there He put the man whom He had formed.

Verse 15: Then the LORD God took the man and put him in the Garden of Eden to tend and keep it.

Verse 21: And the LORD God caused a deep sleep to fall on Adam, and he slept; and He took one of his ribs, and closed up the flesh in its place.

Verse 22: Then the rib which the LORD God had taken from man He made into a woman, and He brought her to the man.

These verses give us an overview of five stages of sanctification or separation that is beneficial for us to go through in order for God to "set" us up for a successful relationship. Let's examine these stages closely.

Step One

The first step of this process can be deduced by looking at verses seven, eight and fifteen. They basically said that God formed Adam from the dust of the ground, planted a garden in Eden, and placed Adam in the garden to tend and keep it. Did you notice that Adam was *put, placed, positioned, moved* into the Garden of Eden? He was set apart from the dust of the ground into the Garden of Eden.

Similarly, in the first stage of the sanctification process, God needs to set us apart from *some things* to set us up for *someone*. He has to take us from an environment like he did with Adam, in order to position us in the environment in which our spouse is located. Eve came from the garden not from the dust of the ground. The difference between the dust of the ground and the Garden of Eden is very telling.

Dust is simply dirt. Eden means *delight* or *pleasantness*. Won't you agree with me that dirt is not pleasant or delightful? If you disagree, how would you like me to pour some dirt on you and see how it feels? Some of us have come from dirt. By that I mean that we have been raised or subjected to filthy things. We've been through the ordeal of unpleasant situations. Such situations stemmed from being in the wrong environment. Some of us are in or came from bad environments. Some of us might have been brought up in dysfunction, chaos, or from a lot of drama. Those undelightful or unpleasant environments or surroundings from which we came might have been an upbringing, a home, a family, a painful situation, or a previous or present relationship.

God has to separate us from such an environment and put us in a surrounding of peace, love, and harmony. A delightful situation. The place where you'll find the person God has for you. In order to merge with that individual God has to first deliver you from that mess.

You might have been shaped in iniquity. If this is the case, God has to cleanse you from that filth by removing you from that relationship, family, background, unhealthy church or community, and place you in a better environment. This is the first step of your sanctification. If this applies to you, let God set you apart from that unpleasant place.

Step Two

We can see the next step of the process in verse 21 where it says that God caused a deep sleep to fall on Adam. Do you know one of the things that intrigued me about that passage, if read from the New King James Version? While the wording of that statement does not really make much of a difference since the bottom line is that God made Adam sleep, I think it's interesting to note that the verse did not say that God caused Adam to fall to sleep. Rather it says that God caused sleep to fall on Adam. I don't know about you, but it seems like Adam was *caused to rest.*

In the second stage of the sanctification process, God has to *set you down* before he can *set you up.* Restlessness is not going to help you find the right mate. Resting and trusting in God, will. One of the reasons why the children of Israel did not enter the Promised Land was because they did not receive God's rest (See Hebrews 4:1-11; Genesis 2:1-3).

Resting in God is mainly about resting in God's finished work. It's about having faith in *His* work, not our work. God's rest is linked to the Sabbath day on which He finished His work and then rested. The Promised Land was kind of a type of finished work or rest per se. All the Israelites had to do to enter the Promised Land was believe that God had done everything that needed to be done to get them into it. But most of them did not believe in Him, or receive His rest, so to speak. So they never made it in. Likewise, if you desire to get married, since God said that He will grant you the desires of your heart, *if you delight in Him*, then you can envision your proposed mate as a promised man or woman. One of His finished work for you (See Psalm 37:4).

We enter God's rest by believing in what He has already done. Be encouraged to know that God is already preparing someone for you. He's working on us to catch up and match up with what He has already done for us. Therefore believe in His efforts to get you a life partner.

After God decided to set Adam up, He set Adam down. He caused him to rest. That was part of the process he put Adam through to hook him up with Eve. The same is necessary for us. Running around like a headless chicken trying to make things happen *on your own* might not necessarily get you hitched. It might get you *ditched*. If you end up with someone by trying to do things solo you might end up *so low*. You can end up so lonely and so broken if the person turned out to be a bad match and bad news.

Rest my friend. This doesn't mean that you turn into a couch potato. It partly means that you focus on living your life according to God's will whether there is someone on the horizon or not, while God focuses on finding you your match. Sometimes resting in the Lord means that you relax and allow God to repair, restore, and refresh you before he can refer you to someone. Sometimes resting in the Lord means that He has to *fix you* before He can fix you up.

Perhaps you're familiar with what happens with a desktop or laptop computer when it's sitting idle for a while. It goes into sleep mode. The screen becomes dark. Depending on your PC, you might see things like stars twirling around on the screen. It appears that nothing is happening in the computer. But on the contrary. There are lots of processes taking place in the computer to conserve its energy, and restore and refresh its power. In the same vein, God needs to put us in "sleep mode" to prepare us for marriage.

It's to our advantage that he reveals and removes things in our lives, perhaps from our past, that can be detrimental to the relationship He's trying to bring us into. Like it looks on that computer screen in sleep mode, it might look like nothing is happening for us in the finding love area, but that is not the case. God is working behind the scenes; in us, and in the lives of our eventual spouses. In the rest stage God is conserving and processing us like he literally did with Adam. This brings us to the third stage.

Step Three

We can also see the third step in verse 21. After God put sleep on Adam the verse also said that God took a rib out of Him. In third step of the process, not only does God have to set you apart from some things, He also has to set some things apart from you. This is necessary because although God might have taken you out of an environment, chances are that you took part of that environment with you.

Again the children of Israel are a perfect example of this premise. Another reason why they did not enter the Promised Land was because, although they let God deliver them from Egypt, they did not let Him deliver Egypt from them. They were no longer in Egypt but they behaved and acted like they were still in Egypt. Despite the signs and wonders that God displayed on their behalf, they still had a slave mentality. The pillar of fire by

night, the cloud by day, the parting of the red sea, and the angel's food given
to them did not stop them from wanting to go back to Egypt each time they
met opposition on their way to the Promised Land.

Unfortunately the same thing happens to a number of us today. Despite
different ways that God has shown His love to us, despite many "signs and
wonders" He has shown in order to protect, liberate, and encourage us,
some of us still go back to same ole, same ole. God might have taken some
of us out of dysfunctional, ignorant, or a detrimental environment, but yet
some of us still act out things we learned in that environment.

The environment might have been a previous relationship or family were
some things were said about you: "You're not good enough; you're ugly;
you'll never get married; nobody would ever want to marry you; you'll
never make a good wife; you'll not amount to anything; if you get married
you're going to get divorced; if your wife acts up you need to smack her; it's
okay to be married and have someone on the side" and the list goes on. We
need to be delivered from those kinds of thinking. That's why God has to
remove those mindsets and other unhealthy habits and relationship-killing
attitudes from us.

After God formed and took Adam from the dust of the ground, placed
him in the Garden of Eden and caused Him to rest, God took a rib, which
was also formed from the dust of the ground, from Him. Like I alluded to in
the previous chapter, what kind of rib does God have to remove from you?
Low self esteem? Shame? Unforgiveness? Ignorance? Prejudice? Whatever
it is, it's beneficial for you to let God sanctify you completely from it.

Step Four

The fourth step can be deduced from the last statement in verse 21. It
said that God closed up the flesh in its place. Over the years I'd never really
understood that statement. It was one of the things I skipped over when I've
read that passage. In fact I thought that closing up the flesh in its place was
the method God used to form Eve. But that is not what that verse was say-

ing. Closing up the flesh in its place had nothing to do with the rib that God took out of Adam. What the verse meant was that God closed the "hole" in Adam's flesh from which the rib was removed.

So the LORD God caused the man to fall into a deep sleep. While the man slept, the LORD God took out one of the man's ribs and closed up the opening. (Genesis 2:21 NLT)

In the fourth step, not only does God set you apart from some things, and set some things apart from you, He also has to *set a* part of you. He has to "set" that part of you that has a hole. He has to *fix* or *adjust* that part in you that has a hole. He has to *fill in* or *fill up* that hole in your heart.

Imagine a soldier fighting in a war zone. Unfortunately for the individual an explosion went off and he was injured. The first step to save that man's life is to get him out of the war zone. This is where we set him apart from that environment. But that is not enough because he has the environment lodged in him. By this I mean the shrapnel, debris, bullets, and bullet fragments from the war zone are lodged in his flesh. The second step is to cause him to rest. This is where the surgeon anaesthetizes him to prepare him for the surgery. The third step is to remove the fragments embedded in his body. This is where they set those harmful things apart from him. The fourth step of course is to close up his flesh. The shrapnel and other sharp objects left a hole in the soldier. That hole needs to be closed after the objects are removed. The soldier is then sown back for full recovery.

Along the same lines, just like God did with Adam, He has to *close* your hole before He brings someone into your life. In other words, before God can bring your mate to you He has to bring *closure* to some things in your life. And before closure (Step 4) is exposure (Step 3). Removing the rib exposed the hole in Adam. Removing the bad habit, hang-up, low self esteem, shame or any other "bone" of contention that might have been lodged in you by the environment you were delivered from will expose any damage that God needs to heal.

According to Pastor Paula White, author and host of *Paula White Today*:

You cannot conquer what you do not confront, and you cannot confront what you do not identify.

By exposing your hole God is helping you to identify the problem. Now that you've identified the problem He will help you confront it, and once you confront it, He'll help you conquer it. I believe that a four-step process that I first learned from Pastor Jentenzen Franklin, which also tackles our shortcomings, coincides with the sanctification process and Pastor White's statement. It is relevant for dealing with our holes. He said that in dealing with an issue as such, we should first trace it, face it, erase it, and replace it.

In order for God to make our parts that have holes become whole He helps us trace them (isolate, expose and identify the problem). Then we face them (confront the problem). Then we erase them (conquer the problem). Finally we replace them (closure).

Step Five

After closure, then we are complete. We are whole. We've been finished for the final step of the process, which is revealed in verse 22. Basically God used the rib he removed from Adam to form Eve and brought her to him. The last step of the sanctification process is when God sets you up with your spouse. This happened right after God set a part of Adam or closed Adam up (closure). Steps one through four was to *prepare* us for step five—set up. God used these five steps to get Adam on his *mark* and *set* him for Eve. The five steps were the "on your mark, set, go" for Adam to receive Eve.

Like Adam, it's to our advantage that we allow God to work out things from us to work out someone for us. We might not realize it, but we are at different stages in this process. Where we are in this process obviously is determined by our circumstances and our willingness to allow God to sanctify us *completely*. It also depends on whether we are even aware that God is working some things out, in us and for us.

Obviously we all don't really have to go through all five steps since some of us were not raised in dysfunction. Some of us, like me, have been blessed to be raised in healthy homes and under the nurture of loving parents. So we don't need to be sanctified from the good habits they taught us. Some others of us were not so fortunate. This is why all the steps are necessary.

You might be in step one, where God has to get you out of something or someone's life. You might be in step two, where God has to cause you to rest. Relax. You might be in step three, where God has to remove some things from you. You might be in step four, where God has to bring closure to some things in your life. Or you might be in step five. You're on the verge of meeting and marrying the love of your life.

I believe that step three is the hardest step. This is where a lot of us get stuck. Why do a lot of us falter in the middle? We are not where we used to be, but we're not where we need to be. It's one thing to have progressed from our past, but it's another thing when we're dragging in our present because of things that we should have left behind us. The Israelites left Egypt, but most of them got stuck in the wilderness and never made it into the Promised Land. Like them, too many of us get stuck in the middle. If we don't allow God to proceed with steps three and four, we'll never get our promised land, step five.

That reminds me of a comment made by Dr. John Maxwell:

Most people who quit don't give up at the bottom of the mountain; they stop half way up it.[77]

Wherever you are in your relationship with others and with God, you have to go through at least one of the processes. You have to be set apart to get espoused to the person God has for you. Even if this only means leaving your mother and your father to cleave with your spouse (See Genesis 2:24).

In a nutshell the five-step process of sanctification necessary for God to make us whole or complete to graduate us into marriage and other things that He has for us are for Him to:

1. *Set us apart* from some things (Put, place, position, move us).

2. *Set us down* (Cause us to rest).

3. *Set things apart* from us (Exposure).

4. *Set a part* of us (Closure—Fix, Adjust, Fill in or Fill up).

5. *Set us up* with and for someone (Preparation).

Revisiting 1 Thessalonians 5:23 again, the scripture said that we should let God sanctify us completely; and that we should let our whole spirit, soul, and body be preserved blameless until the coming of Christ. If you noticed, the sanctification is in three areas: our spirits, our souls, and our bodies. We can think of this as spiritual, emotional and/or mental, and physical. When all these facets of our being are set apart completely, we'll be whole. I believe receiving Christ into our hearts sets our spirits apart. We undergo the spiritual sanctification. Our spirits have been reserved and occupied by the Spirit of Christ. Unfortunately, a whole spirit, with an unhealthy mindset and lack of self control in our body leaves us with Christians that we don't like being around.

I don't believe that you can have a sound mind and body without a sound spirit. Perhaps, from the intellectual's point of view, you can. But from God's point of view, you can't. I believe having Christ in your heart sanctifies your spirit. Changing the way you think, in conjuction with God's Word, sanctifies your mind or soul. Adhering to your new mode of thinking which is in line with God's will, will keep your flesh or human nature in check. It will help you exercise self control and position you to receive the things God has for you. In addition, moving from one physical location to another, I believe, is also a form of physical or body sanctification. In order for us to find the person God has for us, it's to our benefit that we let Him change us completely. Sanctifying us wholly is basically how God gets us on our *marks*, gets us *set*, and ready to *go* to our mates.

CHAPTER FOURTEEN
Get Rid Of Negatives from Your Past

In the previous chapter we talked about the sanctification process necessary for us to allow God to bring someone into our lives. I also mentioned that this process is not limited to getting married. It is applicable to virtually all areas of our lives. It's in our best interest to be separated from some things and some people in order for us to fulfill our destiny. Everyone who was used in a mighty way by God underwent some level of separation.

Joseph was separated from his brothers, Moses was separated from his family, and David was separated from his family during his flight from Saul. Even Esther was separated briefly from Mordecai, her cousin and guardian. But it was all for a purpose. God uses sanctification to help us fulfill His divine destiny for our lives (See 2 Timothy 2:20-21). Even Abraham underwent sanctification to become the father of many nations. His process of sanctification started when God told him to leave his family.

Now the LORD had said to Abram: "Get out of your country, From your family And from your father's house To a land that I will show you. (Genesis 12:1 NKJV)

God told Abraham to set himself apart from an environment. This environment was his family and country. He was told to sanctify himself from the familiar... "family-iar." He obeyed God and left his family. Even so, like I alluded to in the previous chapter, he took part of his environment with him. Abraham took Lot, his nephew, who was part of the family that he was supposed to have separated from.

So Abram departed as the LORD had spoken to him, and Lot went with him.... Then Abram took Sarai his wife and Lot his brother's son, and all their possessions that they had gathered, and the people whom they had acquired in Haran, and they departed to go to the land of Canaan.... Then the LORD appeared to Abram and said, "To your descendants I will give this land."…. (Genesis 12:4-5, 7NKJV)

Abraham partially obeyed God when he left his family. He allowed Lot to come with him. This is often the case with us, too. You might have been separated from something or someone; but, chances are that you took part of the thing, place, environment or person with you. This is going to interfere with what God is trying to do with, and for you. This will also interfere with the person God is trying to bring to you. Let's read on about Abraham, and I'll elaborate further.

Now the land was not able to support them, that they might dwell together, for their possessions were so great that they could not dwell together. And there was strife between the herdsmen of Abram's livestock and the herdsmen of Lot's livestock.... (Genesis 13:6-7 NKJV)

This passage explains a lot about why God, not only has to set us apart from some things but also has to set some things apart from us. The things that He needs to remove from our lives will bring *strife* into our lives. They will interfere and interrupt God's perfect plan for us. Abraham and Lot could *not live* together because their *possessions* were *too great* and the land could *not support* them.

The land of matrimony that God is trying to bring you to cannot support the "possessions" or baggage that you brought with you from the land of heartbreak. Maybe the previous environment from which God brought you wasn't one of heart break. Maybe there were good memories. But that's behind you. That's past glory. Don't let what was supposed to remain in your past interfere with what or whom you're supposed to obtain in your future.

What God has for you in your future cannot and will not support what you had in your past.

Lot's possessions and Abraham's possessions could not cohabitate in the land. There was conflict between Lot's people and Abraham's people. Likewise the person God has for you is incompatible with the memories, memorabilia or souvenirs of your past relationships. Your emotions cannot support the true love of your life and the disappointment that you're holding on to from that relationship that did not work.

In fact, your wound will not give you a clear view of the person God has for you. As a result, that individual whom God has for you will not meet your expectations, even if he or she meets and exceeds them. Unless you let God set past relationships apart from you, you will have unnecessary conflicts in a new relationship—that's if you are even able to get in one.

So Abram said to Lot, "Please let there be no strife between you and me, and between my herdsmen and your herdsmen; for we are brethren. "Is not the whole land before you? Please separate from me, If you take the left, then I will go to the right; or, if you go to the right, then I will go to the left." (Genesis 13:8-9 NKJV)

To resolve the conflict between Abraham and Lot, Abraham had to part with Lot. But notice what happened after Lot separated from Abraham.

And the LORD said to Abram, after Lot had separated from him: "Lift your eyes now and look from the place where you are...northward, south-ward, eastward, and westward; "for all the land which you see I give to you and your descendants forever. "And I will make your descendants as the dust of the earth; so that if a man could number the dust of the earth, then your descendants also could be numbered. "Arise, walk in the land through its length and its width, for I give it to you." (Genesis 13:14-17 NKJV).

This passage completely reveals God's plan for Abraham after He allowed God to sanctify him completely. The promises God made to Abraham came to pass after he fully obeyed God by separating from his family. *All* of them. This passage also reinforces why we should let God sanctify us wholly. It enlightens us on how we can do ourselves a disservice when we don't allow God to fully process us.

Four things jumped out at me in that passage. These things depict what we can receive from God after we are completely separated from whomever and whatever He wants us sanctified from:

1. *And the LORD said to Abraham, after Lot had separated from him* (God spoke to Abraham).

2. *Lift your eyes now* (God opened his eyes).

3. *...from the place where you are* (Abraham was already in the right place).

4. *...for I give it to you* (God gave Abraham the land).

The first thing that happened to Abraham after he separated from Lot was that God spoke *to* him and gave him more direction regarding His promise to him. The second thing was that God opened his eyes to see what God had already prepared for him. In other words, Abraham's eyes were closed, metaphorically speaking, to the thing that God already placed before him. The third was that Abraham was already in the vicinity where his blessing was. He was already where he needed to be; but, he did not know this until God revealed it to him. And fourth, God gave him the land. After Lot left, God gave Abraham what he told him about, opened his eyes to see, and what he was already standing on.

Similarly, sometimes until we allow God to remove things or people from us, God will not speak to us any further pertaining to whom we're supposed to marry. He'll not open our eyes to whom we're supposed to see. He'll not reveal to us that we're already in the vicinity where the person is. And He'll not give us that person. Why? Because the baggage or the "Lot" from our past we'll cause strife between us and the person God has for us. Our proposed marriage cannot support our past. Our past and our future cannot dwell together. There will be unnecessary conflict between emotions, baggage, or negative comments received from your ex, and support, encouragement, and love from your next.

Obviously we're not literally taking ex-lovers with us into a new relationship. However, memories or memorabilia from past relationships like a tee-shirt, perfume or cologne, bed sheet, jewelry, bracelet or even something negative that was said about us, will prevent us from connecting with the ideal person God has for us. In fact, sometimes, those Lots from our pasts we'll prevent us from recognizing and appreciating the angels God has placed before us.

While he was with Lot, Abraham did not perceive the property nor realize that he was already in the place that God had for him. While you are still holding on to your past, knowingly or unknowingly, you can prevent yourself from seeing and receiving what God has for you—be it material or matrimonial. It was after his separation from Lot that Abraham realized and acquired what God had for him. Likewise, it's after we're sanctified completely that we'll also realize and receive whom and what God has for us. Remember the five step sanctification process?

Let's do a recap of what we've just learned from Abraham's situation.

Initially God told Abraham to leave his family, his father's house, and his country in order to go to a place that God would *show* him (See Genesis 12:1). Abraham left but took Lot with him to the land of Canaan. As a result God told Abraham that He *would give his descendants* the land (See Genesis 12:7). Then not surprisingly there was a rift between Abraham's people and Lot's people. But *after Lot had separated from him*; after Abraham was sanctified from his family completely, God did not tell Abraham that He *would show* him the land. God did not tell Abraham that he *would give* him a land. God just *gave* him the land.

My friend, please listen. If you do not allow God to sanctify you completely, then these are the kind of things that you might hear from God: "I have a plan for you, I will bless you, I have something to show you, I have someone for you, I will help you get married." However, when you allow God to set you apart fully, then you're likely to hear things like "Whoop there he is! Here is your spouse. Go ahead and get married. Here is the blessing that I had for you."

When you're separated completely, God does not tell you what He *will do* for you; He just *does it* for you. He won't tell you what He will give you; He just gives it, him, or her to you.

After Abraham separated from Lot God gave him the land. In fact, after Abraham took Lot with him, God told Abraham that he would give the land to Abraham's descendants. At first, God never specifically told Abraham that he would give him a land. He told Abraham that he would show him a land. Then He told him he would give the land to his descendants—not to him.

Sometimes, when we do not allow God to finish His work on us, we will hear Him say what He will do for people related or affiliated with us. We will here Him say what He will do for our family members or our friends. We will hear Him say things like, "I will give your children an inheritance; I will bless your brother; I will do something great for your sister; your friend will get married; I will do a great work in your grand ma's life." You might even hear Him bless your dog, Duffy.

"But, what about me?" You might ask. Yeah, what about you? Well, you would be the maid of honor or groom's man. You will ride "shot gun" in your grandpa's new car. You will be a special guest for the party being held for the startup of your brother's business. And the list goes on. While we should be happy and celebrate the success of our family members and friends, we need to realize that God also has plans for us, too. There are plenty of God's blessings to go around. God wants to generously share His wealth with us, our peers, and our respective families. A major key that needs to be turned in our lives in order for us to experience the promised land of God for our lives, be it marriage, ministry, or industry, is the key of complete sanctification.

When you are completely cleansed, purified, purged or consecrated as God sees fit, then God won't just show you a prospect, He'll give you your spouse. You no longer need to wear *27 dresses*; you'll wear your own wedding gown, "the 28th dress." You're not going to be the maid of honor for the rest of your life, you'll be the maid that was honored with a husband. The words that you hear will change from "you're next" to "you're it!" You're not just going to be congratulating everybody else; everybody else will be congratulating you.

Even Ruth had to be sanctified or set apart completely before she could marry Boaz. She went through some of the five steps of sanctification that I discussed previously before she got set up with Boaz. Let's look at how she was set apart for Boaz.

Her sanctification started when she left Moab to reside in Israel. She set herself apart from her homeland and ended up in the vicinity where her husband resided. Just like Adam was moved from the dust of the earth and placed in the Garden of Eden, Ruth was put, placed, positioned, moved, set in Israel—apart from Moab. That was her step 1.

Her step 3, not step 2, occurred right after her mother-in-law, Naomi encouraged her to hook up with Boaz. She told her to:

...wash yourself and anoint yourself, put on your best garment and go down to the threshing floor.... (Ruth 3:3 NKJV)

Obviously looking and smelling good is important to attract someone. Notwithstanding let's look at some finer points from that statement. If you recall, I mentioned that one of the synonyms for *sanctify* is *wash*. Ruth was told to wash herself. Like I discussed previously, when we leave an environment, chances are that we brought part of that environment with us. Ruth left Moab but she took part of Moab with her. Before she could espouse Boaz she had to wash Moab from herself.

More specifically, she had to get rid of the past that she brought along with her. In this case, I'm talking about the memory of her husband. You see, Ruth was previously married to Mahlon in Moab. But Marlon died in Moab (See Ruth 1:1-5). And in Old Testament times, the way people dressed signified their status. For example, lepers dressed a certain way to indicate to people that they were lepers. Blind people dressed a certain way to indicate that they were blind. Likewise, widows dressed a certain way, to indicate that they were widows (See 2 Samuel 14:2).

Therefore, when Naomi told Ruth to dress up, she wasn't just saying this to encourage her to be presentable to Boaz, but also because she wanted her to shed off her widow's garment. She wanted her to give up her past. It was time to let go of her dead relationship. Along the same lines, if this applies to you, let go of that relationship that didn't work. He or she has let go of you. You are no longer in that relationship. It's dead to you. You also are dead to it. Move on.

Don't be like the women who took spices with the intent to embalm Jesus' *dead* body. They wanted to spice up someone that was dead. Sometimes some of us inadvertently spice up dead relationships. We glamorize and fantasize about things that did not work. We can do this by carrying pictures or souvenirs of old flames. And occasionally, maybe when we're feeling lonely or emotional, bring those old memories up and fixate on them. We reminisce on things of the past. Let them go. Get rid of them! Why are you seeking the living among the dead? Like Ruth, change your garment.

You will be surprised at what can happen for you if you get rid of that Tee-shirt, pen, picture, bed sheet or whatever you know you've held on to, that represents that dead relationship. Throw it away! And let God fill that void; first, with Himself, and then, someone like Himself for you.

After Ruth was told to anoint and wash herself, she was told to go to the threshing floor. Here again is another indirect emphasis to sanctification. The threshing floor was an area where wheat was threshed or separated from grains. And what happened when Ruth got to the threshing floor? She lay beside Boaz' feet. What was Boaz doing before she lay by his feet? After he ate, he was resting.

Did you notice what Boaz and Ruth were inadvertently revealing to us? They were both resting. Boaz was resting, and Ruth joined him by resting—her step 2. And they were both on the threshing floor. Their point of connection was an environment of sanctification. Make no mistake about it friend, God needs to sanctify you completely for your beloved. Your heaven-sent is also undergoing the process for you, too. Just like Boaz was already at the threshing floor before Ruth joined him there, the person God has for you is already undergoing sanctification for you.

After Ruth left Moab and ended up in Israel, washed, anointed, replaced her widow's garment with a beautiful maiden's garment—and went to the threshing floor and rested beside Boaz, she ended up marrying Boaz. She ended up receiving the right mate for her life. She applied the forthcoming passage to her life:

So, come out from among (unbelievers), and separate (sever) yourselves from them, says the Lord, and touch not (any) unclean thing; then I will receive you kindly and treat you with favor, and I will be a father to you, and you shall be My sons and daughters, says the Lord Almighty. Therefore, since these (great) promises are ours, beloved, let us cleanse ourselves from everything that contaminates and defiles body and spirit, and bring (our consecration to completeness in the (reverential) fear of God. (2 Cor-inthians 6:17-19; 7:1 AMP)

Talking about the movie *27 Dresses*, did you notice that Katherine Hei-gl's character *got rid* of the twenty seven *dresses* before she hooked up with the love of her life? Did you also note that she quit her job? She basically *set herself apart* from the things (what the dresses represent), an environment (her job) and her boss, in order to end up with the journalist; the right guy *for her* (someone in *her heart*). Think about it.

At this point you might be wondering how we are to undergo the sanc-tification process. How are we cleansed from our past? How do we let go of bad habits and unhealthy thinking? How do we get the monkey off still clinging on our backs even though we've left the zoo? How do we let go of that relationship that did not work, or the shame and inferiority complex received from that relationship? You might wonder, "How do I get rid of the hurt of what was done to me, said to me, and said about me?"

I'm glad you asked. Here is a possible solution that you're likely familiar with. As familiar as this solution is, too many people don't apply it. Why they don't apply it is often a mystery. Perhaps it's because a lot of us don't really understand its relevance and application. I'll share a few insights that I've learned about this solution—some of which you might have never heard before—and hopefully will inspire you to take this medicine. Let's begin.

Learn to Forgive

Please don't turn off. I know you've probably heard this before: *You need to forgive.* As much as we've heard about forgiveness too many of us don't do it. Why? I believe part of the reason is because we really don't under-stand what forgiveness is. Some of us think that forgiving someone means that we have to hang out and resume our relationship with the person that offended us. This is not true. In a case like this we are misconstruing forgiveness with trust. Just because you forgive someone does not mean that you should trust the person.

To differentiate between forgiveness and trust, let's consider debt. When someone who owes money is "released" from paying the debt, it is said that the debt owed has been forgiven. To drive my point further, envision that you opened a trust fund with $50,000 in a bank. Notice that you opened a "trust" fund. You *entrusted* your money to a bank for future use. Let's say an employee from the bank embezzled your money and as a result you lost all your money. Well, the bank owes you money.

Let's say, out of the goodness of your heart you release the bank from paying you back the money. Guess what? You forgave the debt the bank owed you. You are no longer holding the bank to pay you your money. Even so, that does not mean that you are going to deposit another amount of money in the bank. Why? Because you don't trust the bank. They violated your trust. While you forgave the bank the debt they owed you, you're not going to put money in the bank again because you don't trust them.

Similarly, you might have entrusted valuable and personal things into the lives of others. You might have invested your hopes and dreams, time, desires, maybe even intimacy with someone. Unfortunately for you, your "valuables" were exploited. You might have been used and abused. Someone might have taken advantage of, hurt or fooled you. The personals you entrusted to the person with whom you were involved was embezzled. The individual violated your trust. Maybe someone told your business to others. Perhaps your fears, faults, and failures why divulged. Someone might have said denigrating things about you behind your back. Like the bank, the person defrauded you—so to speak. Forgiveness is releasing the offender from what they did to you. Therefore, when you forgive the person that hurt you, you are letting go of what was done to you.

That does not mean that you will go back and reestablish your relationship with that person to the point it was prior to the individual offending you. Because you don't trust the individual. You're protecting yourself from being hurt again. This is a whole different ball game. Just like you're likely not to entrust your money in a bank that defrauded you, it might not be a good idea for you to entrust your "heart" to an individual that already broke it, and might to do it again, turning it into mush.

Regardless of what anyone did to you, it's in your best interest to forgive. But in order for you to trust someone again, that person has to prove that they are trustworthy. Forgiveness is an imprint of love. If love was a hand, forgiveness is its finger print. The Bible says that we should not owe anyone anything except to love them (See Romans 13:8). Therefore, forgiveness is owed; trust is earned. Forgiveness is unconditional; trust is conditional. Forgiveness is absolute; trust is relative. We're obligated to love everyone; we're not obligated to trust everyone. We should forgive. Depending on your situation and the Spirit of God guiding you, it's up to you to determine if you're going to trust the person who hurt you, again.

Another reason why some of us find it hard to forgive is because we think that forgiveness means letting someone get away with what they did to us. On the contrary. Forgiveness is not about someone getting away with what they did to you; it's about *you* getting away from what was done to you. It does not mean you're letting someone off the hook; it means you're letting yourself *off* their hook.

Remember when I was talking about the bank analogy? Assume that you planned to use the $50,000 to start a business. If you did not forgive that debt, it means that you are holding on to that money because you want to use it to start your business. Guess what happens to your business while you're waiting for the money. It never goes anywhere. It is stuck in your dreams. It will never get off the ground. You are stuck in the same place because you're waiting to get $50,000, without which you can't *move on* with your life.

If you forgave the debt, even though you still don't have $50,000, you can still move on with your life. This is possible because you'll start looking at other avenues to get the capital to start your business. The act of looking for other means to get your investment itself is a sign of progress. It indicates that you are moving on as opposed to getting stuck in the same place. The same is true in forgiving someone. When you let go of a hurt or offense, *you* move on with your life. If you don't, you get stuck in the same place of misery. You are chained to the same merry-go-round.

According to Matthew Kelly: *Unforgiveness is like drinking poison and expecting the other person to die. It's the thief from our past that robs us of our future.*

I recall hearing Pastor Joel Osteen talk about something he realized while going into a building. He mentioned that he was trying to go through a series of double doors that were spaced about fifteen meters apart. He said that after he went past the first double door, the second double door would not open until the doors he just passed closed completely. How those doors operated enlightened him more of our human conditioning. He reasoned that when we don't close the doors to our past, the doors to our future won't open.

Along the same lines, unforgiveness opens the door to your past and closes the door to your future. Forgiveness closes the door to your past and opens the door to your future. Unforgiveness opens the door to your past relationships and the heartbreak that went along with them. Forgiveness closes the door to those broken relationships and opens the door that leads you to the right mate amongst other things that God has for you. Unforgiveness causes you to look back. Forgiveness causes you to look forward.

Unforgiveness keeps you stuck in the same place, with the same type of detrimental thinking, which keeps you in the same type of relationships, with the same kind of drama, with the same kind of person who has been hurting you. The various failed relationships you might have been in, or are in right now, might be with a different person. But ultimately the treatments and results you received or are receiving from the relationships are the same. Heartbreak; discontentment; dissatisfaction.

Unforgiveness is one of the reasons why people who just broke up from a relationship get into another one on a rebound. Did you notice the word "rebound"? In the context of this discussion, it means to be bound *again*. Unforgiveness keeps you stuck in a rut. Forgiveness enables you to make progress. It leads to progression. Unforgiveness leads to regression.

When you forgive, you let go of the past and reach toward your future. You put things behind you while you press toward the things ahead of you. When you walk in forgiveness, your mentality is similar to Paul's below:

No, dear brothers and sisters, I have not achieved it, but I focus on this one thing: Forgetting the past and looking forward to what lies ahead, I press on to reach the end of the race and receive the heavenly prize for which God, through Christ Jesus, is calling us. (Philippians 3:13-14 NLT)

In a sense Paul is saying that in order for him to fulfill God's call on his life, and receive his heavenly reward through his relationship with Christ, he forgets the past and forges ahead toward the future. While we should also have this goal in mind, we should also be aware that in order for us to receive the person God is *calling* us to, we need to let go of the wrongs of our pasts—so that we can make positive strides toward the person—in addition to other things God has for us.

Friend, forgive. Don't let the wrongs that happened to you distract you from what is happening *for* you. Don't allow what is behind you to prevent you from receiving what is *before* you. Don't let your experience(s) in "Egypt" blind you from getting into your promised land.

CHAPTER FIFTEEN
Understand Four Levels of Forgiveness

I hope you now have a better understanding of forgiveness. Something else that is important for you to know about forgiveness is that you are not forgiving from your own strength. The ability to forgive comes from God. You should ask God to give you the strength to forgive. It is His grace that will enable you to forgive the person that has wronged you. To establish our understanding of forgiveness even more, let us look at what I consider as four levels of forgiveness.

First Level

We can deduce the first level of forgiveness from this passage:

Whose soever sins ye remit, they are remitted unto them; and whose soever sins ye retain, they are retained. (John 20:23 KJV)

In the first level of forgiveness, if someone offends or sins against you, you should forgive them. The word used here is remit. It means "to send away."[78] So, to forgive means to send away. In other words, by forgiving someone for what they did to you, the atrocity or hurt inflicted on you is sent away, or dispersed from you. On the other hand if you do not forgive the person, you keep the resentment in you, and that can poison your life. If you note, the passage said:

...and whose soever sins ye retain, they are retained. In the Amplified version of the Bible, this phrase reads this way: *if you retain the sins of anyone, they are retained.*

Did you note that it said that if *you* retain the sins of anyone they are retained?

In other words, if you don't forgive, you are retaining what was done to you. You are retaining the hurt that was inflicted on you. And this is one of the reasons why we have generational curses. When an individual does not forgive a wrong that was inflicted on him or her, that individual retains the experience and passes it down to his or her offspring. If the offspring does not forgive, he or she passes it down to his or her own offspring too. And the pattern continues until someone down the line decides to forgive and remit the experience.

In *Become a Better You*, Pastor Joel Osteen mentioned a military experiment carried out in which a volunteer's white blood cells were taken and placed in a test tube in a room. The volunteer was then placed in another room in which he was asked to watch a war movie. Meanwhile a lie detector probe was placed in the test tube which contained the man's white blood cells. Every time the man reacted to violent scenes in the movie, the probe registered reactions in the man's blood—which was in another room.[79]

Despite being in another room, the man's white blood cells remembered where they came from. As you can see we inherit our genes from our ancestors. We inherit physical characteristics as well as personality traits. We can also inherit and pass down their experiences. Both good and bad—if forgiveness has not been exercised by our ancestors and us. To avoid letting a negative experience prevent you from finding or keeping a healthy relationship with someone that God has for you, forgive or remit any wrongdoing that you might have experienced.

Second Level

We can grasp the second level of forgiveness from Jesus' illustration of forgiveness in Matthew 18:21-35. Jesus talked about a king who was settling accounts with his servants. One of his servants owed him an exorbitant amount of money. The servant begged the king to give him time to pay the debt. The king had compassion over him and forgave him the debt. However, the servant had a colleague that owed him money, too. He went to the individual and grabbed him by the throat and demanded that he pay him back his money. His fellow servant begged him to give him more time, but he refused to adhere to his colleague's request and sent him to prison until he paid his debt. Other servants found out about this and told the king. The king was upset with the servant because the servant did not forgive his colleague like the king did for him. So the king demanded that the servant be given over to torturers.

In the first level of forgiveness, the emphasis is for you to forgive so that you can release an atrocity committed against you. In the first level, the emphasis is on *you* and not the offender. In the second level of forgiveness, the emphasis is on both you *and* the offender. In this second level, not only do you forgive others to release yourself from bondage, but you forgive to release your offender from bondage, too.

When the servant refused to forgive the guy that owed him money, he put the offender in prison. Similarly, when someone has wronged you and that person asks for your forgiveness, but you refuse to forgive him or her, you are inadvertently putting them in bondage. You are uncharacteristically placing them in the prison of unforgiveness. If the person that you're not willing to forgive is not familiar with these principles of forgiveness, you are placing that person in bondage. And when you refuse to forgive, not only will God not forgive you, but He will also allow you to be given over to the tormentors. Traditionally, most have thought that God meant that an unforgiving person would be banished to spend eternity apart from God. Ultimately that might be true; however, there is a passage that says that fear has torment (See 1 John 4:18).

Therefore, if you do not forgive someone, you can end up in fear; whether it's the fear of rejection or fear of commitment. You can live in paranoia and depression. Unforgiveness makes you susceptible to unnecessary insecurities which all have torment. Most people will not want to spend their life with someone who has unnecessary phobias. Besides, it's difficult, if next to impossible, for anyone who has relationship phobia to find and have a healthy relationship. Bearing those things in mind, forgive to free yourself and your offender. Allow God to protect you and answer your prayers—including your petition for the right mate for your life.

Third Level

We can learn of the third level of forgiveness in the Amplified version of parts of James 5:16:

Confess to one another therefore your faults (your slips, your false steps, your offenses, your sins)...that you might be healed and restored (to a spiritual tone of mind and heart)....

In the third level of forgiveness, you are the offender and the one in need of forgiveness. If you've done something wrong against anyone it is to your benefit that you ask them to forgive you. It's also essential that you ask God to forgive you, too. If you don't air out your faults to God and to the person you've wronged, you will hinder yourself from receiving healing and restoration in areas of your life that need them.

Confessing your faults to God and to the person you've wronged will open up the door for you to receive your healing. Maybe you're not in a position to confess your fault to someone you've wronged. Perhaps it's too late for you to ask someone to forgive you. Maybe you can't reach the person that you feel you need to apologize to. In this case, take heart. God knows your heart and is always open to hear you confess your faults to Him. You might also need to share your faults with a professional counselor or someone mature whom you trust to air out your transgressions. Once you've done this, whether by asking God to forgive you or sharing your faults with God and someone else, you'll begin to receive healing and restoration in your life.

Fourth Level

The fourth level of forgiveness can be learned from Matthew 5:23-25 (AMP):

So if when you are offering your gift at the altar you there remember that your brother has any (grievance) against you, leave your gift at the altar and go. First make peace with your brother, and then come back and present your gift. Come to terms quickly with your accuser while you are on the way traveling with him, lest your accuser hand you over to the judge, and the judge to the guard, and you be put in prison.

In the fourth level of forgiveness, someone thinks that you wronged them. You might not think that you've done anything wrong, but God tells us to go and make amends with that person. The altar is a place of sacrifice. The platform or stage in the average church is meant to be a place of sacrifice. Our sacrifices on the altar are our gifts to God. Gifts offered to God range from prayer, praise, confessions of wrongdoing as well as monetary gifts.

While God requires us to do all those things, it is more important to Him that we have right relationships with others. Those deeds do not mean much to Him nor will they bring blessings to us if we know that there is someone who has a grudge against us. That passage is saying that if we *know* of someone who has a spat with us, it's more important to halt on offering our gifts, and go and reconcile or ask for forgiveness from that person. If we don't do this God will not accept our "offerings." In addition, just like the person thought to be at fault was prone to be given over to the judge, to an officer, and to prison, not asking for forgiveness from someone who thinks you've wronged them even though you feel that you are not guilty, can lead you to be "judged" and imprisoned.

Obviously unless it's a crime, you are not going to be sent to lockup because someone thinks you did something against him or her. Notwithstanding, imprisonment is confinement. It's restriction. It's immobilization. Maybe you're trying to make progress in an area of your life, at work or in an endeavor—or perhaps you need a big break in your life. Not reconciling with someone who thinks you're his or her problem could halt your progress. You can end up stuck in a rut because you refused to make amends.

That is the kind of imprisonment that can befall you. The judgment can be God taking His hands off helping you out in an area of your life where you need assistance. And if this area is in your relationship, I hope you can understand even more why it is important for you to learn to forgive—or ask for forgiveness. If applicable to you, forgiveness plays a vital role in helping you find and marry the right person for your life.

Endeavor To Be At Peace with Your Family

The following narration begins to tell us the story of Ruth. Peruse this biblical text with me and let's note some things revealed about her and her interaction with her mother-in-law, Naomi. As we do this, we'll draw nuggets from Ruth's relationship with her mother-in-law. The importance of letting go of the past will also be reinforced.

Long ago, in the days before Israel had a king, there was a famine in the land. So a man named Elimelech, who belonged to the clan of Ephrath and who lived in Bethlehem in Judah, went with his wife Naomi and their two sons Mahlon and Chilion to live for a while in the country of Moab. While they were living there, Elimelech died, and Naomi was left alone with her two sons, who married Moabite girls, Orpah and Ruth. About ten years later Mahlon and Chilion also died, and Naomi was left all alone, without husband or sons. (Ruth 1:1-5 GNB)

During Old Testament times only the Israelites were God's people, whereas the other nations were not. There was a famine in Israel and this led Naomi, her husband, Elimelech, and their two sons, Mahlon and Chilion, to leave Israel. They went to Moab and dwelt there. While there, their sons married the Moabites, Ruth and Orpah respectively. Since they left Israel and since God was in Israel, in a sense they went out of God's Will by leaving His jurisdiction. I believe this is akin to a child of God leaving

God or backsliding because of some kind of persecution. They left because of the famine in Israel.

Did you note what happened after they left Israel? Naomi's husband and sons died. This could happen to anyone who backslides, leaves God, or gets out of His will. The person might not necessarily face physical death; however, it might be that the individual would be unfruitful, or things would not work out for the person. Perhaps you're being persecuted as a believer. Perhaps you feel like you have too many restrictions as a child of God. As a result you might decide to leave in search of greener pastures but face the consequence of ending up on meaner pastures. Israel was where they should have stayed. However, the famine made them look for greener pastures. God's place for us isn't always easy. But leaving the will of God is never the right decision.

Some time later Naomi heard that the LORD had blessed his people by giving them good crops; so she got ready to leave Moab with her daughters-in-law. They started out together to go back to Judah, but on the way she said to them, "Go back home and stay with your mothers. May the LORD be as good to you as you have been to me and to those who have died. And may the LORD make it possible for each of you to marry again and have a home." So Naomi kissed them good-bye but they started crying and said to her, "No! We will go with you to your people." (Ruth 1:6-10 GNB)

Naomi is now stuck with her daughters-in-law, Ruth and Orpah. Naomi learned that God had visited His people. God provided food for them and things were much better. So she decided to go back to Israel. Meanwhile, she insisted that her daughters-in-law remain in Moab and get married again. But they refused.

"You must go back, my daughters," Naomi answered. "Why do you want to come with me? Do you think I could have sons again for you to marry? Go back home, for I am too old to get married again. Even if I

thought there was still hope, and so got married tonight and had sons,
would you wait until they had grown up? Would this keep you from mar-
rying someone else? No, my daughters, you know that's impossible. The
LORD has turned against me, and I feel very sorry for you."Again they
started crying. Then Orpah kissed her mother-in-law good-bye and went
back home, but Ruth held on to her. (Ruth 1:11-14 GNB)

Naomi kept on insisting that her daughters-in-law stay home. She felt
they wouldn't be gaining anything by going to Israel with her since she
was convinced that God was against her. Orpah eventually gave in to her
insistence and not only went back to her folks in Moab, but also *went back*
to worshipping her god. Remember? The Israelites were the only ones who
had the true and living God, whereas other nations like Moab worshipped
other gods. Despite Naomi's appeal to her Moabite in-laws to stay home,
Ruth rebuffed her plea.

So Naomi said to her, "Ruth, your sister-in-law has gone back to her
people and to her god. Go back home with her."But Ruth answered, "Don't
ask me to leave you! Let me go with you. Wherever you go, I will go; wher-
ever you live, I will live. Your people will be my people, and your God will
be my God. Wherever you die, I will die, and that is where I will be buried.
May the LORD'S worst punishment come upon me if I let anything but
death separate me from you!" When Naomi saw that Ruth was determined
to go with her, she said nothing more. (Ruth 1:15-18 GNB)

Ruth on the other hand refused to return to her people and her old way of
doing things. She stuck with Naomi and with equal vehemence insisted on
going back with her to Israel. She earnestly desired to be with Naomi. She
wanted Naomi's people to be her people and most importantly, she wanted
Naomi's God to be her God. She was seeking God first, and this eventually
led her to God's best. She took advantage of her relationship with Naomi to
get to know God. She wanted to date God. She wanted to be around God's
people. If you're not already, it's proper for you to be around people who are
dating God. This will assist you in finding the right person.

Did you notice that Naomi acknowledged the fact that Ruth was still in her prime to have a husband? And as a result, insisted that she stay in Moab and get married again? But Ruth declined vehemently! She insisted in sticking with her. In spite of Naomi's hysteria courtesy of the loss of her husband and sons, Ruth saw something in her, her people, and her God that she needed, that she wanted, that she craved. Maybe you feel the same way. Maybe you are not a Christian. But there is something about the Christian faith that intrigues you, grips you, and draws you. Yes, you might be aware of some believers who appall you by conducting themselves contrary to their beliefs, but don't let that deter you from getting your blessing, salvation, and eternal life from God.

Ruth declined to stay in Moab and look for another husband. She chose to stick with Naomi who definitely needed support. She was more concerned about Naomi who had now become her only family. She was also more interested in having Naomi's God in her life. Drawing from this, before you get married, there might be more important fishes for you to fry.

While you are single, get your priorities straight. As priorities I've mentioned knowing what you are getting yourself into. Understand what love is and what love does. Practice save sex. Avoid, resist and flee temptation. Date God first. Find out what makes relationships successful, the purpose of relationships, and how to find the right person. Get a job by finding out God's will for your life. Let God do His job. Get on your mark to get set to go to your mate. And get rid of negatives from your past.

Furthermore, like Ruth, supporting your family especially your parents, guardians or whoever raised you, and endeavoring to have a good relationship with them, is essential. Did it occur to you that your time with your family may be an on-the-job training for your own family? If you take for granted your parents, brothers or sisters who you may have lived with for eighteen years, more or less, how will you treat the person you'll meet in the near future?

While you are single, as much as possible, try to ensure that you are at peace with your family. Show them some appreciation. I hope that the last time you expressed gratitude to your parents was not the last mother and father's day. Mother and father's day should be every day because they're still your mother and father everyday. If you have a good relationship with your parents or whoever raised you, I hope they feel appreciated by you. If they hardly hear you say "thank you" to them, or get a sense of value from you, I suggest you begin to show them some very well deserved gratitude. Thank them for taking care of you, feeding you, housing you, and whatever else they've done to ensure your welfare.

I urge you to go to them now or call them up and tell them you love them, appreciate them, and are grateful for all they've done for you. If you live with them, give them a good, fat, mushy hug. Let them know you care, like Ruth did for Naomi. If they're surprised and touched by your homely gesture toward them, don't exploit the situation either. Don't seize this opportunity to empty their wallets. Let them know you appreciate and value them.

On the other hand, if you have a dysfunctional relationship with your family, especially your parents, my heart goes out to you. Try and do as much as you can in ironing out any misunderstanding with them, or anyone else. You don't want to bring that burden into your marriage. Ask God to give you the strength to forgive them. Do whatever is in your power to get things right with them. Do your best and let God take care of the rest.

It's in your best interest that you forgive your parents or guardians for whatever they might have done wrong to you. If you don't, you can carry that resentment into your marriage. You cannot afford to lose the special person God has for you, or spoil your relationship with him or her because of the feud you have with your parents. It's not about them; it's about you.

And whenever you stand praying, if you have anything against anyone, forgive him, that your father in heaven may also forgive you your tres-

passes. But if you do not forgive, neither will your father in heaven forgive your trespasses. (Mark 11:25 NKJV)

You have to forgive. If you don't, God won't forgive you, either, for anything you do wrong to Him. I hope you recall that love forgives. Begin to cultivate this quality of love toward those who are closest to you because you're going to need it in maintaining your upcoming marriage. Whatever grievances you have against your family—your parents in particular, please let them go. It's not up to them to ask for forgiveness from you, it's up to you to forgive them.

In the words of Bishop T.D. Jakes:

Forgiveness is not about how the person responds to you, it is about releasing anger out of you.[80]

Furthermore, we are to honor our parents, not because they've always done the right thing, but because it's a mandate from God and it's just the right thing to do.

Children, obey your parents in the Lord, for this is right. "Honor your father and mother"—which is the first commandment with a promise. (Ephesians 6:1-2)

That doesn't mean we should condone any ungodliness on their part. Notice the passage said obey them "in the Lord"—not out of the Lord's will. We're not to obey anything they tell us to do if it's against the Word of the Lord. All the same, we're obligated to respect, value, appreciate, and esteem them for their position as parents. When we do this, we can expect:

"that it might go well with you and that you might enjoy long life on the earth."(Ephesians 6:3)

That is God's promise to us when we honor our parents. I believe you want everything to go well with your relationship with the person God brings to you. Moreover, I believe you'll also desire to live a long life with this individual. Therefore, drawing strength from the Lord, do your part in forgiving and respecting your parents even if they don't seem to deserve it.

I sympathize with the fact that Naomi was still grieving for the loss of her family and bitter toward God. God bless her heart, she did not know any better by saying that she left Israel with plenty, but blamed God for bringing her back empty.[81] Faced with her situation we may have acted the same way, if not worse. Nevertheless, she was going back with Ruth who ended up being her jackpot, her priceless lotto. Ruth ended up marrying a very wealthy and distinguished Israelite man named Boaz. Her marriage to him helped restore Naomi's property inherited through her marriage to her deceased husband.

That took place after she arrived in Israel with Naomi. Ruth's unflinching decision to come to Israel with Naomi definitely paid off. I believe that because Ruth honored Naomi, things went well with her as promised by Ephesians 6:3. In chapter ten, I began to discuss how Ruth met Boaz when she ended up on his field while searching for work. She found favor with Boaz and this was her response to the kindness he bestowed on her when they first met on his field:

So she fell on her face, bowed down to the ground, and said to him, "Why have I found favor in your eyes, that you should take notice of me, since I am a foreigner?" (Ruth 2:10 NKJV)

How often do you see a woman prostrate (not that she needs to) because she is overwhelmed by the kindness and thoughtfulness of a man? Rare isn't it? Be that as it may, Boaz was such a man for Ruth. I believe God wants to bless us with spouses that'll inspire us to humble ourselves as a token of our appreciation like Ruth did. If you're seeing someone right now, can you say this about him or her? Do you praise God often for blessing you with such an individual, or do you fast and pray in tongues that God will slay the person in the spirit out of your life? Do you often ask yourself why God gave you such an outstanding person, considering that you feel you don't deserve the blessing?

If you're single but involved with an individual who you know is not God's best for you, what are you doing playing around with this individual's emotions? Is the person just an "appetizer" for your "main course"? I hope you're aware of how appetizers often spoil one's appetite for the main course. Sometimes appetizers prevent you from having a main course meal when you're stuffed full of them. God help you if those appetizers are "ribs" because like He did to Adam, He needs to yank those ribs out of you to prepare you for your "entrée."

Ruth was astonished that Boaz took notice of her. Trust God, if God takes notice of you, a man, or woman, after his own heart, will, too. In fact, if you recall when I talked about how God sanctifies us in chapter fourteen, I mentioned how Ruth had to shed her widow's garment and freshen herself up before she could go and be with Boaz. But prior to changing her cloths, Ruth already met Boaz. Despite the fact that she looked "jacked up" Boaz still noticed her. Hmmm, isn't that something? She was not looking her best, but he noticed her. And as the scripture above attests, she was surprised and asked Boaz why she found *favor* with him. This statement reinforces a profound truth about ending up with the person God has for you:

Finding the right person for your life is not based on fervor, but on favor. Trying to make things happen with your efforts is not going to bring you a suitable life partner. God's efforts, will. It's not about your fervor but God's favor.

The man who finds a wife finds a treasure, and he receives favor from the Lord. (Proverbs 18:22 NLT)

If you're a lady, you don't have to dress risqué for a Godly man to notice you. You don't need to show off your cleavage and expose your thighs to be noticed by a Godly man. If this is how you advertise yourself, then don't be surprised in attracting the wrong guy who will take advantage of your promo and jet! Not that his justified to exploit you. I believe that what you draw attention to, in yourself, determines who you get. If you draw attention to your "assets," you'll probably get a man who's only after your assets. However, if you exude a Godly character, you don't need to draw attention to yourself because your wholesome demeanor will do the job for you. It will endear a man of character to you, just like Boaz was transfixed with Ruth.

Charm is deceitful and beauty is passing, but a woman who fears the Lord shall be praised. (Proverbs 31:30 NKJV)

In the words of Dr. Ed Cole:

When the charm wears off, you have nothing but character left.[82]

Truly speaking, even a man only after your assets will be captivated with you. Nevertheless, a virtuous woman would repel such a man by telling him to buzz off and let the Lord deliver him from his lasciviousness, while she continues to preserve and reserve every facet of her irresistible, invaluable and incomprehensible being for her man—God's best man for her.

You should become like whom you're trying to attract. You should concentrate on becoming the right person to be found by conducting yourself like Christ. Be Christ-like. If this applies to you, please show some appreciation for yourself and gracefully cover up your bosom and thighs.

Ruth may have been *hot* like pico de gallo, but Boaz noticed more than that about her as the scripture reads:

And Boaz answered and said to her, "It has been fully reported to me, all that you have done for your mother-in-law since the death of your husband, and how you have left your father and your mother and the land of your birth, and have come to a people whom you did not know before. (Ruth 2:11 NKJV)

Boaz was given a comprehensive report about Ruth, and what he heard was remarkable. She supported her mother-in-law despite circumstances that compelled her to do the contrary. Despite the demise of her father-in-law, brother-in-law and husband, Ruth stood by her mother-in-law. She left her family, and came to Israel; a land and its people that were foreign to her. It is wise to find out how an individual treats their mother—or any other close relative, as a way of ascertaining their character—and how the person will treat you. This was part of what caught Boaz' attention about Ruth. This is why you should endeavor to be at peace with your family because this will be necessary to maintain your impending relationship.

So, what kind of report do people give about you? Most importantly, what kind of report does God have about you? People in general, be it parents, other family members and friends, can be spiteful, misunderstand you and tell lies; however, God can't. So, you have no excuse. After all, God knows your heart, right? Is your heart right with Him? Are you obedient to Him? Are you dating Him? If not, I encourage you get with His program. And it's not MTV or BET, but B-I-B-L-E.

Why does a woman like Ruth leave her family, home, culture and comfort zone, with a lady who had lost everything, and attributed her loss to the same God that Ruth is now trying to know? Boaz helps us answer this question when he said:

The Lord repay your work, and a full reward be given you by the Lord God of Israel, under whose wings you have come for refuge. (Ruth 2:12 NKJV)

Ruth was seeking after God. She was putting God first. In doing so everything else she needed was added to her (See Matthew 6:33). She got Boaz and Bo's cash (though not her focus). I hope you see that it's imperative to put God first in your life. He'll add Jason or Jessica later. He wants to deal with your heart, first, courtesy of His words to you. He wants to sprinkle the necessary ingredients in the stew of your heart that'll emanate the irresistible aroma, which will draw a Boaz or a Ruth to you—not a bozo or a ruth-less.

If you're a man, He wants to give you someone who is like Ruth, not someone who is like—rude. If you're a woman God wants to bless you with a guy like Boaz, a Godly man that will embrace you with love and lift you up. Not a guy like a Boa, a snake that will squeeze you to death and eat you up.

CHAPTER SIXTEEN
Let God Make the First Move

You may call me old-fashioned, old-school, anachronistic, archaic, medieval or a naiveté; nevertheless, if you're a lady, I don't think you should make the first move on a man. Relax, and take it easy. Please, don't castigate me on this statement. This is just my take, and you're not obligated to accept it. Besides, I haven't finished my statement—I don't think a guy should make the first move on a lady either.

Let God make the first move. After God makes His move, you should make your move—after God gives you the green light. You should make your move after God has moved. And how do you know when God has moved? Well, God would have been way ahead of you before you figured that out.

When God moves by drawing your attention, somehow, someway, to someone, and placing a desire in your heart for the individual, you and the individual will be *willing* to get to know each other. Sometimes, this might not happen initially but it will eventually. The individual will also be someone who will help you fulfill God's purpose for your life—and for your lives together. There might also be an element of surprise, an element of unexpectedness—as in knowing the person all along, or being around or connected to the individual one way or the other, and finding out later that, that person was God's best for you.

For example, Eve had always been close to Adam all along—under his nose—close to his heart—from his side—and Adam had no clue, until he woke up from his sleep to discover her come seemingly from nowhere. Rebecca was related—connected to Isaac, but neither knew the other—until God made the first move. I didn't know Dana was for me until 4 years after I met her. So for 4 years we served together, hung out and prayed with mutual friends together. And yet I wasn't aware that my mate was right under my nose.

So, expect the unexpected by watching out for your desire for someone who's affiliated with you. And perhaps, someone you disliked previously. Also, someone you meet by accident, and who'll help you fulfill God's purpose for your life—not take you out of it—before you make your move. The move you make should be in response to the move God made on your behalf. The move you make, at least initially, should be a "choice-move"— choosing to accept or reject whomever God presents to you. And if you're a man: ASK HER OUT AND BE CLEAR THAT YOU'RE INTERESTED IN HER!

God made the first move by "moving" or relocating Adam from outside the garden into the garden and bringing Eve to him. Adam responded to God's move by declaring Eve as his mate. God made the first move when He revealed to Rebecca through Abraham's servant that she was the one for Isaac. In response, she made the choice-move to accept Isaac as her husband.

Prior to releasing Rebecca to go with Abraham's servant to adjoin with Isaac, Rebecca's mum and brother asked Rebecca if she wanted to go with the servant.

And they said "we will call the girl and ask her (what is) her desire." So they called Rebecca and said to her, "will you go with this man?" And she said "I will go." (Genesis 24:57-58 AMP)

Please note, though Abraham's servant told Rebecca's family that she was the answer to his prayer, they still gave Rebecca the choice to respond.

In spite of being told about God's revelation to Abraham's servant they still asked Rebecca if she was willing to go. This was very smart! Much kudos to Becky's mum and brother for their foresight and courtesy toward her.

Friend, please listen. Don't be fooled by getting in a relationship with someone just because the individual said that God told him or her that you are the person's husband or wife. It doesn't matter if the person went to heaven for thirty seconds and while there, Jesus gave him or her that so-called revelation. It doesn't matter if the individual saw you marrying him or her in a dream— saw Moses appear from nowhere to tell him or her that you are the person's spouse—or a Prophet prophesied to the individual that you are the person's mate.

What matters is that you have a *choice* to accept or reject anything as such. If God really had anything to do with it, just like with Rebecca, you'll have the desire to be in a relationship with whomever He advocates for you. At times, this might not be the case at first impulse, but as time goes on and as you continue to yield to God's will, everything will fall in place accordingly.

On seeing Rebecca, Isaac also responded to God's first move by accepting and taking her to be his wife.

Then Isaac brought her into his mother Sarah's tent; and he took Rebekah and she became his wife, and he loved her. So Isaac was comforted after his mother's death. (Genesis 24:67 NKJV)

God also made the first move when he allowed Ruth and Boaz to get hitched. They responded to God's move by accepting and marrying each other. I've heard some say that Ruth made the first move on Boaz. I beg to differ. Naomi tried to prevent Ruth from coming to Israel. She insisted that Ruth stay and get a man, but Ruth refused. Rather, she chose to come to Israel and seek God Almighty. She had her priorities straight. A man was not on top of her list at that point in time. Besides, she wanted to support her mother-in-law. Meanwhile, I believe God was already moving. Ruth got to Israel, got a job in Boaz' field and met Boaz, too. I believe God already made the first move. Furthermore, Boaz inquired about Ruth *first*. He also approached Ruth first.

He was impressed with Ruth by complimenting her regarding her dealings with her mother-in-law, feeding her, providing for her and making her work in the field very much easier.[83] I believe God already set the deal up. It was just a matter of it getting sealed by the parties involved—Ruth and Boaz. Let's see how this develops.

Then Naomi her mother-in-law said to her, "My daughter, shall I not seek security for you, that it might be well with you? Now Boaz, whose young women you were with, is he not our relative? In fact, he is winnowing barley tonight at the threshing floor. Therefore wash yourself and anoint yourself, put on your best garment and go down to the threshing floor; but do not make yourself known to the man until he has finished eating and drinking. Then it shall be, when he lies down, that you shall go in, uncover his feet, and lie down; and he will tell you what you should do."And she said to her, "All that you say to me I will do." (Ruth 3:1-5 NKJV)

Did you notice that Naomi said Boaz was a relative? They already had some kind of connection to each other, unbeknownst to either of them. Furthermore, Naomi told her to wash and anoint herself; in essence, look and smell nice for the guy. I don't think I need to overemphasize that. Although, an attractive physical appearance is necessary—for both men and women, let's not forget the spiritual attractiveness—Godly character. This is where your date with God also comes to play. Jesus would have washed and anointed you. Know what I mean? But if you get dirty again, He's willing to forgive you. Just ask Him to, and endeavor to stay clean.

Naomi also gave Ruth instructions to lie beside Boaz as a gesture of her interest in getting hitched with him. Please note that although the stage had been set, Ruth didn't initiate this idea—her mother-in-law did. Quite obviously she must have been interested in Boaz since she adhered to Naomi's instruction. Furthermore, Ruth was told that Boaz would tell her what to do. Naomi didn't tell Ruth to tell Boaz what to do. She told Ruth that he would tell her what to do. I'm just presenting the scripture as it was written. However, you can draw your own conclusions. Ruth's job was to be in position while Boaz' job was to do the inquisition.

Naomi is giving Ruth some invaluable advice here. This is the same woman that could have prevented Ruth from being in this position, had Ruth listened to her and remained in Moab. Drawing from this, I'm getting more understanding on why God wants us to honor our parents. They may not always do the right thing. They may not always make the right decisions. However, God, sometimes through their life experiences still places some invaluable wisdom in them that we can tap from, if we have the proper attitude toward them. Let's read on.

So she went down to the threshing floor and did according to all that her mother-in-law instructed her. And Boaz had eaten and drunk, and his heart was cheerful, he went to lie down at the end of the heap of grain; and she came softly, uncovered his feet, and lay down. Now it happened at midnight that the man was startled, and turned himself; and there, a woman was lying at his feet. (Ruth 3:6-8 NKJV)

Wow! "*...there, a woman was lying at his feet.*" This is profound. Boaz was startled on seeing a woman at his feet. Please note the element of surprise. Similarly, Adam probably felt the same way initially when he found his woman too—after he woke up from his sleep. Also, Isaac was probably surprised on seeing Rebecca come from nowhere after his meditation. The dude was not even thinking about Ruth, but there she was—by his feet.

If you're a guy, why would you want to stress yourself by looking for a woman when God can do the job of simply placing her by your feet? In other words, simplify the whole process for you by placing her close to you.

Out of courtesy we often say things like: "You found a wife," or "she found a husband," or "when are you going to find somebody?" But in all honesty, If God wasn't involved, we couldn't find a booger if it was right under our noses. God allows us to find the person He already found and intended for us probably the same way parents allow their children to find them when playing hide and seek. So, when you do find your mate, or if you already found him or her, make sure you give the Almighty His due.

Ruth followed her mother-in-law's instruction. I hope you noticed that she came to him "softly," not rambunctiously, not obnoxiously, and not pro-miscuously. Boaz found her by his feet. He did not find her on top of him. In addition, she was instructed not to reveal herself to him until he finished his repast. You can position yourself to be noticed; however, your positioning should be done by God and in His *timing*.

It would have been bad timing for Ruth to reveal herself to Boaz while he was in the middle of getting his "grub on." Her timing was on the money when she approached him cautiously and lay beside his feet—which, I be-lieve, signifies her humility. By that time he was in a good mood. His mood could only get better when he discovered the sweetheart by his feet. Ruth lay quietly beside him and *waited patiently*. She was in the right place, with the right guy, at the right time, waiting for him to acknowledge her the right way. It was left to Boaz to discover Ruth lying beside him. Ruth did not smack him upside his head to get his attention.

If the character of God is resonating in you, you do not have to show some drama to get a guy's attention. God will grab his attention for you. He might be sleeping now; he might be in la-la land; he might be preoccupied with his education, his goals, his business, or even with some other lady. Don't let this faze you. If he is the one God intends for you, just yield to God's leading. Let God relocate you beside your man. While there, relax, and don't say anything. Be courteous, humble and patient. Watch him wake up to the scent emanating from God's fragrance on you. And when he does, and he makes the inquisition—inquires about you, then you can sing to him like a canary. Then you can pour out your heart to him, depending of course on the manner of your conversation with him. Then you can respond to him like Ruth did below.

And he said, "Who are you?" So she answered, "I am Ruth, your maidservant. Take your maidservant under your wing, for you are a close relative." Then he said, "blessed are you of the LORD, my daughter! For you have shown more kindness at the end than the beginning, in that you did not go after young men, whether poor or rich." (Ruth 3:9-10 NKJV)

You don't have to take my word for it. You just heard it from the horse's mouth. Boaz said it himself. Ruth was not about chasing men, regardless of their financial status. Certainly not first. With that, I rest my case. Even so, let's finish the chapter.

"And now, my daughter, do not fear. I will do for you all that you request, for all the people of my town know that you are a virtuous woman. Now it is true that I am a close relative; however, there is a relative closer than I. Stay this night, and in the morning it shall be that if he will perform the duty of a close relative for you, good; let him do it. But if he does not want to perform the duty of a close relative for you, then I will perform the duty for you, as the LORD lives! Lie down until morning." So she lay at his feet, and she arose before one could recognize. Then he said, "do not let it be known that the woman came to the threshing floor." Also he said, "Bring the shawl that is on you and hold it." And when she held it, he measured six ephahs of barley, and laid it on her. Then she went into the city. (Ruth 3:11-15 NKJV)

Notice that he gave her more gifts. There was no one nightstand, no hanky panky, and no *sex in the city* of Bethlehem.

When she came to her mother-in-law, she said, "is that you, my daughter?" Then she told her all that the man had done for her. And she said, "These six ephahs of barley he gave me; for he said to me, 'Do not go emp-

ty-handed to your mother-in-law.'" Then she said, "Sit still, my daughter, until you know how the matter will turn out; for the man will not rest until he has concluded the matter this day." (Ruth 3:16-18 NKJV)

As I alluded to previously, the suggestion that women in particular should note how a man treats their mother might be ingenious after all. Boaz was kind enough to be thoughtful about Ruth's mother-in-law by giving her those measures of barley even though she was just a close relative to him. This was not even his mother and this was not the first time he did this for their welfare.[84] You may need to be vigilant enough to see how a potential prospect treats their mother, father and even your parents. Does the individual treat them like in-laws or out-laws? Though some mothers and fathers do act like outlaws, we should still honor their office as parents.

Moreover, Naomi told Ruth to *sit still*, or be patient, and watch how everything turned out. It's essential that you're patient and continue to do God's bidding while He does your hitching. You shouldn't force your way into anyone's heart. As long as you've done all God has instructed you to do, take a chill pill, relax and be about God's business while He's about yours. Evidently, according to their custom the closest relative was required to grant Ruth her request. In following the proper protocol and displaying his integrity, humility, and respect for his custom, Boaz thought it necessary and justifiable that the man who was in a better position than him as a relative to Naomi, be given the opportunity to buy back Naomi's property inherited from her deceased husband and sons, and marry Ruth.

With that in mind, not every Christian man or woman is for you. The first Christian man or woman that notices you or that you might be attracted to, may not be the one. Neither may the second or third, but the one God approves for you. Apparently, Boaz did not marry any of the women that worked for him. I guess he knew that just because they were Israelites and around him didn't mean that they were the best for him. Even when he had the chance to have Ruth, he went through the required process to make sure everything was done right. Despite his influence and opulence, he humbled himself and sought counsel with regard to Ruth. You should also seek counsel before you proceed to the altar with anyone. It turned out that the other guy on given the opportunity to marry Ruth turned it down, even when he had the advantage.[85] This should not be a surprise because the other guy was not the best man for Ruth. Boaz was. So, how did the story end?

So Boaz took Ruth and she became his wife; and when he went in to her, the LORD gave her conception and she bore a son. (Ruth 4:13 NKJV)

After God set the deal up, Boaz closed it by marrying Ruth. I believe that God should make the first move and the man should make the next move. The move the woman should make is to *move* right into the arms of her beloved, like Eve moved to Adam and Rebecca to Isaac. Even Jesus made the first move for His woman, the church. He made the move when He came and died for her. I, and many others like me made the choice-move by accepting what He did for us on the cross. Now, the church is His bride and we're going to have the official wedding ceremony sometime in the future, yippeeeeee! I hope you responded positively to His move, too.

You might be familiar with people who moved before God did and seemingly have a good relationship. You really don't know the struggles they had to overcome to arrive at that point. Therefore, you shouldn't use them as an excuse to move ahead of God. Because faced with their situation you might not survive. You may not have the kind of support system they had, which held them together before they cried out to God who came through for them. They may have gotten married without checking with God first, but they survived the corresponding consequences thanks to the Almighty, Who, through His mercy and grace saved their marriage.

Nevertheless, my exposition is more about prevention than treatment. It's about going for the best-case scenario in a relationship. It's about shooting for the best. I heard Dr. Price articulate it something like this:

I would rather shoot for one hundred percent and only make fifty, than to shoot for nothing and make all of it.[86]

I'd rather make the effort to obtain and maintain the best relationship attainable and get something close to it, than not make the effort at all and end up in a less than mediocre relationship. Thanks to excuses such as: "Nobody is perfect, life is hard, most marriages are not like that," and blah, blah, blah. It's been said that experience is the best teacher. I agree with this only from a positive standpoint. Perhaps the best way to learn about anything that is to your benefit is by experience. But the best way to learn about anything that is to your detriment is not by experience; rather, it's by having and applying the information that will help you avoid such a situation.

For example, the best way to become a very good physician is by experiencing or practicing the theory taught in class in the clinic, by interacting with patients and perfecting surgical skills in the lab, depending on one's medical expertise. On the other hand, the best way to avoid being in prison is to obey the law. I don't need to disobey the law and *experience* excruciating friction between my medulla oblongata and a police baton—have my body do the electric bugaloo to the beat of hundreds of volts of electricity from the officer's taser—taste my blood, the sole of the officer's boots, and the dust from the concrete—while my face is smack down on the pavement thanks to the big burly cop's knee on my back. Neither do I need to end up behind bars with some guy or guys who think I'm the next best thing to Vivica Fox!

Just like Jesus said that blessed are those who have not seen and yet believed, blessed are those who have never experienced a bad situation, and yet believe that being in a bad situation is a bad experience.[87] Being in a bad relationship is a bad situation and a bad experience. In this discourse, part of the objective is to avoid being in such a predicament. Nevertheless, God can and does repair bad relationships. This is possible when we do things God's way.

Therefore, let God make the first move while you *checkmate*! Check your mate—tick or check *right*, as a signature of accepting your mate—and check to see if the individual computes with the profile of the right mate for you. You'll only be able to checkmate if you allow God to teach you how to play His "dating game," courtesy of the time you spend with Him. Besides, you need the King (Jesus), to checkmate.

CHAPTER SEVENTEEN
Are you dating online or "offline"?

In recent years the search for a soul mate has landed on the Internet. Nowadays pop-up windows advertising singles' dating services are a common occurrence. There are online dating services that cater to singles from all works of life, diverse ethnicities, and religions. So it's no surprise that there are matchmaking sites that cater to Christians, too.

The idea is that Christian singles' sites help singles who are believers meet other believers. And to ensure successful setups, Christian singles are required to fill up questionnaires so that their compatibility with other believing bachelorettes or bachelors are accessed. If there is a match, singles with compatible profiles are supplied with the relevant contact information that would help them get together.

Christian online dating services sound like a good idea. But are they God's idea? Are single believers supposed to use such services to find their respective mates? Instead of seeking God—theology, some single Christians have ignored Him and gone to technology. Without going to God first, is it sensible to seek a life partner online? Or, is it "offline"—out of line with God's Word?

I do understand however, that not everyone who patronizes Christian dating sites or other sites for that matter go online to find a spouse. Some log on for the purpose of camaraderie. Some just want to chitchat, meet new friends, share their faith and fellowship. This is good and well. But, honestly, is that the reason why *most* people go to Christian dating sites?

Are they *just* trying to make friends and fellowship with other believers? There is nothing wrong with desiring to have a life partner. We just need to be careful on how we go about finding that person. For singles who desire to go beyond fellowship to courtship and then marriage, *bypassing* God and heading straight to the net is not the right way to accomplish the quest for the right mate.

Just because websites providing dating services for single believers claim that they are *Christian* doesn't mean that *Christ is in* it. Before the world-wide web was the Worldwide Word—the Bible. Before internet search engines was The Holy Spirit who *searches* all the things of God, the creator of the universe. In essence, finding the right mate is *best* realized through God's help.

Please do not misunderstand me. I am not saying that God cannot bring someone across your path via the Internet since all things are possible with Him. It's possible that individuals that found each other through the web were successful because they independently went to God *first*. Perhaps through God's guidance they unwittingly stumbled across each other. In some cases, couples initially met online for completely different reasons: E-banking, long distance education, wrong email address, bulletin boards, non-dating chat rooms, or while responding to an online article. They did not just use the Internet as a method to get hitched. They sought God first, and through the net, He hooked them up. Other than such scenarios, it stands to reason that going online to find a mate "without seeking God first" is offline. The only way that you can go online to find God's best for yourself is if your approach is online with God's Word—God's way of doing things.

The questionnaires that singles are required to fill are supposedly designed to access compatibility. If you are thinking of filling such a questionnaire, or if you've filled one already, did you consider whether the results of the questionnaire are valid? When filling behavioral test questionnaires necessary for job applications, some applicants resort to answering the test questions the way they think the employer would want them to, so that they could land a job. Did you consider that singles do the same on online questionnaires by giving false information about themselves so that they could get hitched with a Christian single? What are the chances that some of the singles who patronize Christian online dating services are non-believers? Do the questionnaires detect false information? Are the questionnaires laced with lie detectors?

Proverbs 20:6 says that most men will proclaim their own goodness but who can find a faithful man? Most singles will present the best of themselves on the questionnaires, but only God knows the validity of their claims. No one, not even the best professionally arranged questionnaires can find someone faithful for you. Only God can. Proverbs 19:14 says, "... But a prudent wife is from the Lord." Also, Proverbs 31:10 starts off by saying, "Who can find a virtuous wife?" Truth be told, no one can, except God.

You will find a man exclusively through the Internet; but you will not find a Godly man apart from God. You will find a wife online; but you will not find a prudent or virtuous wife strictly by the click of a mouse. Such a precious woman only comes from the Lord. Through God's help you can click with a man or woman without going to the web.

You might argue that when you meet your prospect in person you'd soon find out if the person was lying to you. That might be true. But why go through all that trouble only to find out that the person you were chatting with online was actually offline—out of line with his or her alleged profile and therefore out of sync—incompatible with you. Sadly, some singles who've gone to technology often find that out too late. Doesn't that add to your frustration?

According to an article displayed on CNN.com, false profiles, bad behavior, and mismatches were some of the growing complaints mentioned by various individuals who solicited online dating services. Similar complaints were given by users of Christian dating websites as revealed by eDateReview.com, an online dating review site whose services have been featured on CNN.com/Reuters and CBS Marketwatch.

At eDateReview.com personal testimonies of individuals who used various online dating services can be viewed. Although there were a few individuals who gave high marks for a Christian matchmaking service reviewed on their site, even more individuals were disgruntled about the Christian site's service. Having viewed eDateReview.com myself, I gathered that some users of Christian sites have either used secular sites or are using Christian and secular sites simultaneously.

That suggests that some of the members of online Christian dating services are either not Christians, or are Christians seeking life partners on criterion not based on Christian values. Users' complaints range from people lying about their profiles, incompatible matches, the services were expensive and just a business scam. They also complained that their applications were rejected at one time and then accepted at another. Furthermore, while it's important to evaluate all aspects of a person in order to match the individual appropriately, it seems that the Christian sites based their matches more on professional, educational, emotional, and psychological criteria more than on spiritual values.

Dr. Robert Epstein, a long time researcher, professor, West Coast editor of *Psychology Today* and contributing editor for *Scientific American Mind*, does not believe that tests that will help people find their soul mates exist. He drew this conclusion based on his thirty years of research experience, about half of which he spent designing tests. He questioned the veracity of the tests claimed by some online services designed to help people find their soul mates.

Dr. Epstein said that for such tests to be credible, they have to be reliable, meaning you can count on them to produce stable results, and they need to be a valid measure of what they are supposed to be measuring. In this case, the tests should show that romantic pairings are successful. In addition, the results of the tests are to be submitted to the scientific community for evaluation, and a peer-reviewed report about the tests analyzed by other knowledgeable researchers in the field is ultimately published in an academic journal. According Dr. Epstein, not one of those tests purported by some online services have undergone the criteria he described in order to establish their authenticity.

Dr Epstein also referenced a report published in 2005 on an online white paper by Dr. Philip Zimbardo, former president of the American Psychological Association, after he and other researchers evaluated statistics published by an online matchmaking service. According to Zimbardo, when the online service recommends a compatible match to you, there is a 1 in 500 chance that you will marry that person. Since the online service under review facilitated 1.5 matches a month, if you dated all their recommendations, it will take you 346 dates and 19 years for you to reach a 50% chance of getting married. The team also involved in the review also concluded that "there is no evidence that … scientific psychology is able to pair individuals who will enjoy happy, lasting marriages."[88]

In truth, your success in finding the right person for your life is not based on *how* you approach this goal, but *who* you approach for the goal. If you don't approach God for help you will be disappointed, whether you look for love online or not. You don't have to compute user membership to marriage ratios, and analyze tests and individual testimonies to draw conclusions on the pros and cons of exclusively soliciting online dating sites to seek your mate.

Though online dating offers you the opportunity to meet more prospects, it also gives you more opportunity to be rejected, frustrated and depressed. Why waste all that time online when you can conserve your energy and maximize your time doing other things. You can enjoy, empower, enlighten and discover yourself by spending time with God, the undisputed best matchmaker in the world. A lie detector comes standard with the Holy

Spirit since He is the Spirit of truth. His services are at your disposal only if you seek God to direct you to the right person. And, check this out: He offers his services pro bono. The only "price" you pay for His services is following His instructions—obey Him.

Before Compatibility is Eligibility

Compatibility is a key to having a successful relationship. But before compatibility is eligibility. You might be compatible with someone, but are you eligible to marry the person? Are you mature enough to be in a relationship? Are you prepared for matrimony? Are you ready to be someone's wife or husband? Instead of trying to find the right person, it is more important for you to let God prepare you to be the right one to be found. Instead of looking for a mate, you should let a mate look for you. Better still, look out for you.

God was the one who took it upon Himself to create Eve and bring her to Adam. Adam was sleeping. So was Boaz, until he woke up at midnight to discover Ruth by his feet. Rebecca was going to the well to fetch water when she met Abraham's servant who eventually brought her to Isaac. Similarly, you need to be about your business while God is about His business of either bringing you the right mate or bringing the right mate to you. You should go on living your life as best as you can. Go to sleep—rest in God. Have your mind somewhere else while God places someone beside your feet. Or, let Him place you beside someone else's feet. At midnight—a set time—God's time not yours.

What strikes me about how God orchestrated Adam and Eve, Boaz and Ruth, and Isaac and Rebecca is that none of these couples had any overly significant part in their espousal. All they did was be in the right position in relation to God and accept the person God brought across their paths. Genesis 2:15 informs us that God put Adam in the garden. God positioned him in the place from which his wife emerged. Also, God positioned Adam in a deep sleep. He was in a state of dormancy while God was sculpting his wife whom he accepted after God brought her to him (See Genesis 2:21-23 NKJV).

Isaac was in a position of meditation from which he looked up and saw his queen coming toward him. Later on, he received his wife who prior to her trip from the City of Nahor to Canaan "chose" to be Isaac's wife (See Genesis 24:3, 10, 58, 63-67 NKJV). Ruth was positioned in the right place when she moved to Israel. She was also in position when she was instructed by Naomi to lie beside Boaz who was also in position when he was sleeping (See Ruth 3:1-5). God brought Eve to Adam. Abraham tasked his servant who sought God to set up Rebecca and Isaac. Ruth relocated from Moab to Israel not to find a husband but because she wanted to be with Naomi, and she wanted Naomi's people to be her people and most importantly, she wanted Naomi's God to be her God (See Ruth 1:16-19).

God was the common thread that knitted all the aforementioned biblical couples together. It is in your best interest that you allow God to do the same for you in His own time. The timing of placing individuals together is an important factor that online questionnaires cannot ascertain. An electronic paper can never tell if it is the proper time for you to get married. Even if it predicts your compatibility it cannot predict your eligibility. Only God knows both.

I believe the Holy Spirit subtly placed in the scriptures the timing of the hitching of the biblical characters. Abraham's servant who brought Rebecca to Isaac came to the well at evening *time*, the time the women came to draw water from the well (See Genesis 24:11). Boaz woke up at *midnight* to discover Ruth by his feet (See Ruth 3:8). Adam was in a deep sleep, a period of time after which he saw Eve. There is a time for everything. Only God knows the best time for you to discover and marry the person suitable to be your spouse.

Until then, if you are not in position with Him—online with Him, you might be prolonging the time He could have brought someone into your life. One way you can be offline with God is by disregarding His help but going online by surfing the web for a mate, instead of deep-sea-diving into the water of God's Word for the right mate. You might be distracted from discovering the person God is presenting to you because you're out of position, out of line, offline, on the web, when you could have been online, in position with Him to discover the person right in your neck of the woods.

CHAPTER EIGHTEEN

It's Not About Where You're From, But Whom You're From

I found it interesting that God had no qualms with Boaz marrying Ruth. One of the most wealthy, prominent, and eligible bachelors in Israel married a foreigner. God had no problem with it. In all of Israel, wasn't there a woman good enough for Boaz? I believe there was not; at least, no one good enough for Boaz as Ruth was for him. God allowed a *foreigner* from an ungodly nation, Moab, to be Boaz' wife. Ruth, a Godly lady, was relocated from an ungodly nation to a Godly nation to meet a Godly man—the right mate for her. This left me with the conclusion that all Naomi went through was really an opportunity that God seized to get Ruth from Moab to Israel, to receive her blessing and be a blessing to Boaz.

Don't Let the Wrongs of Your Past Determine Your Future

Ruth was surprised that Boaz took notice of her. In fact, she said:

At this, she bowed down with her face to the ground, She exclaimed, "Why have I found favor in your eyes that you notice me—a foreigner?" (Ruth 2:10)

I believe Ruth is saying a whole lot more here than just the fact that she was a foreigner. I believe she was also referring to her background, which was nothing to write home about. She was a Moabite, a descendant of Moab. Do you recall my brief discussion on Lot, Abraham's nephew in chapter five? He was the man who impregnated his daughters while in the drunken stupor orchestrated by them.[89] His firstborn daughter gave birth to Moab. This means that Ruth was a descendant of a child conceived illegitimately. Furthermore, the people of Moab like all other non-Israelites indulged in idolatry. That was the kind of background Ruth had, and yet, Boaz married her. Why?

Because Boaz said it was *fully* reported to him how she treated her mother-in-law, who was not a happy camper when they came back to Israel from Moab. It was also reported to Boaz that she left her family—her background—the lawless deeds of her past—and came to Israel to seek refuge under God—Boaz' God, too. Furthermore, Boaz acknowledged her reputation as a virtuous woman. She wasn't in Israel long, and yet, she was already known as a virtuous woman. Ruth was an outstanding woman. She fits the description, *the right one*.

Their story even gets better. Do you know what they had in common— from their past? If you haven't figured it out yet, let's explore this together. Boaz was an Israelite. This means that he was a descendant of Israel—a descendant of Jacob—whose name was later changed to Israel. Jacob was one of Isaac's sons, and Isaac was Abraham's beloved son. Moab was the son of Lot, Abraham's nephew.

Lo and behold, Boaz was a descendant of Abraham, and Ruth was a descendant of Abraham's nephew—or Abraham's brother's son. Haran was Abraham's brother and Lot's father, and Terah was Abraham and Haran's father.[90] In essence, Boaz and Ruth are descendants of Terah. They came from the same genealogy. Therefore, they were related to each other.

Just like Abraham through prayer to God rescued Lot from God's judgment on Sodom and Gomorrah, Boaz rescued Ruth, too—from her past. More precisely, he redeemed Ruth just like Jesus redeemed believers from sin by His blood. That's why Bible scholars often describe Boaz as a type of Christ. He redeemed Ruth by marrying her and restoring her inheritance to her.[91]

Boaz redeemed Ruth—he restored her—revitalized her, despite her past. He knew she was a Moabite. He knew her background and yet he married her. Her impeccable character and hunger for God evidenced by leaving her background against all odds must have alerted this wise, understanding and humble man that—*she's the one.*

Dear reader, if your background is nothing to write home about, if you were conceived illegitimately or if you're a product of a dysfunctional family, as long as you're not practicing the ungodly deeds of your past and/or family members and old friends—but moving out of that lifestyle toward refuge under God's wings, you're on the right track. If you were raised in a horrible environment, as long as you're not living there anymore—you're not allowing it to influence you and determine your conduct—but allowing your conduct produced by your relationship with God to influence and control the ungodly circumstances encircling you from that environment—you'll not be hindered from obtaining God's best. He'll give you someone who'll give you a breakthrough, not someone who'll break you—or mess you up.

Don't let your heredity stop your destiny – Pastor Joel Osteen

Don't let the wrongs of your past determine your future. Don't let what you went through hinder you from where you're going to. Just make sure that where you're going to is under God's wings. Ensure that your destination is God's arms—His embrace—His love—His compassion—His protection. You know what? Ruth wasn't even a virgin when she married Boaz. This was because she was married before. Nonetheless, like I alluded to in chapter four, if you're not a virgin, *physically*, that doesn't mean God can't hook you up. Just unhook the grips of your past, hook up with Him, and He'll make you a virgin again, *spiritually.*

In a way, Ruth's espousal to Boaz is an olden day version of the movie, *Maid in Manhattan.* The difference is that Ruth and Boaz' story is better, *very real,* and not a *fairy tale*—since God orchestrated it. Better still, yours will be the same, since it'll be *Made in Heaven*—provided you let God do the setup.

Ruth was from an ungodly nation. Boaz was a child of God of great wealth from Israel, and God let both of them get together. God allowed a foreigner from another culture, ethnicity, and background to marry Boaz. Ruth's marriage to Boaz should disqualify all myths and fabrications about interracial marriages. In fact, after being more enlightened by Dr. Frederick Price's expose on race, religion, and racism in the church, in the first volume of his book, *Race, Religion & Racism*, I began to dislike using the term "interracial." The term as it applies to people implies different races. It sounds ludicrous since there is only one human race. Consider this:

For all flesh is not the same, for there is one kind for humans, another for beasts, another for birds, and another for fish. (1 Corinthians 15:39 AMP)

Notice the *one kind* for humans? There is one kind of flesh for humans because there is only one kind of human race. In this regard, I prefer to use the term "intercultural" in lieu of "interracial." God doesn't have a problem with a relationship between two believers from different cultures, ethnicities or backgrounds. This is because, with God it's not the cultural heritage that matters but the spiritual. With God, the issue is not about where you're from, but whom you're from.

Being from North America, South America, Africa, Asia, Europe, or Australia is not the issue. Being from Christ or another is the issue. Those who have accepted Jesus are born again and are not just from their native countries but from Jesus Christ. But those who have not accepted Him are not from Christ. With God, it's not about whether you're American or African; it's about whether you're Christian or not.

In light of this, God doesn't have a problem with a relationship between two people just because one is Chinese and the other is Korean. It's not

God's best for one to be a believer and the other an unbeliever. It's not God's best for someone who believes in God to have a relationship with someone who doesn't. Simply put, a relationship between two people God didn't put together, even if they are both believers, is not God's best. However, God through His book, admonishes believers not to be unequally yoked with unbelievers. So, why is there still a fuss about intercultural relationships, even in the church? Well, if you're not careful, you'd think the Bible encouraged this. Thanks to scriptures like these:

After all these had been done, some of the leaders of the people of Israel came and told me that the people, the priests, and the Levites had not kept themselves separate from the people in the neighboring countries of Ammon, Moab, and Egypt or from the Canaanites, Hittites, Perizzites, Jebusites, and Amorites. They were doing the same disgusting things which these did. Jewish men were marrying foreign women, and so God's holy people had become contaminated. The leaders and officials were the chief offenders. Ezra the priest stood up and spoke to them. He said, "You have been faithless and have brought guilt on Israel by marrying foreign women.... (Ezra 9:1-2;10:10 GNB)

If you take that scripture at face value without understanding the reasoning behind it, you'd be left with the conclusion that God hated intercultural relationships. I hope you noticed that "Moab" was one of the nations mentioned that the Israelites were not supposed to intermarry with. If God despised intercultural marriages as a whole, how come He allowed Ruth who came from Moab, to marry Boaz, an Israelite? It doesn't make sense, does it? Before I shed some light on this issue, let's look at another passage.

But King Solomon loved many foreign women, as well as the daughter of Pharaoh: women of the Moabites, Ammonites, Edomites, Sidonians, and Hittites from the nations of whom the Lord had said to the children of Israel, "You shall not intermarry with them, nor they with you.... (1 Kings 11:1-2 NKJV)

Here we go again. If you read this and stopped at this juncture, you would be left with the impression that God frowned on intercultural relationships. But that isn't the case. There is a reason in these particular instances why God was upset with those Israelites who intermarried with foreign nations. The reason is addressed in the concluding statement of the second verse of *1 Kings 11:2,* which I did not include above.

...Surely they will turn away your hearts after their gods." Solomon clung to these in love.

That was why God didn't want the Israelites to intermarry with other nations—they would turn the Israelites away from God. In doing so, they would cause the Israelites to worship their gods and practice their ungodly deeds. This point is reinforced in Moses' address to the children of Israel prior to them entering the Promised Land.

*"When the LORD your God brings you into the land you are about to enter and occupy, he will clear away many nations ahead of you: the Hittites, Girgashites, Amorites, Canaanites, Perizzites, Hivites, and Jebusites. These seven nations are greater and more numerous than you. When the LORD your God hands these nations over to you and you conquer them, you must completely destroy them. Make no treaties with them and show them no mercy. You must not intermarry with them. Do not let your daughters and sons marry their sons and daughters, **for they will lead your children away from me to worship other gods**. Then the anger of the LORD will burn against you, and he will quickly destroy you. (Deuteronomy 7:1-4 NLT) Emphasis mine.*

Like the aforementioned Israelites, anyone that has accepted Jesus as their Lord and Savior is a child of God—a believer—a Christian. Just like God in Old Testament times didn't want His children, the Israelites, to intermarry with other nations—those who had other gods and would lead them astray, nowadays God still doesn't want His children to marry those that would lead them astray.

Do I need to elaborate how often a child of God who was active in his or her church suddenly stopped being involved in the things of God after they got involved with an unbeliever? Are you familiar with someone who was on fire for God, but got his or her flame fanned and eventually quenched after the individual got acquainted with someone who was not serious about God—or didn't even believe in Him? Do you know anyone who used to be involved in *prayer* service in the church, but after having a relationship with a non-believer or a believer living like an unbeliever, got involved in *player* service in the nightclub?

No well-informed parent in their right mind would sanction their child to be involved with someone who would draw their child away from loving and respecting them. How do you think God feels when His children are drawn away from him by anyone? He's not trying to pair you up with that kind of person. That's why He doesn't want you to be unequally yoked with unbelievers. Please don't think that you're Godly enough to change the other person either. Despite God's instruction to Solomon and all the things He did for him, Solomon still married women from foreign nations, and what was the result of this?

For it was so, when Solomon was old, that his wives turned his heart after other gods; and his heart was not loyal to the LORD his God, as was the heart of his father David. For Solomon went after Ashtoreth the goddess of the Sidonians, and after Milcom the abomination of the Ammonites. Solomon did evil in the sight of the LORD, and did not fully follow the LORD, as did his father David. Then Solomon built a high place for Chemosh the abomination of Moab, on the hill that is east of Jerusalem, and for Molech the abomination of the people of Ammon. And he did likewise for all his foreign wives, who burned incense and sacrificed to their gods. So the LORD became angry with Solomon, because his heart had turned from the LORD God of Israel, who had appeared to him twice, and had commanded him concerning this thing, that he should not go after other gods; but he did not keep what the LORD had commanded. (1 Kings 11:4-10 NKJV)

Solomon strayed away from God. Did you notice when this happened? It happened when he was old. Solomon did not err in the beginning of his relationship with the foreign women. It happened later in his life. A relationship with someone who does not believe in God might not lead you astray immediately. But in the long run, it will. Everything might be fine at the beginning of the relationship. But watch what happens as the relationship progresses. Sometimes, you won't see the elephant in the room until after you've said "I do."

There is a way that appears to be right, but in the end it leads to death. (Proverbs 14:12)

Notice the scripture above reveals that death comes at the *end*, and not in the beginning of the path. Having a relationship with someone who is not living for God might look and feel right in the beginning, but eventually the death of the relationship is inevitable. God didn't take issue with Solomon's wives because of their ethnicity, but their spirituality, which led him astray when he was old. If it was strictly a cultural thing, God would be angry with Boaz for marrying Ruth or Moses for marrying an Ethiopian. Perhaps you never knew Moses married an Ethiopian woman. If this is the case, the following text presents this information.

Then Miriam and Aaron spoke against Moses because of the Ethiopian woman whom he had married; for he had married an Ethiopian woman. So they said, "Has the LORD indeed spoken only through Moses? Has He not spoken through us also?" And the LORD heard it. (Now the man Moses was very humble, more than all men who were on the face of the earth.) Suddenly the LORD said to Moses, Aaron, and Miriam, "Come out, you three, to the tabernacle of meeting!" So the three came out. Then the LORD came down in the pillar of cloud and stood in the door of the tabernacle, and called Aaron and Miriam. And they both went forward. Then He said, "Hear now My words: If there is a Prophet among you, I, the LORD, make Myself known to him in a vision; I speak to him in a dream. Not so with My servant Moses; He is faithful in all My house. I

speak with him face to face, even plainly, and not in dark sayings; and he
sees the form of the LORD. Why then were you not afraid to speak against
My servant Moses?" So the anger of the LORD was aroused against them,
and He departed. And when the cloud departed from above the tabernacle,
suddenly Miriam became leprous, as white as snow. Then Aaron turned
toward Miriam, and there she was, a leper. So Aaron said to Moses, "Oh,
my lord! Please do not lay this sin on us, in which we have done fool-
ishly and in which we have sinned. "Please do not let her be as one dead,
whose flesh is half consumed when he comes out of his mother's womb!"
So Moses cried out to the LORD saying, "Please heal her, O God, I pray!"
(Numbers 12:1-13 NKJV)

Moses married an Ethiopian woman, and his brother and sister criticized him about her. Evidently God was not upset with Moses because he had a foreign wife, who also didn't turn Moses away from God. However, God was upset with Aaron and Miriam, a priest and a prophet respectively, for speaking against Moses regarding her. God was upset because they had the effrontery to speak against the man he placed as authority over them, and who was faithful and perhaps more humble than both of them put together.

It's sad that it was his brother and sister, his own relatives that criticized him about his wife. This is somewhat similar to how some family members, brothers and sisters in Christ, even leaders in the church, criticize their other family members—brethren or colleagues in clergy about the foreigner they married—if applicable—and other things pertaining to ministry that don't follow their religious traditions. Regardless, the bottom line is that God was not upset with Moses for marrying an Ethiopian wife.

I am of the view that Zipporah was the Ethiopian woman that Moses married. I believe this because the Bible does not mention any other person as Moses' wife. If Moses had another wife, I don't see why the Bible would not mention this considering that it clearly reveals other prominent Bible characters like Abraham, David and Solomon who had other wives. However, some scholars like Herbert Lockyer have a different view. He suggests that the Ethiopian wife being referred to was not Zipporah but a second wife of Moses.[92] Even so, whether Zipporah was the Ethiopian woman or not, the fact remains that he had a foreign wife.

There is also the concern that when people from different ethnicities intermarry there will be mixing of blood, which will facilitate the spread of diseases from one culture to the other. That argument does not hold water because the human race, which has one kind of flesh, came from *one* blood as substantiated by this scripture:

And He has made from one blood every nation of men to dwell on all the face of the earth, and has determined their preappointed times and the boundaries of their dwellings. (Acts 17:26 NKJV)

God created us all from one blood, starting with Adam. But you know what? The *only* way by which the argument about blood mixing can hold water is *strictly* from a spiritual and *not* a cultural and natural point of view. From this spiritual perspective, God doesn't want blood mixing either. What do I mean? God does not want anyone who has the *blood of Jesus* marrying someone who does not. Anyone who has accepted the Christ is covered with the blood of Jesus. Non-Believers are not. In this context only, believers should not intermarry with unbelievers. Rather, they should marry within God's family, regardless of the cultural heritage of the individuals they marry, since they are all covered with the blood of Christ.

Although by principle, God advocates a marriage between two believers, regardless of their cultural heritage, the ideal marriage is still based on God's direction. You still need God to help you know if that other believer, whether foreign or from your neck of the woods, is the best one for you. God gave Isaac, Rebecca, and they were both Israelites. God also allowed Boaz to marry Ruth, an Israelite and Moabite respectively, an intercultural marriage.

A marriage that was not sanctioned by God is not the end of the world. Although not the best case scenario, believers and non-believers, and unbelieving couples have married before and survived, thanks to God's intervention, forgiveness and willingness to adopt *any* unbeliever into His family. God makes a way out of no way. He can fix anything. It doesn't matter how bad you messed things up. God can fix it for you—as long as you ask and allow Him to, and commit yourself to obey Him from henceforth.

By the way, I'm not proposing that you marry someone foreign to your culture. Neither am I sharing this because I'm in an intercultural marriage. I first published this book 12 years ago. I also addressed the intercultural issue in that first edition. At the time, I was very single, and the prospect of marrying someone that was not African or African American was the last thing on my mind. I didn't fathom that I would be marrying a white Hispanic American. Ten years later, God flipped my script. I am not promoting intercultural marriages. That is completely besides my point. I am promoting *God-directed* marriages.

I am also not talking about *preference* but *ignorance*. I understand that some, if not most people, have preferences for someone from their culture. Sometimes our preferences are influenced by our experiences. Without thinking less of another ethnicity some people just prefer someone from their background. That's understandable and good. However, if someone shuns other cultures because the person thinks other ethnicities are *inferior* to his or hers, then the individual is misinformed.

I am proposing that you marry whomever God wants you to marry based on His guidelines in the Bible, even if it is against man's traditions. Who should you obey? Man or God? Who's going to help you maintain your marriage? God or the people who may also lambaste you for failure in upholding the marriage they recommended you to have in the first place? Whenever you seek counsel to make any decision, always remember that:

It is better to trust in the LORD than to put confidence in man. (Psalm 118:8 NKJV)

Let God have the final say-so. If you have to choose between God's advice—which is in the Bible, and man's, choose God's. He knows best—and He knows who's best for you.

Continuing on Boaz and Ruth, there were other women that Boaz could have taken as wife, but he chose Ruth over them.[93] Ruth worked in the field just like the other women. In fact, they had been working there long before she showed up. But what was so special about her that Boaz took notice of her and eventually married her? I already discussed what I believe are the answers to this question in chapter eleven. In addition, it's possible that she was more dedicated than the other women.

Perhaps she did her work more heartily, thoroughly and submissively. Perhaps she did it with all her might. Perhaps her heart was in the right place, whereas the other women were going through the motions and only trying to impress Boaz. Whichever case, Boaz chose a foreigner over a native. I suppose he figured she was God's best for him and didn't allow his tradition to constrain him from receiving his woman.

In spite of the hype about Boaz did you notice that the name of this book in the Bible is not named after Boaz, but Ruth? A woman who was a foreigner from an ungodly nation has a book written after her name in the Holy Bible. Furthermore, Ruth is the great great great … grandmother of Jesus. After Boaz took Ruth as his wife she conceived and gave birth to Obed who begot Jesse. Jesse also begot David. And as you continue down David's lineage, Joseph the husband of Mary the mother of Jesus came from this line.[94]

So, there is a foreign woman in Jesus' ancestry. Hmmm, she's not the only one either. It doesn't matter where you are situated, God will find you.

If you need to change course, go somewhere else, or relocate, don't get upset. Your mate may be waiting for you wherever God directs you to go.

Crossover

If you recall the story about the land of Canaan, which God gave the Israelites, there were twelve guys assigned to spy out the land. After they checked out the Promised Land, other than Joshua and Caleb, the remaining ten claimed that they couldn't take the land because the people who lived in the land looked bigger and stronger than they were. Joshua and Caleb could have probably made the journey into the Promised Land in less than eleven days. But thanks to the other ten, it took them forty years to obtain God's promise.

If you are like those ten guys, then you are affecting your mate. Your mate might be ready to roll, ready to conquer the world, ready to be married, ready to have kids, ready to accomplish God's vision for your home. But because you are straddling along with fear, unbelief, and not really trusting God for him or her, it takes longer for you to be espoused to God's gift to you. If you're not careful, you might end up losing the person intended for you just like those ten, and a generation of Israel lost out from entering the land of Canaan.

If the land of Egypt represents a relationship in which you were enslaved—a relationship of bondage, pain and anguish—a relationship in which you were oppressed—a relationship that was just mediocre—a relationship that was not God's best for you, I suggest that you crossover the red sea to the land of milk and *your* honey.

Considering Ruth and Rebecca's relocation to meet their respective husbands, if you're a lady, I don't want you to think that only a woman can be moved around to meet her man of valor. I recall this lady whose man was relocated to her. Her man was full of integrity and wisdom. He was handsome in form and appearance. In other words, "He look gooood!" He was Jewish; she was Egyptian. Another intercultural relationship that God didn't have a problem with. She was the daughter of a priest in Egypt, and her man was the pharaoh of Egypt's vice, having come up the ranks.

Her man's rise from obscurity to authority was prompted by his relationship with God. Her man went from rags to riches, from the pit to the palace, from humiliation to elevation, from having nothing but God, to having control over everything with God. Her name was Asenath, and her man was Joseph, Jacob's most beloved son. Through captivity, Joseph "crossed over" from the land of Canaan where he lived, into Egypt. However, it's not about what he dealt with; rather, it's about getting Joseph to be where God wanted him to be.[95]

Esther's marriage to King Ahasuerus is another intercultural marriage in scripture (See Esther 2). I've heard very little said about the fact that she was married to a Persian. Most commentaries about her rise from being a peasant to a princess suggest that God was behind the whole setup. And it was a blessing to her and the Jews. I agree. Her position as wife to her husband played a significant role in delivering the Jews from perhaps the first recorded act of anti-Semitism, and gave rise to one of the Jewish celebrations, which is known as the feast of Purim (See Esther 8 & 9).

In our present day, Esther's marriage to Ahasuerus is equivalent to an Israelite marrying an Iranian. Ahasuerus did not turn Esther away from God. In fact He supported their relationship. That's the kind of relationship God wants for you. This can be accomplished with any God-fearing believer regardless of his or her culture. If this applies to you, don't miss out on someone God brings to you just because the person is not from your culture.

God is trying to set you up with someone who'd blow your mind. Look at some of the attributes of His elite mentioned in the Bible. Esther was lovely, beautiful and a virgin. Abigail had understanding and was of a beautiful countenance. Ruth was virtuous. Boaz was wealthy. Joseph was handsome in form, appearance, and was successful. And David was a psalmist, good looking, and a man after God's heart.[96]

Need I say more? These are some of the attributes you should ask God to develop in your mate—and especially in you! It's sad to say that sometimes, out of ignorance and/or unbelief, we prevent God from blessing us with such remarkable mates. Instead, we settle for less, we settle for mediocre, we settle for animals, we settle for pets.

You might think that I'm contradicting myself for including David. Considering the atrocity he committed, how can I include his character as one to be desired in a husband? Good question. The attitude of David that I admire is the one attributed after God's own heart. The attitude of David that was discussed previously in chapter four, was the one attributed after his own flesh. I pray women don't end up with men that have no qualms in sinning like he did.

My earlier discussion on David was strictly concerning the mistake he made, courtesy of yielding to his fleshly desires. However, that was one side of the story. The other side is one that is worth mentioning and validates the character to be desired in a man. Yes he messed up, but he took responsibility for his actions. Women should desire husbands who are accountable and take responsibility for their actions, rather than those who make lame excuses for them.

When God called David on the carpet for his transgression through the Prophet Nathan, he wasted no time in admitting his misdeed. He didn't give a cock and bull story like some men by saying that he's just a man. He didn't act like he had amnesia by saying that he didn't know what the Prophet was talking about. He didn't act like he didn't know Bathsheba. He acknowledged to God his sin and the Almighty spared his life, but told him the child conceived from his adulterous episode with Bathsheba would die.

In spite of that, David interceded for the child. David had enough compassion to pray for a child that was conceived illegitimately. My goodness!
He fasted for "seven days," praying that God would spare the child. How
many Christian men in this day and age would pray to God to prevent the
death of a child conceived by their unfaithfulness, talk less of fast for the
child? Some Christian men hardly fast for themselves, how much more for
a child they don't want anyone to know about.

Furthermore, despite David's sacrifice of fasting seven days—which
doesn't justify his sin, the child still died. And what did David do? He got
up from his fasting, took a bath, "worshipped God," and went to eat.[97] He
worshipped God even after He refused to grant David's request. How many
believers have become atheists because God did not grant them a request
made in a thirty seconds prayer made unabashedly? David's commitment
to God did not falter even when God didn't save the child. A man or woman
who has that kind of commitment to God, will have that kind of commitment to you.

Lastly, David took care of Bathsheba who'd become his wife after Uriah
died.[98] He didn't excommunicate her like some men do after sleeping with
her. If some of us men were in David's shoes, after the child died, we would
probably declare ourselves home free and tell the lady we exploited "*sayo-
nara!*" But David did not kick her out of his life after the child died. He did
not discard her like a toilette after its purpose had been fulfilled. He embraced her and took care of her. As his wife she gave birth to other children
for them, one of which is Solomon. Another was Nathan (not the prophet)
who was also one of Jesus' great great great grandfathers.[99]

Pray that God gives you a mate with such a Christ-like demeanor, and
develop that character in you, so that you'll be a person after God's own
heart for the person, too. It's unfortunate that David sinned. This is not an
endorsement for ungodly behavior. Unfortunately this kind of thing happens to the best of us. This is why the Bible says:

For a righteous man might fall seven times and rise again.... (Proverbs 24:16 NKJV)

He might fall, but he gets up again because he's righteous. With this in mind, don't be quick to write off anybody who makes a mistake regardless of how many times the person falls short. Needless to say, this is not a license for anybody to sin. Some people often exploit this scripture as a reason to fall. Notice it says that a righteous man—or woman if I might add, *might* fall, not *will* fall. Moreover, the individual will rise again or get up, not stay down wallowing in the sin.

All the same, while you are single, know that God is not giving you a mate based on where you're from, but whom you're from. And if you're after God's best, it's in your best interest to hook up with God, since the right mate for you is from Him. If you're an unbeliever, I beseech you to relocate—crossover the blood of Jesus—to God, and let Him mold you for your precious who's waiting patiently for you in Him.

CHAPTER NINETEEN
Trust God More than Anyone Else

If you're a lady and you attend church, other ministry-related and social events, you might be discouraged by the frequency of seeing more ladies than guys. Not only are there few guys, fewer still are really gentlemen. By gentlemen, I'm referring to guys whose character and conduct reflect their relationship with Christ.

You might be a woman who has a heart for God. You're probably also aware of other ladies who love and seek Him, too. With that in mind it might be difficult for you to fathom your chances of getting any of the few Godly men in your circle. For example, let's say the ratio of ladies to the guys in the church, Bible study, single's fellowship or social events that you attend are about 5 to 1. In addition, let's say there are about 4 guys that are really God-fearing gentlemen. But also affiliated with them and you, are 19 other ladies who are also decent, chaste, and fear God. Looking at this scenario you might be disheartened about your likelihood of landing any one of those guys.

Sometimes due to the fewer number of men compared to women, some guys exploit their numerical leverage or monopoly over the women. Usually in business, a monopoly is a situation in which a company or a group has exclusive control over the supply of a particular service, which is often in great demand. One of the disadvantages of a monopoly is that, because the company is the only one supplying the service, even if their service is below par, the company still does not do a better job because their service will be solicited anyway. It's kind of like that with some men.

A guy might feel that he does not need to better himself, grow in the Lord, have a proper attitude and behave respectfully toward a lady because, though the woman who demands this kind of character from him might not want him, there are plenty other women who would jump on him before he snaps his fingers. Therefore, why does he need to improve himself? Unfortunately, as a result, some ladies compromise their high standard so that they could end up with one of those jokers.

Stay Focused

If you fall in that category of women faced with the scarcity of real good men, what you might not understand is that your man might not be in your vicinity. He might not be in your neighborhood like Mr. Rogers. He might not be in the social events you attend. He might not even be in your school, ministry, Bible study, church, city, state or country. Besides, you have your focus in the wrong place and on the wrong man. Your focus should be in heaven, on the Lord, the true Lover and guide to finding and keeping the right mate for your life.

Maybe God has a guy for you undergoing serious character training somewhere else. God will not bring him to your vicinity, at least not yet, because the guys already in your neck of the woods might compromise him. So, God wants to finish His work on him and in him, and when the time is right, He'll import him to you or export you to him.

If you're a man and perhaps one of the few good men without being related to Tom Cruise, despite the number of women around you, perhaps none of them light your candle. Well, maybe your woman is not in your circle of influence. Do you recall Joseph ending up in Egypt where he got married? And Asenath, Joseph's wife, got a man that was not from her vicinity. The same applies to Boaz and Ruth. Both ended with each other and not with spouses from their respective hometowns. This might also be the case with you.

Another possible concern of yours could be that while you're still trusting God for a mate, some friends who you might have been instrumental in bringing to the Lord, and who probably are not as committed as you are to Him, already got hitched. You try to be cheerful, but deep down you are disconcerted and you feel cheated and overlooked on learning that they found someone and are about to get married.

You lament to God, possibly saying, "How come? What about me? I helped them know You. And now You bless them with mates and leave me hanging. What's up Lord? Why? What have I done wrong? I am more mature in the faith. I pray often, they hardly pray. I fast often, but the only fast they know is slim fast … not that they patronize it either. I also minister to them often. How come they got hooked up? Not only did they get hooked up, they got hooked up before me. Did I sin? What did I do wrong? Why lord? Why?"

Why don't you get a hold of yourself! You might want to check your attitude. If this applies to you, maybe pride has something to do with it. God needs to humble you before He honors you because:

Before his downfall a man's heart is proud, but humility comes before honor. (Proverbs 18:12)

God knows what He's doing. He has it all planned. He has it all laid out. He might be trying to give you a mate who has more responsibility than the ones your peers have. Besides, you don't know if God truly orchestrated your friends' espousals. They might have done their own thing. They might not have allowed God to really do what He needed to do in them like He desires to do in you. Yes, they might be married but God's intention might be that your marriage should be the model. You're the clay and He's The Potter. Continue to yield yourself to Him so that He can show off His flawless craftsmanship in you, and through you.

Without undermining anyone's profession, perhaps your peers have spouses that basically work a 9 to 5. This is good and well. They might not require as much spiritual fortitude for the champion, first-class, world changer spouse that God desires for you. God desires to fully prepare you for the visionary He has for you. You shouldn't be flaky. You shouldn't be inadequate for your mate. You shouldn't be medium rare. In retrospect, your main purpose as a partner to your beloved is to help him or her. God wants to fully arm you to the teeth for this life long task. He will let you cook longer to toughen you up to prepare you and set you apart for the person he has for you.

Another reason could be that the person God has for you is not ready. The person God has for you might still want to live and enjoy the single life. You should, too. Your mate might still be undergoing surgery from God. Your mate might still be spiritually immature. God's timing is the best. You still need to wait patiently. You don't want to be involved with anyone who is not ready to be married to you. If God gave you someone who is not ready, you might be forced to lament by saying what Jesus said on the cross: "eli eli lama sabachthani," translated "My God My God, why have you forsaken me."[100]

Relax and let everything fall in place like God intended it to. There is somebody out there for you. Stay focused on the Lord and let Him do what he needs to do in you, with you, and for you. When the time is right the person will show up.

Put More Confidence in God than Man

Perhaps you're involved with someone but you feel like there is something wrong with the relationship. You can't put your finger on it, but you feel like your relationship with this individual is not right—it's not God's best for you. Perhaps you question yourself saying: "Is this it? Is this how relationships are supposed to be? Is this God's best for me? Is this the right person?"

Even so, you still remain in that relationship. Why? Possibly because people you look up to, like friends, confidants, mentors, Pastors, and even parents, approve the person you're involved with. They seem to endorse your relationship. Based on the facade you and your boyfriend or girlfriend display, your friends who are still single and not involved with anyone might have complimented you both by saying that they wished they had what you both had going on. Perhaps I should adjust the last part of this statement by saying that they wished they had what they "thought" you both had going on. Sometimes your parents support your relationship. Quite naturally, if your parents sanction it, you are inclined to make it happen. This passage of scripture is relevant in dealing with this issue.

Now the LORD said to Samuel, "How long will you mourn for Saul, seeing I have rejected him from reigning over Israel? Fill your horn with oil, and go; I am sending you to Jesse the Bethlehemite. For I have provided Myself a king among his sons." ...So Samuel did what the LORD said, and went to Bethlehem. And the elders of the town trembled at his coming, and said, Do you come peaceably?" ...So it was, when they came, that he looked at Eliab and said, "Surely the Lord's anointed is before Him!" But the Lord said to Samuel, "Do not look at his appearance or at his physical stature, because I have refused him. For the LORD does not see as man sees; for man looks at the outward appearance, but the LORD looks at the heart." ...Thus Jesse made seven of his sons pass before Samuel. And Samuel said to Jesse, "The LORD has not chosen these." And Samuel said to Jesse, "Are all the young men here?" Then he said, "There remains yet the youngest, and there he is, keeping the sheep." And Samuel said to Jesse, "Send and bring him. For we will not sit down till he comes here." So he sent and brought him in. Now he was ruddy, with bright eyes, and good looking. And the LORD said. "Arise, anoint him; for this is the one!" Then Samuel took the horn of oil and anointed him in the midst of his brothers; and the Spirit of the LORD came upon David from that day forward. So Samuel arose and went to Ramah. (1 Samuel 16:1, 4, 6-7, 10-13 NKJV)

We see the Prophet Samuel, a Prophet that God ordained from a young age. He was a man of God. A true one. One of the major prophets in the Old Testament. A man that was God's mouth piece. A man that heard from God. A man that God asked to go to Jesse's house to find a king for Israel. He went to Jesse's house and saw Eliab first. Eliab "looked" like what you would expect a king to look like. He was probably tall and strong-looking. He probably had a tough disposition. And the Prophet Samuel who you would have thought knew better, thought Eliab was the one God wanted to be king based on what he saw. To add insult upon injury, Jesse, the father, who you would think would know more about which of his sons should be king, did not consider David as a candidate for the position.

In the same way, your mentor, confidant, friends and/or parents, who you trust and whose opinions you value—and should value, might have made the same mistake by telling you he or she is the right one for you based on what they "thought" they saw, and probably heard about you two. With regard to Jesse's ignorance about his son's competency for the job, I thought to myself, "Does he really know David? Did he know that David killed a bear and a lion?"[101] I wouldn't be surprised if David didn't tell his father about killing the animals. David might have done this to prevent his father from stopping him from tending his sheep.

We don't tell our parents everything, do we? They don't know everything about us and what we go through. They see the part of our lives that we want them to see. We allow our friends to see the laughter galore and the joy. But sometimes they don't see what is really going down between you two, away from the public. You don't *think* what you see, you *know* what you see. You know what you see about the person your friends, relatives, church members and parents don't see. You know what you hear from the person that they don't hear. You know what goes on behind the scenes that they don't know. They really don't know that person, but you do.

Although you feel the relationship is not right, the pressure you feel from the endorsement of those you look up to might compel you to think that you're just too picky about how you want the relationship to be. You might feel you are the problem. You might feel that everybody else knows better and you don't. You might feel that you are not appreciative that you have a man or a woman that your friends don't have, that your mentor thinks is the best for you, and your parents cherish to be a son or daughter-in-law.

And as for the issues that you feel are unacceptable to you based on your standard as a man or woman of God, seeking God's best for your life, needing God's peace in your life, you overlook them perhaps claiming that you are going to have problems when you get married anyway. You might ponder saying, "I guess this is the way it's supposed to be. Other than these *minor* incidences that make me question if this person is for me, I enjoy their company, he or she is really not like this. It's my fault. I need to be more appreciative of what God gave me." Maybe who you have in your life now, is not who God thinks is best for you.

Another possible reason why you haven't left the relationship that you sense you're not supposed to be in, might be pride. Perhaps you were revered. You were distinguished amongst your peers. You were the poster child for your ministry or profession, amongst your friends and peers. People looked up to you. They cherished, blessed, complimented and envied you. They spoke extremely well of you and held you in high regard.

When your friends needed counseling they came to you. They valued your opinion and insight on delicate matters. You certainly ought to know the right person for you. You certainly know better than everyone else. You hardly made mistakes, especially when it came to relationships. You were never in a relationship until recently. Surely you must have made the right decision. Did you?

How would it look to your peers? How would they perceive you now that you made a mistake? "I guess he ain't all that." "I guess she ain't all that." "I thought he would have known better." "I can't believe she broke up with him." "I thought she posted on facebook that God told her he's the one." "I thought he said God showed him in a vision that she's the one." "I thought they were supposed to get married." "So, all the time they were seeing each other was just a waste." "Does he really hear from God?" "I guess she's just a phony, acting all spiritual, when she's just as carnal." These might be some of the ridicule you dread from receiving from your peers.

You might feel like you disappointed them. You might feel like you let people down. You might feel like you humiliated yourself, dented the confidence your friends, confidants, and Pastor had in you. You might also feel you embarrassed your parents. It feels like a fall from grace. It feels like it's easier to stick with Mr. or Miss "not really the right one," rather than face the music which evidently is not *Amazing Grace*. So, you try to make it happen by sticking with the wrong person. I know it feels hard. It's hard to break away, especially when you now feel attached to the person—especially now that you've developed ties with the individual. Ties which might have been developed through constant communication, association, fellowship, praying together—and unfortunately, perhaps, sexual intimacy.

Maybe you tell yourself "I don't want people to think I messed up. I'm just tripping, there is nothing wrong, God has to be in this, after all everybody says we look good together." Looking good together and being good together—and to each other are two different things. For your betterment, don't make excuses for yourself and the other person. Don't sink any deeper than you already have. Cry out to God for help and He'll stretch out the arm of His strength, and catch you and lift you up out of your ocean of depression, dejection, and discontentment like he did for Peter.[102]

Yes, it feels hard. But it's harder staying in this predicament. You think it's bad now? I hope you don't wait till you get married to the wrong person before you find out how really bad and disastrous it could be. Please don't give in to the pressure of staying in the wrong relationship, and end up regretting that you should have gone by your intuition, courtesy of God's still small voice. Don't let your attachment to the individual coupled with the unfounded endorsements of the people you look up to, skew the mediocrity of your relationship with the person—if that is the case. Don't let them make you think everything is alright, when you *know* it is not.

Dr. Sam Hamburg, a clinical psychologist and marital therapist addressed the fact that some people get married even when they have bad vibes about the person they're about to marry. All the time invested in the relationship, and the risk of starting over again by looking for someone else, were some of the reasons the marital therapist gave about why people still marry, despite their hunches to do otherwise.

He also reasoned that people get married because they confuse their attachment to the person with their love for them. They think they are in love with the person, when in actuality they are just attached to the individual. Dr. Hamburg said that we form attachment bonds to those we feel close to. Our attachment to someone makes us feel that having the person around is important for our welfare, but when the person is separated from us there is a sense of grief characterized by sadness, and sometimes fear and panic.

The clinical psychologist, however, acknowledged that, naturally, we'd be attached to those with whom we have positive, affectionate, relationships like family members and love interests. He also acknowledged that we could be attached to people with whom we have negative and hostile relationships too. He cited as examples, attachments between prisoners and their jailers, hostages and their captors, and if I might add, slaves and their masters—if applicable, you and the person with whom you're involved.

By now, I hope you understand even more why you should not misconstrue your feelings for someone as the sole indicator that you are in love, and as a result, conclude that, that person is the right one for you. Considering that some prisoners *felt* attached to their jailers, and some slaves felt bonded to their masters, we both know that those relationships were not healthy. Certainly not God's best for you, me, or anyone else.

Dr. Hamburg also elaborated that the pressure of getting married is another reason why people marry erroneously. He said that they experience this pressure through embarrassment, guilt or both. For example, couples marrying because of the guilt or embarrassment of an accidental pregnancy. Another example is that of couples getting married despite feeling like doing the opposite because invitations to their wedding had been sent out.

In order to avoid the embarrassment of canceling the wedding, and ensure that the costs and the efforts put into the ceremony were not in vain, they get married anyway. This should not be the case. The costs of a disastrous relationship, especially if kids are now involved, far exceed the cost of canceling the wedding. A cost that still ends up in vain if the marriage that shouldn't have happened in the first place becomes annulled. Besides, the couple will still be embarrassed, even more so, if it's a nasty divorce settlement—where they'll incur more emotional and financial costs.

If you're about to get married to someone you sense or know is not God's best for you, what should you do? I recommend Dr. Hamburg's prescription. I'm for this because it's in line with the Great Physician's prescription—His guidelines in the Bible. This is what the marital therapist prescribes, and he calls it *The Bad Vibes Rule*:

"Listen to your bad vibes and take them seriously. If you have any doubts, hesitations, or second thoughts, then at least postpone the wedding. If it's become clear to you that entering into this marriage is a mistake, cancel the wedding—and don't let anything or anyone stop you."[103]

God, The Great Physician, simply says you should abstain from all appearance of evil. Avoid anything that doesn't look right. The Bible is an inexhaustible reference of what's right and what's evil. Through it, you'll know what's right and what's evil. It's also through it that God primarily talks to us. If you're not at *peace* with the person you're about to marry, abstain from marrying the individual. God might be speaking to you through your spiritual sensors—your sensitivity to God's voice, developed during your date with Him, as you read, meditated, and assimilated His words to you transcribed as biblical text.

You should not marry someone when you do not feel right about the individual. You might wonder how you can hear from God. How can you distinguish between what your emotions are saying, what God is saying, and what the devil is saying to you? It is by intimacy with God. It is by dating God. It is by spending time with Him. If you don't know God you are in bad shape. Only those who are seeking God diligently will benefit more from this advice.

How can you discern if God is speaking to you if you do not know His voice? How can you hear God if you are not standing close to Him? How can you hear from God if you are not inclining your ear to His words, which are in the Bible? If you want to hear from God, draw close to Him and He will draw close to you.[104]

You can recognize His voice by knowing what He said to you through His sayings in the Bible. And for those secret things pertaining to you, you just have to draw closer to Him to open the eyes of your heart and whisper them in your ear by His Spirit.[105] Do you recall that God's children perish because of a lack of knowledge? The knowledge comes from His Mouth, by His Word, in His Book. If you're not reading, if you're not listening, and if you're not receiving from your guide to the right person for you, unless someone is dating God on your behalf, you stand a reasonable chance of ending up with the wrong person.

If you date God, He will tell you what love is. He will tell you not to get in a relationship with someone who does not believe in Him. You will be directed not to get involved with someone who might believe in Him, but purposely live a lifestyle that contradicts his or her belief in Him. If you know God intimately you will know what inappropriate conduct is. In public, the person might act like a Christian but behind the scenes live like a pagan.

You might have decided to axe the relationship several times, but lo and behold, the person on the wrong end of the blade all of a sudden took a turn for the better. The individual changed overnight. The person who used to come late to church, that's if he or she even came in the first place, suddenly came to church early—even before you did. The person who hardly whispered in service suddenly sings A*mazing Grace,* and even gives a testimony. The person suddenly showed interest in biblical scriptures, even memorized one or two.

If the person is a woman, perhaps she mentioned how awesome you are and fed your ego by quoting the first part of Joshua 1:5 NKJV; *No man shall be able to stand before you all the days of your life....* If the person is a man, he possibly quoted Proverbs 18:22 NKJV; *He who finds a wife finds a good thing, and obtains favor from the Lord.* The person seemed to have met, even exceeded your reasonable demands contingent on God's word— at least, until the individual went back to—same ole, same ole.

Maybe they didn't do all that, but you get my point. Such changes can be genuine and are necessary for someone who God truly has for you. Even so, if you have some serious misgivings about the person with whom you're involved, don't let the individual's sudden saintly act mislead you. Besides, if the person reverts to his or her old ways after they've tickled your fancy and caused you to change your mind about rescinding the relationship, that might be something for you to think about.

The Bible does say that *in the multitude of counselors there is safety.*[106] Please understand me. I'm not saying that you should ignore the counsel of your mentors, Pastor, parents, and friends. Qualified ones I might add, not just anyone that comes up with their 2 cents. Someone who dates God like you do or are trying to do.

You should seek counsel before you proceed to the altar. In fact before you go that far, you need to seek Godly counsel. They will help you screen out those who are not worthy of tying the knot with you. They will help ensure that you marry the right person. Their counsel will help protect you from being hoodwinked. Counsel includes marital counselors, your Pastor, parents, successful married couples and good friends, who will keep you accountable with your best interest in mind. More often than not, good counsel will save you from getting involved with the wrong person—that's if you heed their advice.

At least, listen to what your parents or guardians have to say about whomever you're befriending, courting, or thinking of dating. You can draw some invaluable lessons from their life experiences. They've "been there done that" so they know a few things. They might not be as cool as you are. They might not know what time it is. But they know the grief that results from being involved in a bad relationship; a grief that they're trying to prevent you from experiencing.

Abraham, Isaac's father, was instrumental in helping Isaac get a good wife. Naomi was instrumental in getting Ruth a good husband. All things being equal, your parent's counsel is important. So is a marital counselor's, Pastor's, church ministers', mentor's and good friends' (who are not trying to snatch your prospect).

Nonetheless, counsel can *cancel.* Counsel shouldn't decide whom you should marry; they should help *you* decide who you should marry. They shouldn't make that decision for you; they should help *you* make that decision. They shouldn't make the choice for you; they should help *you* make the right choice. The choice is yours. Their help includes what they think about your prospect, which should be based on what the Bible says. It also includes their prayers and advice on how to ensure a happy marriage, should *you* choose to proceed to the altar with the person.

Rebecca's mum and brother helped Rebecca make the right choice. They simply gave her the choice to marry Isaac—and *she chose* to marry Him. She wasn't coerced into making that decision. She made it of *her own volition.* She made an excellent choice. After all is said and done counselors should allow you the choice to go with what's in your heart. Let's just hope they're God's words of approval.

The good book also says it's better to trust God than put confidence in any man. God might begin to show you things that go beyond other people's comprehension. God might be so close to you that He trusts you to hear His voice and give heed to it regardless of what others say if they are contrary. Depending on your sensitivity to God's voice, He might reveal things to you and expect you to have the backbone to ignore what others say when it contradicts what He said to you. He might spoon-feed you some-times through your Godly advisors, but after sometime He'll know when you're spiritually seasoned enough to handle His revelations to you.

Babies need to be carried in their parent's arms for some time. As they grow older, parents stop carrying them all the time, but encourage them to walk by themselves. Sometimes they force them to walk by themselves, use the potty by themselves, and eat by themselves. This is akin to how God deals with us sometimes.

The bottom line is, what is God telling you? What did He reveal to you? What did He show you? You can only answer these questions if you've been spending time with God. If not, I encourage you to start now. Discard any-thing distracting you from God. Never stop dating Him. If you're already seeking Him, continue to do so. Don't stand Him up and don't cancel your dates. When you spend time with Him, I encourage you to worship Him. Tell Him that you love and appreciate Him.

Samuel the Prophet made a mistake the instant he thought Eliab should be God's chosen. He drew this conclusion based on Eliab's looks. But thanks be to God who alone is wise, Samuel ended up choosing the most unlikely candidate, David, who became king and was the greatest king in Israel. Jesus is even called his son. In spite of his faults, God considered him a man after his own heart.

Who's that lady who's the most unlikely candidate to others, which might include your parents, brothers and sisters, but not to you? Who's that guy who's the most unlikely candidate to your Pastor and friends, but not to you? If there is somebody, put more confidence in what God placed in your heart than in what anyone else says to you.

Learning from the Prophet Samuel's error, it's possible that any of the people you esteem and hold in such high regard—like you should, can make a mistake by encouraging you to have a relationship with someone who's not the best for you. This is not a license to say that they *never* know what they are talking about. This is not a license to say that your Pastor does not know how to shepherd your church, or your parents are not good parents.

Please don't exploit this discourse. These last few paragraphs are for you if the shoe fits. If it doesn't, keep reading, you might come across this shoe later or know someone wearing it. And if it does, this is by no means an endorsement for you to denounce your Pastor, parents and friends. Everybody makes mistakes. I have. Some made their recommendations thinking deeply that they were helping you out. They thought they were demonstrating their love and welfare for you by advocating someone they thought would complement you well.

Besides, you might not have given them the whole gist. You might have only given them the part you wanted them to hear. They probably fed into this, and knowing that you had never been so excited about anything in your life, bought into your enthusiasm and embraced your prospect. Or, their desperation to see you get married got the better of their judgment.

They didn't do it to spite or despise you. They did it in love. Their mistake doesn't make them incompetent as your Pastor, parents, friends, mentors or confidants. It certainly doesn't mean God can't use them to bless you. Samuel eventually chose the right person. If you ostracized your friends and family just because they encouraged you to have a relationship with the wrong person, I suggest you go to them, apologize, and ask for their forgiveness.

Even if God reveals things to you that the average person doesn't grasp, I believe that there is someone to whom you're accountable—somebody, somewhere, who somehow catches your vision, and who would also encourage you to go with what you believe God placed in your heart.

Sometimes the individual you are seeing might not have done anything wrong; yet, you just don't feel like that's the person for you. Don't settle for Mahlon when you can get Boaz.[107] Don't settle for okay, when you can get *whoa*! Don't settle for bronze when you can get gold. Don't settle for less; settle for the best.

Even though you made a mistake in getting involved with the wrong person, despite your embarrassment, the faster you get out of this situation, the better. Marriage is a serious God-ordained institution. It is a covenant relationship. You should not go into it half-stepping. You should not go into it hoping things will work out when you *know* things are definitely not working out. You should not go in hoping he or she would change for the better when the person is already changing for the worse—or does not want to change for the betterment of the relationship. You want to get things right as much as you can from the start. At the end of the day, you will be relieved.

Bearing all that in mind, while you're single, stay focused on the Lord and trust Him more than anyone else. Especially when everybody else is encouraging you to get in a relationship or any other thing that God doesn't want you to be involved with. On the other hand, if you're at peace with the person with whom you're involved, you believe the individual is God's best for you, and your courtship with the person has been a blessing to you and definitely in concert with God's ways, then, go for it! Go for the gusto! Go for the whole enchilada!

CHAPTER TWENTY

If God Spoke It, He Will Bring It to Pass

I was watching a popular Christian program in which a minister was being interviewed. This man was revered and popular in a major segment of the church. The gentleman mentioned how God brought his wife to him. He simply said that God revealed to him that a particular lady was his wife. He went ahead and divulged this information to the woman in question. In essence, he told her that God said she was his wife. This, of course freaked her out, and she ran for the exits. She bolted! She must have thought he was crazy. I don't blame her. Eventually, she came back to him. They got married. They seem to be a very happy couple. Apparently, He was right about what God told him.

Notwithstanding, I believe that most people who *have to* tell individuals that God told them they are supposed to marry them are often off base. The guest in that program, as time has told, was right, on his assessment. His experience in getting his wife is not the norm; it's the exception.

In life there are certain slangs that we use in order to look cool. In Christendom, there are certain lingos that Christians also use to make them look cool or spiritual. One of those lingos is: "God told me…." It is a wonderful thing to be used of God. It's self-fulfilling to know that God told you to do something, you did it, and it came to pass. Wow! It's awe-inspiring. Although God can, and does, speak to us personally, it is not always that clear. At least, for me, it isn't. Especially when the alleged speech from God deals with spending your life with another human being—with a mind of their own.

I think one of the things that get some of us in trouble, especially when it comes to finding a mate, is thinking that God told you something when He did not. It seems God speaks very loudly about someone for you if the person is very attractive to you. Is that God or is it your hormones? Is it the God of love talking to you, or your natural "love concoction" whispering sweet *nothings* in your ears? Is the Holy Spirit prophesying to you or is your emotional soul "prophelying" to you?

A lot of singles want to do what the guest in the show did to get his spouse. But, they're not willing to do what he did to get to the point where he could here God clearly enough to make that bold declaration. He dated God to find his mate. Some of singles just want to date to find a mate, and then throw God in the mix. It doesn't work like that. Are you trying to find a date to mate? I think the best approach is to find a mate to date; not the other way round.

By date to mate, I mean actively *looking for* just *anyone* available to date and then marry. By mate to date, I mean *looking out* for not just anyone, but someone who demonstrates the characteristics of a husband or wife, a mate, to date and then marry. Perhaps this explains why Proverbs 18:22 starts up by saying *he who finds a* wife—not he who finds a girlfriend. I believe this also applies to *she who finds—or is found by a husband*, not she who finds, or is found by a boyfriend. The same passage ends up by saying, *obtains favor from* the Lord. In other words, God makes this happen. He gives you the favor to find the mate to date. Apart from Him, we exert the fervor to find the date to mate and often end up irate and filled with hate.

The bottom line is that finding the right mate for your life is through God's help. And if God ever told you that someone was your spouse, it will happen. If God spoke it, He will bring it to pass like He did for the man in the program. I will not recommend that you tell your prospect what God told you though. Not unless God explicitly instructed you to use that approach.

If God told you anything, He would also tell the prospect in question. God usually sends a go-between to connect you two. God was the go-between between Adam and Eve. God through Eliezer, who somewhat symbolizes the Holy Spirit, was the go-between between Isaac and Rebecca. Naomi was the go-between between Ruth and Boaz. An angel was the go-between between Joseph and Mary, the mother of Jesus.

Part of the problem is that some people begin a relationship with God today, and begin to talk about God telling them to marry someone, yesterday. In fact, some people who've had a relationship with God for years err regarding God telling them to marry someone or do something. How much more those who are just starting a relationship with Him? Furthermore, sometimes God brings someone to your heart just for you to *pray* for the person, not for you to *prey* on the person. At times He brings someone to your attention not as your life partner but for another purpose.

Maybe you are an individual who has been dating God by consistently studying your Bible, praying, praising, and worshipping Him. Maybe you are someone who is spending time with God like I suspect the Bishop did. As a result, you've developed a sensitivity for hearing God's voice. Furthermore, in the course of your time with Him you believe that He revealed to you who your mate is. This revelation to you might have been placed in your heart while you were conversing with Him, or perhaps through circumstances or coincidences you deem to be divine.

In other words, you believe that God revealed the individual to you through situations that only God could control. Although you question if this revelation is of God, or of you, you're inclined to think it's from God because the person meets, even exceeds your expectation for a Godly mate based on God's Word.

However, you have doubts. You have doubts not because you thought this up yourself, not because the person does not conform to the character of a Godly person, but because the person is seeing someone else. Your doubt is mainly amplified because the person in question seems to be head-over-heels in love with another individual.

By the way, I'm talking about a situation where you believe that God showed you someone who is single as your proposed mate, but is seeing someone else, not someone who is married to somebody else. If you have feelings for a married person, this is a very serious issue that you need to resolve with God. I doubt that God will show you a married person as your spouse. Didn't He say that no man should separate what He has put together? Why would He then instigate you along those lines? If this applies to you, I pray that you allow Him to deliver you from that situation.

Having clarified the subject of my current conversation, let's proceed with the discussion. Perhaps you feel that if this is God's doing, the single person in question should not be seeing anybody else. If this is God's doing, that person should be ready for you at the time God gave you this revelation. Nope! Not necessarily. Remember when God told the children of Israel to possess the land of Canaan? Guess who were in it—giants in the land. Is there a giant in the life of the person you believe God has for you? If there is, and if God truly showed you that that person is yours, you need to keep trusting God to turn that person's heart to you. He might be turning that person's heart to you, even right now.

The king's heart is like a stream of water directed by the LORD; he guides it wherever he pleases. (Proverbs 21:1 NLT)

First of all, let's get real. Like I alluded to previously, you could have made a mistake about what you *think* God is showing you. You could have missed it like the person who got to the airport at 8am for his flight which left at 5.30am. The coincidences that connected you to the person you thought God gave you might have just been coincidences and not *God-incidences.* Just because you have similar syllables in your names, have birthdays in the same month, both like to eat sushi, both loved to watch *Teenage Ninja Turtles* as toddlers, both ended up in the same class in college, both had a mutual friend who went to high school with you, and both approved by each other's parents, doesn't mean you're meant for each other.

If that person is not for you, then somebody else is. And that somebody else will make you thank God that you missed it. God has someone for you that would make up for the loss you think you suffered by not having the wrong person. Don't be discouraged but be thankful that God closed that door, so that he'll open another for you—or direct you to the door that He already opened for you.

You were just too preoccupied with the door that was closed, locked, bolted, and wired with God's ADT alarm system to notice the other door that had been opened for you. Perhaps this explains why you might have felt so humiliated and embarrassed when you tried to open the door, but the security system blazed resoundingly and alarmed others about your attempt to hook up with someone whom you thought God showed you, but He didn't. In other words when you tried to hook up with the person, the individual rejected you.

On the other side of the spectrum, that person might be yours. That person might be your milk and honey, your wedding cake, your baby, virtuous woman or man of valor. Unfortunately, that other person who your beloved seems to be in love with, makes you question if you really heard from God, and conclude that God's promise to you was just a figment of your fantasy. Listen carefully, if God said that that person is yours, that person is yours. If God spoke it, He will surely bring it to pass.

Trust in the Lord and don't rely on your understanding of the situation. Conduct yourself by what God said to you and not by what you "think" you see; because everything is not what it seems. Don't get me wrong, your heaven-sent mate at this point might truly think that the other person they have feelings for is the one for him or her. Notwithstanding, watch God flip the script on your behalf. Watch God snap his fingers and snap your beloved out of his or her temporary romance into your arms.

You might feel that if you had expressed your feelings to her first or if he had approached you first, then the other person would not be in the equation. In other words, you might feel that you missed out because you didn't have the opportunity to share your feelings, or you were slow to confirm your heart's desire—a slowness which might have been prompted by your cautiousness to make sure that it was God leading you to the prospect and not your emotions leading you to the person. If this is the case, I have good news for you.

The race is not to the swift.[108] This is not on a first-come, first-served basis. Just because someone got into the life of your proposed mate first, doesn't mean that your prospect will end up with the individual. Just because you're late doesn't mean you missed out. Don't forget that receiving a spouse from God is not based on your fervor, but on God's favor.

So then (God's gift) is not a question of human will or human effort, but of God's mercy. (It depends not on one's willingness nor on his strenuous exertion as in running a race, but on God's having mercy on him.) Romans 9:16 (AMP)

Don't worry. You will have your time and your chance. And when that time comes, like Bishop T.D. Jakes often says: "Get ready! Get ready!! Get ready!!!"

The Bible tells us about a certain sick man who had an ailment for thirty eight years. There was a pool in Jerusalem around which people suffering from all sorts of diseases lay. This man was among them. It was alleged that a certain time an angel came and stirred the pool and the *first* sick person that got into the pool after it got stirred received his healing. Unfortunately for this guy, there was nobody to help him into the pool, and even when he attempted to get to the pool, somebody always got there before him. In essence, this man thought he was not able to get his healing because he always got to the pool late.[109]

The man was in a helpless situation. Given his circumstances, what was he to do? But, lo and behold, his time and chance came when the Head Honcho showed up. Jesus Himself showed up and healed the man. The poor guy didn't lose out because others got to the pool before him. If that person is yours, you're not going to lose out just because somebody got to them before you. God would take care of it for you—in His own time. It might look like a miracle is required for you to obtain your promise. Well, just like God miraculously healed the man, God will lead your prospect to you provided you let Him do His job while you do yours.

With that in mind, don't try to make things happen on your own. You don't have to make any superficial changes to yourself. You don't have to advertise yourself to your spouse-to-be obnoxiously. You don't have to tell him or her "verily verily sayeth the Lord, thou art my beloved, so come on thither my love!" No, no, no! Don't mess things up. That might be why God allowed that giant in your prospect's land. God will take care of it in His own time.

You don't have to do anything, except whatever God tells and teaches you. Like, understand how to love and practice save sex for the person. Date God first, find out what will make your relationship successful, as well as the purpose of your relationship with the individual. Find out how to find that person for your life, get a job, find out God's will for your life, and let God do His job in bringing the person to you. In addition, get on your mark, get set, and get ready to go to the person. Learn to get rid of negatives from your past, understand four levels of forgiveness, and let God make the first move to set you both up. Whether you're dating the person online or offline, trust God more than anyone else. And if He spoke to you that that person is your spouse, He will bring it to pass.

You might wonder why God showed you your mate when you're really not ready to tie the knot, and evidently not on the person's top 100-priority list. God might be showing you a glimpse of His plan for you as an incentive that will motivate you to get yourself together. The revelation of your spouse-to-be could be a means through which God urges you to clean up your act and get with His program. Furthermore, God might want you to pray for your mate, considering that he or she doesn't seem to be falling in line with God's will for you both. There might also be other things that the person is dealing with, and God is asking you to intercede for him or her. In doing so, you're practically on the job-training to be a Godly husband or wife who supports and encourages his or her mate through tough times, thereby preparing yourself for marriage.

The situation might look even gloomier to you if the relationship between the person God promised you and your circumstantial competitor seems to be going very well and lasting longer than expected. Given this scenario, you might be forced to question God by saying something like, "Lord, are you sure this is the person for me? They look like they're good together, and they've been on it for five years now." I hope it doesn't take that long, because five years is a *loooong* time. Nevertheless, if for five years nobody has stolen your heart away from your mate, although you might have tried to get others to, out of frustration, but to no avail, you might just be on the right track.

So why is the giant in the land of the mate of your life? For one, maybe God is trying to keep you and others away for the mean time so that He can set it up in His own time. Until God is satisfied that you're ready to proceed to the altar, that giant might be there to keep every other suitor, including yourself, away from your beloved. In addition, your mate might not be ready for you, neither are you ready for the individual. If God allowed you both to see each other now, you might get sick with each other, break up, and alter God's perfect plan for you two. It's all about timing. I believe God wants to ensure that you both have the right chemistry and ministry.

You might even be more flustered on acknowledging that the person in your prospect's life is amiable, likable and a Godly person. As far as you know, the person looks adequate for the job of betrothing your beloved, a conclusion unanimously drawn by your peers. Let's look at some examples in the Bible that I believe will help alleviate your stress about this issue, and encourage you to hold fast to God's promise to you, regardless of the prevailing circumstances prominent in your proposed mate's life.

I'll proceed with the lovely lady Esther. There was a certain king named Ahasuerus who threw a party for his officials, workers, and royal guests. In his enthusiasm, he asked that his queen, Vashti, grace the occasion with her beautiful presence. I guess her name was proper for her since it meant "beautiful woman."[110] But Vashti refused. The king was upset, consulted with his advisers who encouraged him to dethrone her and look for someone who was better than her to take her spot. Guess who took her spot? Esther.[111]

Now, consider the story this way: Whether you're male or female, assume you're Esther, assume the king is your prospect, and assume that Vashti is the other person in your prospect's life. King Ahasuerus did not know Esther nor needed her, since he's got a beautiful Vashti. Similarly, your beloved doesn't know you nor need you since that other remarkable person is in your prospect's life. When Vashti declined the king's invitation, she aroused his anger and was demoted by him. This opened a door for Esther who was equivalent to a nonentity at the time to come into the picture.

Esther was already prepared spiritually and physically before she met the king. And when the king saw her, he was enthralled with her, and approved her on the spot. The Bible says Esther was lovely, beautiful, and a virgin. Most importantly, she was a Godly woman. There were other beautiful virgins evaluated for Vashti's vacated position; however, the favor of God on Esther gave her the advantage over them to secure her God-given spot.

Your beloved might not know you but when the person does, hallelujah! When your prospect begins to see God in you, when the individual begins to see your love, kindness, meekness, gentleness, submissiveness, and joyfulness or fun, you will almost make it to the number one spot on the person's priority list. You should be number two, since Jesus should be number one in the person's life.

As of now, your proposed mate might not be seeing you because he or she does not really know you. As of now, that other person in your mate's life might be everything to your mate. But at the set time your beloved will discover that the other person is not cutting it. There will be a time when your prospect will need that other person to come through for them, but that other individual will disappoint them incredibly. When this happens, at God's prompting, get ready to take your rightful spot. The favor of God on you will mesmerize your mate and filter the scales from his or her eyes to behold your true self, their true help—mate.

Before Esther met the king and assumed her ordained position, she went through a preparation process. The same is required of you before you assume your position as your mate's beloved. It took about four years before Esther actually became queen. This is four years after Vashti was banned from the royal palace. In reference to this, it's to your benefit that you allow God to prepare you for your mate. Furthermore, a cooling off period might be necessary after your love interest decides to part ways with your competitor. Meanwhile, don't do squat until God gives you the green light.

Let us also look at David, Saul, and Israel. As before, regardless of your gender, see yourself as David, the other person as Saul, and your prospect as Israel, which brings me to another interesting point. Perhaps a reason why your prospect has someone in his or her life was because your beloved was impatient and demanded that God bring someone to him or her. God granted the individual's request. Instead of getting God's best, David or you, the person got *God's less* or godless, Saul or the other person.[112]

Just like Israel demanded for a king so that they could be like other nations, your mate could have demanded to be in a relationship so that he or she could be like his or her other friends who were in relationships, too. Considering the fact that the other nations did not have God and most likely had kings that oppressed them, your mate's friends might have had boy-friends or girlfriends who weren't Godly, either. Accordingly, your mate ended up with the same since your prospect asked to be like his or her friends.

Saul was given to be king of Israel.[113] He was the *people's* choice, not God's. He was the tallest and most handsome. In addition to the looks of the person going out with your love interest, the individual's personality might be so enchanting that you think you stand no chance in winning your prospect's heart away from the person. Don't be dismayed as God allowed Saul to be king of Israel until he messed up. Then, God went to get His real deal, someone who was better than Saul. Someone that He really wanted to be king. This person was David. He was *God's* choice, not the people's.

While Saul held the position as the king of Israel, David was anointed as the true king of Israel. That other person in your mate's life is just holding that position for you, while you are undergoing preparations that will help you assume your proper role as your "Israel's" true king or queen.

David was the man. God began to set things up when David fought Go-liath. Israel was paranoid about the philistine's top fighter. Saul was clue-less about what to do to defend Israel. David's pops, Jesse, sent David to his brothers who were fighting in the war against the Philistines. David was sent to give them and their captain food and see how they were doing. While David was there, he heard Goliath mouthing off.[114]

Just like Israel, your mate, might be dealing with a situation, a storm, a trial or a Goliath, he or she would look up to the other person for help to arrest the predicament but the individual would be incompetent for the job. This is when God pulls from His bag of infinite omnipotence and makes you aware of the situation that He has equipped only you to solve. The revelation of the storm in your promise's life, just like the revelation of Go-liath's threat to Israel was heard by David, is for you to know what to pray about. Ironically, the Goliath in your beloved's life could also be the other person your prospect is involved with. It's up to you, in the name of *Jesus*, to bind the spirit of Goliath and loose your beloved.[115]

Please don't misunderstand me. I'm not saying that you should pray maliciously against the person in your mate's life by saying things like: "Lord kill her!! Kill her!! Lord I pray she falls down and die! Father I pray that He ends up in a ghastly motor accident! I call down fire from heaven to burn him up!" Don't do this! If this is your attitude, you are off base and this calls into question if you truly are the right mate for the person you mistakenly thought God showed you. If you have ill-will, it's likely that you're not on God's "Soon To Be Married" list.

Since you are holding on to what you believe God said to you, it won't hurt to borrow a nugget from what is considered the Lord's prayer.[116] Just pray that God's will be done with regard to your prospect and the other person in his or her life. David subdued Goliath, and in essence got high praise from his Israelite people. I find this comment in the scriptures very interesting:

When the victorious Israelite army was returning home after David had killed the Philistine, women from all the towns of Israel came out to meet King Saul. They sang and danced for joy with tambourines and cymbals. This was their song: "Saul has killed his thousands, and David his ten thousands!" This made Saul very angry. "What's this?" he said. "They credit David with ten thousands and me with only thousands. Next they'll be making him their king!" (1 Samuel 18:6-8 NLT)

You never know, as you begin to intercede for your mate as God leads you, and as a result help the person out of helpless situations, your prospect's heart for some reason unbeknownst to him or her might begin to turn to you despite the presence of the other person. Your mate might begin to absent-mindedly give you more praise than the person involved with your beloved. Your prospect might begin to mention your name more often than necessary even in conversations with the other person.

Even Moses and Joshua present an interesting scenario. Think of yourself as Joshua, Moses as the other person, the Promised Land as your promised life—your marriage, and Israel once again as your love interest. Moses was God's best man for delivering the Israelites from Egypt but Joshua took them to the Promised Land, the land of Canaan. Moses was used to get Israel out of the land of bondage but Joshua was used to get them into the land of bounty.

That other person could make you question God, "Why you?" After all that other person is one to be revered. He or she is the cream of the crop, why does God want to give you your proposed mate who at present is involved with the other person. At this juncture, let me reemphasize that these are not a married couple. They are singles seeing or courting each other.

At this point in your heaven-sent mate's life, the other person might be the best for the job of helping with your mate's personal relationship with God, and eventually with you. That other person might be putting up with issues in your propect's life that you cannot handle now. The other person might be doing the dirty work for you, saving you a lot of heartache and energy that you should use in developing your relationship with God, and your adequacy for your spouse-to-be.

In a sense, Moses dealt with the dirty work—at least, most of it, while Joshua obtained the finished work. Moses had to put up with an ungrateful bunch of Israelites, who complained, murmured, and talked about him and God like dogs. Overtime, Israel's ungratefulness took its toll on Moses and contributed to him not entering the Promised Land. Furthermore, that generation of Israelite men, eligible to fight, twenty years and older, didn't enter the land of Canaan.

Your prospect might be immature and needs to grow up. God might be sparing you the ordeal the other person is going through with your Israel. By the time God is finished with your beloved, the other person and the old ungodly and immature behavior in your mate's life will be discarded. The new, fresher, submissive person is presented to you. Now you both can go into your land of milk and honey—your marriage.

You both can now walk together since you're in agreement. You both can now put ten thousand to flight since each of you had been individually trained by God to put a thousand to flight. You both can now take your land of promise, your promised life, and overcome it's trials by truly loving, supporting, uplifting, and submitting to each other while standing on the foundation, the Rock of your marriage, Christ.

Be encouraged and trust God to fulfill His promise to you. Don't interfere with God's job. Don't go mouthing off that God told you this and God told you that, because if He did, He'll bring it to pass.

Do you know what Ruth, Esther, David, and Joshua had in common? None of them had anything to do with God's promise to them. Mahlon, who was Ruth's husband, had to die, before Ruth was given the opportunity to meet and marry Boaz who had nothing to do with Mahlon's death. Esther had nothing to do with Vashti getting kicked off the throne. Although he had opportunities to kill Saul, out of respect, David spared his life and had nothing to do with Saul's botched suicide and eventual execution.[117] Joshua did not have anything to do with the death of Moses. Moses died before the Lord gave Josh the green light to lead Israel to the land of Canaan.[118]

Therefore, it's not your job to make things happen, but God's because:

Promotion does not come from the east or the west, but God puts down one and lifts up another. (Psalm 75:4 NKJV)

Your transition from being single to being part of a couple is a promotion that only God should give you, if you're after His best. You let go, and let God take care of your marital business in His own time. Don't mess things up. God and not the beneficiaries orchestrated the marriage between Boaz and Ruth, Esther's rise to power, David's kingship, and Joshua's leadership.

Boaz did not get into a bar fight with Mahlon using broken miller lite bottles and yelling obscenities at him because of Ruth. Esther did not take out her jewelry, and pull Vashti's hair while bludgeoning her with her stilettos, and waving her hands in her face in a mud fight for the queen's position. David did not assassinate Saul who played a suicidal role in his own death.[119] The other person might just of their own accord leave your mate or do something that will make your beloved let go of him or her.

Joshua didn't go behind Moses' back telling God how he's a better candidate to lead Israel into the Promised Land. In the same token, you're not supposed to verbally lambaste the other person in your proposed mate's life. Don't speak evil about the other person. Don't be spiteful and don't harass the other person for being involved with your prospect. Don't belittle your beloved because he or she chose to be involved with the other person. Just like David had the opportunity to kill Saul, but didn't, you shouldn't kill the other person's reputation by exploiting God's revelation to you. You shouldn't be telling your beloved about any inadequacies you might have noticed in the other person's compatibility with your prospect.

Rather, continue to pray God's will. I urge you to learn some humility by praying for the other person. Joshua supported Moses. Pray that God will reveal and lead the other person to His will for him or her. Of course, you should pray that God prevent the other person from having any inappropriate relationship with your mate. David encouraged Saul when he was distressed, and still respected him even when he was after David's life.[120] Why don't you borrow a leaf from David? If given the opportunity, encourage the other person whichever way you can. You should also support the other person in any Godly effort to develop your mate. After all, your beloved's spiritual, even physical development is ultimately to your benefit.

If that person is for you, just like Naomi, Ruth's mother-in-law, told Ruth that Boaz would not rest until he took care of the business that pertained to Ruth's welfare, I believe that God will not let the person He has for you rest until the individual comes to the realization of the truth that you are God's best for him or her.[121]

If the person is not for you, even if you missed it, even if you discovered that your belief about what you thought God revealed to you was only a figment of your imagination, don't berate yourself for your error. Learn from it and thank God that you discovered your mistake—while you were single. You're still in a win-win situation. God will still give you the hook up—with somebody else. Whichever case, while you are single, if God told you who your mate is, trust Him to set you both up together.

CHAPTER TWENTY ONE

Learn to Protect Your Mate

When I published this book 12 years ago, little did I know that I was going to be seriously tested on one of the insights I discussed in it. In April of 2012, I was driven to take the medicine I gave in chapter 19. This advice dealt with not making relationship decisions based on third party influences. There was a lady that was very dear to me. In order to be discreet, I'll give her the name, Venus. On hearing of my relationship with Dana, she recommended I see a prophet to get counsel regarding our relationship. Venus wanted to make sure that I was making the right decision.

I didn't want to see any prophet. It wasn't necessary. Dana and I had already had plenty of counsel. Colleagues and leadership of ministries in our church where we served were aware of our relationship and gave us their support. But out of respect for Venus who had been an invaluable blessing in my life, I obliged to her request. Keeping on with my discretion, let's just say the name of the prophet that I agreed to see, was Liam.

When I met Liam, the prophet told me that it wasn't the prophet's place to tell me who to marry. I noted that in mind. This was true. Liam said it would be my choice to decide. Also true. Liam told me that Dana was good, but she had anger issues. That was odd, but I didn't say anything to the prophet. Liam said she was good, but in the future her anger issues could be a liability for the ministry God entrusted me. Though Liam reinforced that it was my choice to decide whether I wanted to move forward with Dana, I was disturbed and confused by Liam's word of knowledge.[122]

Venus was also influenced by Liam's insight on Dana because she allowed it to cause her to have reservations about her. To Venus' credit, she encouraged me to pray about Liam's comments, which of course I did. On the day I met Liam, I also brought Dana along with me. So, after Liam spoke with me privately, the prophet also met and prayed for Dana. Later on, Venus told me that Liam said, after praying for Dana, it was detected that she was hardhearted. Venus told me that Liam said I needed to stay far away from her. In my mind, after I heard that, I felt like a line was crossed. That was the third sign that the revelation was *off.*

The first sign that helped me deduce that the prophet's comments were amiss, was that what was said did not line up with what was in my heart. It did not bear witness with what was in my spirit about Dana. To be honest, between Dana and I, if there was anyone more prone to anger, it would be me. Dana puts others first. She's selfless, loving and very flexible. Hardhearted and Dana don't exist in the same sentence. The second sign that things were off was that the word of knowledge left me troubled and confused.

For God is not the author of confusion but of peace .... (1 Corinthians 14:33 NKJV)

A confusing prophecy or revelation is not authored by God. Therefore, the prophe-lie came from something else. The third sign was Liam going against the principle of telling me what to do regarding Dana. In chapters 16 and 19 I mentioned that you don't make decisions based on a third party's influence. It is better to trust God than any man, woman—or prophet (See Psalm 118:8). Remember that Liam had said it wasn't the prophet's place to tell me what to do. To give Liam the benefit of the doubt, Liam did not tell me directly that I needed to stay far from Dana. I received the message from Venus who claimed that that was what Liam told her. A few days later, Liam left me a voicemail, wanting to speak to me. I reluctantly returned the call. In our conversation Liam said "people like her are hard to marry." This was the fourth sign.

What did Liam mean by people like her? Liam meant that she was white. To the unsuspecting observer, my wife looks white, though she is also Hispanic. Therefore, was the prophecy about her, or about her ethnicity? Was the prophet being led by the Spirit or by the prophet's flesh? Was this revelation or fabrication? That comment by Liam confirmed my suspicion that the prophet's advice was based on prejudice, not on divine revelation.

Despite those four signs, I still needed to seek God personally for clarity. Though I doubted the allegations against my woman, I wasn't foolish not to know that sometimes you can be so in love with someone that you're not seeing straight. Though I felt like I was clear about my relationship with Dana, I wanted to reconfirm that we were on the right track.

Prior to the prophet's comments about Dana, she and I had been dating for close to a year with relatively no hiccups. I deliberately didn't tell Dana what the prophet said about her. I wanted us to seek God independently first. I told Dana that we needed to be apart for a month. I told her we needed to pray for clarity on whether we needed to move forward. Though Dana was receptive, she wondered why all of a sudden I needed clarity after a year of dating. She cried, wondering why I came up with the idea. Much to my chagrin, again, I was on the lookout for any flashes of anger from her.

My reflexes were on the edge ready for any sudden movements by her to plant a frying pan on my head. Not surprisingly, this didn't happen. She didn't curse me out. She didn't attack me. She just sobbed profusely. She didn't like that the month we were taking off from seeing each other was May, the same month for our one year dating anniversary. It was a very long month. I didn't tell her about Liam's prophecy. I just told her we needed to be apart, and pray.

The day after I gave Dana the bad news, she came to see me. She told me she was restraining herself from being very upset with me, but wanted clarity about our relationship. I told her I had no intention on breaking up, but we needed to be apart for the whole month. She cried some more, but she agreed to my request. She recalled advice given to her by her Godly mentors several years prior when she was in college. They had said that sometimes being apart for a while to seek God was not such a bad thing. It will help determine whether a relationship should halt or move forward. Dana and I agreed not to see each other for a month. We hugged, and then she went home. During this fiasco I also sought the counsel of two Godly and dear friends. They basically encouraged me to pray. They prayed for Dana and me, as well.

Our hiatus didn't last 2 weeks. In that time, while seeking God desperately for clarity, I received two more signs. After threatening God that I would hold Him responsible if I ended up marrying or not marrying Dana and it was not His will, I got two more confirmations—not that my childish threats had anything to do with them. The first was listening to Pastor Joel Osteen preach a message. In the sermon He advised that a person shouldn't do something just because somebody else said the Lord told them to tell the individual to do it. The second was a tag I received on facebook. The tag was a picture sent by a mutual friend of Dana and me. The friend had no clue of what was going on between us. In the picture I was holding Dana close to my side. Through that picture, I felt that God was telling me to hold on tight to her. Finally, before the misinformation about Dana, I was at peace with our relationship. After I confirmed that the comments about her were misguided, I was still at peace with our relationship.

The peace that Christ gives is to guide you in the decisions you make … (Colossians 3:15 GNB)

After I received the confirmations that Dana and I were on the right track, I told Venus I was moving forward with Dana. I didn't bother telling Liam. I cut my separation from Dana, three weeks short. I apologized to Dana about what happened and told her what the prophet said about her. Dana chuckled at the thought of being described as hardhearted. We shared the story with a few of our friends, and they were all amused that the prophet said she had anger issues.

One of those friends was one of Dana's best friends. She, her siblings, and her family had known Dana since they were in college. This is about 9 years before I met Dana. If she was prone to anger outbursts, they would have known this. They, as well as other friends and individuals acquainted with Dana and I, all know her to be a sweetheart. We also know her passion for social justice. It is usually only in this context that my laid-back Dana might perk up, rise up, and speak up voicing her reservations about any injustice she feels inflicted on anyone.

On hearing what Liam said about her, the "hardhearted" Dana gave the prophet the benefit of the doubt. She said that perhaps the prophet misinterpreted the revelation. At the time, Dana's profession as a mental health specialist in school often required her to work with students with anger issues. She suggested that perhaps the prophet got it all mixed up. Dana reasoned that the correct revelation may have been that she was good and worked with students with anger. Does Dana's response to someone who insinuated that I break up with her, make her sound like someone with anger issues? Is this how a hardhearted person responds to borderline slander?

Despite what was alleged about her, she kept assuring me that Liam and Venus were trying to protect me because they loved me. Though Dana was hurt by the allegations against her, she was more forgiving than I was. We both let it go, but she was more understanding than one would expect of someone who had the issues claimed by Liam.

Several months later I bumped into the prophet. Somehow Liam found out that I was continuing my relationship with Dana. You wouldn't believe what Liam told me. The prophet wanted to be informed of our wedding so that the prophet could attend. Really?

Conclusion

Considering what happened to me, and what happened to Adam and Eve, it's necessary for you to know that just because you find the right person doesn't mean you both are going to live automatically happily ever after without working at it. Just because the person is perfect for you doesn't mean the person is perfect. Neither are you. In fact, you both are being perfected through your relationship with each other, and any other means God deems necessary. Perhaps you might have wondered why I used Adam and Eve as an object lesson knowing how they messed up.

Well, nobody can refute the biblical truth that Eve was custom-made for Adam. Yet, they got kicked out of their house shortly after they got married. They foreclosed their domain to the devil. Even so, their banishment had nothing to do with whether or not they were compatible with each other. God already took care of that. Their eviction was as a result of their disobedience, which could have been prevented had Adam denounced the conversation the serpent had with his wife. It seems like as soon as Adam got the blessing, he lost the lesson. He lost focus like Peter did when he took his eyes off Jesus while walking on water, and began to sink. Adam and Eve began to sink when Eve took her eyes off God's instruction, and placed it on the fruit from the forbidden tree courtesy of the devil's instruction. Adam also took his eyes off God's instruction and perhaps placed it solely on Eve.

With that in mind, don't lose focus when God blesses you with your spouse. Don't stop dating God. Don't stop spending time with Him. Don't stop seeking Him. In fact, you need to seek Him more for direction for this newfound relationship. Just because you find the right person doesn't mean that you can now discard everything you learned while you were single, which helped you in your quest for your mate. You're to build on it.

An intern should not ease back after obtaining the promotion. Usually promotion means more money, more privileges, and also more responsibility. To whom much is given, much is required (See Luke 12:48). Getting the promotion is easier than keeping it. Getting your man or woman will be easier than keeping your relationship with the person. This is why you shouldn't let your guard down. Let it up even more. Since it is two of you, then it's beneficial for you to extend your reach to embrace your better half and fend off intruders like that nincompoop, the devil, who'll try to cause division between you two, and between you and God.

Be advised about modern day serpents that come in a variety of shapes, colors, and flavors. They can be disguised as friends, family, church members, music, magazines, and television programs. Their mission: to seduce you to eat the forbidden fruit of disobedience, which can separate you from God, from your spouse, and ultimately from reaching your destiny—God's purpose for your life.

Drastic changes often take place during corporate mergers. Sometimes people get laid off and personnel get moved around in the name of doing what's best for the company. In the name of doing what's best for you two— your company—your companionship, you might have to make changes to your habits, philosophies and even friends. You may have to lay some of them off and renew others.

If you don't want to get exiled from your marital garden, if you want to keep your house intact and in order, it's to the benefit of your forthcoming union that you and your beloved keep yourselves accountable to God and to each other. You both have to communicate and make things clear to each other. You cannot afford to *assume* that your mate will do what is right without you exemplifying what is right, and communicating it to him or her clearly, respectfully and lovingly.

According to Dr. Cole:

Assumption is life's lowest level of knowledge.[123]

So, while you are single, know what you are getting yourself into, understand what love is and what love does. Practice save sex. Avoid, resist, and flee anything that will prevent you from doing so. Date God first. Find out what makes relationships successful. Find out the purpose of relationships. Find out how to find the right person. Get a job. Find out God's will for your life. Let God do His job. Get on your mark ... get set ... and get ready to go to your mate. Get rid of negatives from your past. Understand four levels of forgiveness. Let God make the first move. Are you dating online or offline? Whichever case, keep God first. It's not about where you're from but who you're from. Trust God more than anyone else. If God spoke it, He will bring it to pass. And learn to protect your mate.

God has someone special for you. He never overlooked you. You might know who the person is. You might believe you know who the person is. You might hope who the person is—or you might not have the faintest idea of who the person is. Whichever case, God the True and Best Matchmaker will guide you to the right mate for your life.

I hope this book has been a source of encouragement for you. Let God guide you to the right person. Meanwhile allow Him to develop your character and teach you how to love the person He has for you so that you'll be the "right one" for the individual, too. Let God *invest in you* the returns you desire to receive from *His best for you*. Until next time, *Adios*!

Envision the Dream

If you haven't trekked the path to your beloved yet, watch out! One day, you'll be going to see God at the restaurant where you both usually meet for a date. The name of the restaurant is called *The Private Place*.[124] You quicken your pace to the restaurant and begin to salivate as you think of sinking your teeth in the restaurant's special delicacy, and your favorite dish—*The Daily Bread*.

You walk into the plush eatery dimly lit with a tint of blue, while a soft jazzy ballad by Ben Tankard, Kenny G, and Kirk Whalum are alternating in its background. Occasionally, the music genre switches to worship, and likewise, the jazzists are replaced by the psalmists: Darlene Zschech, Israel Houghton, Pastor Marcos Witt, Martha Minuzzi, Cindy Ratcliffe, Steve Crawford, Deidra Greathouse, Hillsong, Pastor Donnie McClurkin, Karen Wheaton, Fred Hammond, Yolanda Adams, Angelo & Veronica, Rebecca St. James, Monica Pollard, Lori-El and Ryan Bell. Their respective, heart warming, and heavenly lyrics also play alternatively. These songs engulf the restaurant with an atmosphere of warmth, love, and *Eldora do*.

Your feet bounce slightly on the soft, thick, *crimson red* carpet as you advance toward your favorite booth by the window, overlooking the French Rivera in France, Rio de Janeiro in Brazil, droves of light emanating from the sky scrapers and moon lit night, which together form a radiant glow that illuminates the downtown business district of Houston, Texas, USA, or whatever strokes your imagination.

On getting to your booth you are puzzled not to find God there. Instead, you find a gentle man or lady. You wonder if you got there late and proceed to inquire from the enchanting and familiar looking stranger the where-abouts of God, your *First Date*, from the stranger. This scenario further intrigues you when you learn from the stranger that he or she was also sup-posed to meet with God but was surprised to see you instead. Could this be a God-incidence?

By this time you've sat down across from this individual. You've both taken occasional sips of the *living water* placed before you in the *new wine* glasses.[125] As you and this person begin to untangle this mystery, you begin to realize that you sort of know each other and have at least the one most important thing in common: your first date, Jesus! This is when the server who goes by the name, "First Move," comes to your table. The server asks how you like your order and you both look at him bewildered saying, "But we didn't order anything." But the server says that your order had been placed when each of you independently dated God. He placed the order for you two, and He also paid for it. You know what I mean?

Moreover, the server tells you that you're the order for the other person and the other person is the order for you. The server also tells you both to check your *Bible* menus and confirm that your orders were right. The server also tells you in a display of impeccable brilliance that, just like people order steaks, medium, medium well, well done and so forth, you ordered yourselves, "Equally yoked."

The server now draws your attention to the table on which was placed a tip. Ironically, the tip was not for the server but was left by God for both of you. Since waiters get tips, and since you and the stranger who's becoming more attractive every time God unveils your eyes through this server from heaven, have been waiting—patiently like "waiters," God gave you both a tip. You both glance at the tip and on reading it you both catch your breath and shed tears of joy as a sign of relief and mutual accomplishment. It was a *Kodak* moment. Guess what the tip said? *Checkmate*!

Let the Date Begin

If you haven't found the right mate for your life, here is your opportunity to find Him. At this point I am only talking about Jesus. He is the right lover for anyone. No one is right for you until the person is right with Him. Since you are preparing for someone else, it's only fitting that you put yourself in right standing with Him too. He already made the first move on you; perhaps, through this book and other circumstances. He is, "The Right One." Invite Him into your life and He will make you the right one, give you the right one, and together with the person He gives you, you two become "one." So, I encourage you to say this prayer to invite Jesus into your life and let your date with God begin.

Dear Jesus, thank you for dying on the cross on my behalf. In so doing, you took away my sins. Forgive me for not acknowledging what you did for me. I confess you, Jesus, as my Lord. I believe with my heart that God raised you from the dead. Lord Jesus come into my heart. I believe and receive you as my Savior. Since I now believe in you, I am saved and have eternal life. Thank you for saving me. In your name I pray, Amen.

If you have already accepted Jesus Christ into your life, but you went astray and you would like to get back in fellowship with Him I encourage you to pray this prayer:

Father, forgive me for my sins that lured me away from you. I repent, and ask you to help me continue to live for you, and be like you from hence-

forth. Thank you for being faithful and just in forgiving me and cleansing me from all unrighteousness .[126] In Jesus' Name I pray, Amen.

If you don't have a home church, I encourage you to find a good Bible-based church in your area where you can develop your relationship with God. He will help you in every area of your life.

To contact the Author, please email: toks@ojtoks.com

Endnotes

Chapter One

1 Pat Love, Ed.D, *The Truth About Love* (New York, NY: Simon & Schuster, 2001), 28-29, 39-41, 60-61, 150, 165.

2 Mark 11:23.

3 See John 1:1, 14.

4 The Merriam-Webster Dictionary (Springfield, MA: Merriam-Webster, 1997) 32.

Chapter Two

5 Tommy Barnett, *Hidden Power* (Lake Mary, FL: Charisma House, 2002), 122.

6 M. Scott Peck, *Road Less Travelled* (New York, NY: Touchstone), 119.

7 See Matthew 5:1-12.

8 Ephesians 3:20.

9 Gregory Witt, *Rolling Stocks* (Seattle, WA: Lighthouse, 1998, 1999), 124.

10 Barnett, 126.

11 Matthew Kelly, *The Seven Levels of Intimacy* (New York, NY: Fireside, 2005), 104

12 Frederick K.C. Price, Ph.D., *The Christian Family* (Los Angeles, CA: Faith One, 1996), 219-220.

13 Kelly, 102.

14 Matthew 26:36-40, 42, 67; 27:26, 28 AMP, John 19:30.

15 Genesis 29:1-11.

Chapter Three

16 Barnett, 124.

17 Barnett, 138.

18 Genesis 29:18, 20; 31:41

19   Edwin Louis Cole, *Communication, Sex & Money* (Tulsa, OK: Albury, 1987), 19.

20   Cole, 78-79.

21   Dr. Robin L. Smith, *Lies at the Altar* (New York, NY: Hyperion, 2006), 153.

Chapter Four

22   I John 1:9.

23   Edwin Louis Cole, *Irresistible Husband* (Southlake, TX: Watercolor, 2001), 92.

24   Jentezen Franklin, *Right People Right Place Right Plan* (New Kesington, PA: Whitaker, 2007), 155.

25   Cole, Communication, Sex & Money, 98.

Chapter 5

26   Romans 16:20 GNB.

27   Luke 4:1-13.

28   Joseph was 30 years old when he became governor. He died when he was one hundred-and-ten. Genesis 39:6-23; 40, 41:37-46; 50:22.

29   2 Corinthians 5:17 AMP.

30   Romans 12:2

31   Cole, Irresistible Husband, 96.

32   Genesis 19:23-38.

33   Galatians 5:9.

34   2 Samuel 11:4-27; 12:1-18.

35   1 Corinthians 6:18-20.

36   2 Corinthians 5:7 AMP.

37   Romans 10:17.

38   Source obtained from the Internet: http://dictionary.reference.com/search?q=kingdom.

Chapter Six

39   Hebrews 12:29.

40   Matthew 6:6 KJV.

41   Proverbs 11:16; 12:4; 14:1; 31:10, 17, 30; Genesis 24:16-20; 1 Samuel 25:3.

42   Genesis 25:21; 39:6-12; 1 Kings 11:28; Proverbs 20:6; Daniel 1:14-20; Matthew 1:19; Luke 2:52; Acts 13:22; 1 Corinthians 11:1; 2 Thessalonians 3:10.

43   Ephesians 5:25-33.

Chapter Seven

44   Myles Munroe, *Single, Married, Separated & Life after Divorce* (Shippensburg, PA: Destiny, 1992), 25.

45   Smith, 1.

46   Joshua Harris, *Boy Meets Girl* (Sisters, OR: Multnomah, 2000), 106.

47   Kelly, 15.

Chapter Eight

48   Kelly, 22.

49   Ephesians 5:23, 30; Colossians 1:18; Revelations 19:7-8.

50   John & Stasi Eldredge, *Captivating* (Waterville, ME: Thorndike, 2005), 351-352.

Chapter Nine

51   John C. Maxwell, *The 21 Irrefutable Laws of Leadership* (Nashville, TN: Nelson, 2007), 104.

52   Dr. Fuchsia Pickett, *Cultivating the Gifts & Fruit of the Holy Spirit* (Lake Mary, Fl: Charisma, 2004), 2; James Strong, *The New Strong's Exhaustive Concordance of the Bible* (Nashville, TN: Thomas Nelson, 1990), 64.

53   Pickett, 1-5.

Chapter Ten

54   Genesis 26:6-11.

55   Genesis 20.

56   Genesis 29:9.

57   Genesis 29:18-20.

58   John 6:35.

59   Genesis 22:14; Psalm 18:2; Isaiah 10:27; 60:16; Matthew 13:54, 16:16, 17:18, 19:16; Luke 23:44-46, 24:1-7, 24:50-53; John 6:4-12; Acts 2:33, 10:38; Romans 5:19; Philippians 4:19; Colossians 2:15; Hebrews 2:14-15; Revelations 1:18, 11:15, 12:10-11, 19:11-16.

Chapter Eleven

60   Kelly, 29.

61   Munroe, 29.

62   Exodus 7:7; Deuteronomy 34:7.

63   Exodus 2:11-22.

64   John 19:3

Chapter Twelve

65   2 Corinthians 6:14.

66   Hebrews 4:12 GNB, AMP.

67   James 1:4.

68   Genesis 12:1-5,10, 13:1, 15:1-4, 16:1-4,15 GNB (Abraham was 75 when he went to Canaan, left for Egypt, came back to Canaan. When he was 86 he had Ishmael).

69   Genesis 16:12.

70   Genesis 17:1-2.

71   Numbers 13:1-2.

72   Deuteronomy 1:2 AMP.

73   Numbers 13:25-33; 14:1-10.

74   Numbers 14:26-38.

Chapter Thirteen

75   James Strong, "Delight,"*The New Strong's Exhaustive Concordance of the Bible* (Nashville, TN: Thomas Nelson, 1990), 89.

76   Strong, "Eden," 62.

77   John C. Maxwell, *17 Indisputable Laws of Teamwork* (Nashville, TN: Nelson, 2000) 189.

Chapter Fifteen

78   Robert Young, *Young's Analytical Concordance to the Bible* (Peabody, MA: Hendrickson, 2005), 805.

79   Joel Osteen, *Become a Better You* (New York, NY: Free Press, 2007), 60-61.

80   T.D. Jakes, *The Great Investment* (New York, NY: G.P. Putnam's Sons, 2000), 129.

81   Ruth 1:21.

82   Cole, *Irresistible Husband*, 41.

Chapter Sixteen

83   Ruth 2:5-17.

84   Ruth 2:14-23.

85   Ruth 4:1-12.

86   Price, 94.

87   John 20:29.

Chapter Seventeen

88   Dr. Robert Epstein, *The Truth About Online Dating*, http://drrobertepstein.com/pdf/ Epstein-TheTruthAboutOnlineDating-2-07.pdf, Scientific American Mind, www. sciammind.com, February/March 2007, 33-34 (accessed November 19, 2009).

89   Genesis 19:35-37.

90   Genesis 11:27.

91   Ruth 4:10.

92   Herbert Lockyer, *All the Women of the Bible* (Grand Rapids: Zondervan, 1967), 168.

93   Ruth 2:8, 22-23.

94   Ruth 4:13, 21-22; Matthew 1:5-16.

95   Genesis 41:37-45.

96   Esther 2:7, 17; 1 Samuel 16:18; 25:2-35; Ruth 3:11.

97   2 Samuel 12:1-20.

98   2 Samuel 11:26-27.

99   Luke 3:23-31.

Chapter Nineteen

100   Matthew 24:46.

101 1 Samuel 17:34-35.

102   Matthew 14:30-31.

103   Sam R. Hamburg, PH.D., *Will Our Love Last* (New York, NY: Scribner, 2000), 55-58.

104   James 4:8 AMP.

105   1 Corinthians 2:9-10.

106   Proverbs 11:14 NKJV.

107   Mahlon was Ruth's first husband, one of Naomi's sons who died after they left Israel.

Chapter Twenty

108   Ecclesiastes 9:11.

109   John 5:1-9.

110   Strong, 208.

111   Esther 1:2-3, 10-22.

112   1 Samuel 8:1-22.

113   Joshua 1:1-2; 1 Samuel 10:17-27.

114   1 Samuel 16:1-13.

115   Matthew 18:18.

116   Luke 11:2.

117   1 Samuel 24:1-10; 26:7-10 ; 2 Samuel 1:1-10.

118   Joshua 1:1-2.

119   1 Samuel 31:4-5.

120 1 Samuel 16:21-23.

121 Ruth 3:18.

Chapter Twenty One

122 1 Corinthians 12:8. A word of knowledge is a gift given by the Holy Spirit, which enables a person to receive information about someone supernaturally. You can read examples of this gift, in operation in the following scriptures: 2 Kings 5; John 1:43-50; Acts 5:1-11.

123 Edwin Louis Cole, *Maximized Manhood* (Springdale, PA: Whitaker, 1982), 91.

Envision The Dream

124 Matthew 6:6 KJV.

125 John 4:10; Acts 2:1-4; Ephesians 5:18.

Let The Date Begin

126 John 1:29; John 3:16; Romans 10:9; Colossians 2:13-14; 1 John 1:9.